INFORMATION INDIA : 1996-97

About the Author

S.P. Agrawal (*b.* 1929) was Director, National Social Science Documentation Centre, ICSSR, Government of India and Member Secretary, Indian Association of Social Science Institutions. He was also the Vice-Chairman of the Asia and Pacific Information Network in Social Sciences (APINESS). In 1988 he was awarded the degree of Doctor of Philosophy in Education (*Honoris Causa*) by International University Foundation. Presently, he is Member, IFLA Round Table on Research in Reading, International Committee for Social Science Information and Documentation, Board of Studies of National Archives of India. He is also Fellow of the Society of Ethnobotanists. Born and brought up in the cradle of freedom movement, which he joined at the tender age of twelve, he gained an insight into political problems and developed a sense of responsibility which bore fruit as an information scientist. He has written extensively on various aspects of Education. Indian Polity and Library and Information Science.

CONCEPTS IN COMMUNICATION
INFORMATICS & LIBRARIANSHIP—82

General Editor : **S. P. AGRAWAL**

INFORMATION INDIA : 1996-97 Global View

S.P. AGRAWAL
former Member Secretary
Indian Association of Social Science Institutions, and
Director, National Social Science Documentation Centre,
ICSSR, Government of India

Assisted by
M.W.K. SHERWANI
former Asstt. Educational Adviser
Ministry of Human Resource Development, New Delhi

CONCEPT PUBLISHING COMPANY, NEW DELHI-110059

ISBN 81-7022-786-0

First Published 1999

Published and Printed by
Ashok Kumar Mittal
Concept Publishing Company
A/15-16, Commercial Block, Mohan Garden
New Delhi-110059 (India)

Phones: 5648039, 5649024
Fax: 091-(11)-5648053

GENERAL EDITOR'S INTRODUCTION

Today we stand on the threshold of a new age. Information technology is the third revolution in the history of mankind after agriculture and industrial development which are the first and second revolutions respectively. "Knowledge is power, information is liberating, education is the premise of progress in every society, in every family . . . Information and freedom is unthinkable without democracy and democracy is unimaginable without freedom of information." These are the sovereign words of wisdom spoken by UN General Secretary Kofi Annan in 'Global Knowledge 97' Conference held in Toronto (Canada) in June, 1997.

In the modern explosion of knowledge information has assumed a great importance in the progress of present-day society. It is nerve centre of every field of activity, be it economic, political or social. We cannot take proper and judicious decisions on any field of knowledge without having basic facts about it. The newer forms of information technology has revolutionised our life by providing users with rapid access to rest amounts of knowledge.

There are a number of ways in which information is stored or packaged for exchange. These are books, audio tapes and discs, microfilm in the form of microfiche, video tapes, etc. Of these the oldest way for information retrieval is the book. It is so efficient and inexpensive that in the developing countries like India it is still used widely as a form of information storage and exchange. It will continue for long for conveying the information and it will not be easy to be supplanted by electronic Communications systems. In the developed countries where information technology has made a tremendous development the information in the form of a book is still relevant.

The focus of the present volume is on India as it was in 1994-95 and 1995-96. In this compilation every effort has been made to give all important facets not only of India but also of the world as a whole. The challenges facing the world global economic and social development and significant international reports have been included. Relating to India it has been attempted to provide almost all embracing facts and figures with regard to various sectors of development. Detailed account has been given about important aspects as well as other social areas which are of significance in any discussion on India.

It is of great consolation that previous editions of this publication placed in the hands of the discerning readers as also of the reviewers have been received well. It is hoped that like the previous editions the present volume would also be of equal interest to a large category of readers from different disciplines and professions, administrators, business magnates, economic analysts, journalists, planners, researchers, students and those preparing for various competitive examinations.

It is observed that the data collected by various national and international organisations from different sources and also used here, do not necessarily relate to the same year in a few cases.

S. P. AGRAWAL

CONTENTS

PART ONE

WORLD OVERVIEW

1

RESPONSIBILITIES TOWARDS FUTURE GENERATIONS : UNESCO RESOLUTION, 1997

The General Conference of UNESCO on 12 November 1997 at its 29th session adopted the following Declaration on the Responsibilities of the Present Generations towards Future Generations

UNESCO DECLARATION

Article 1— Needs and interests of future generations

The present generations have the responsibilities of ensuring that the needs and interests of present and future generations are fully safeguarded.

Article 2— Freedom of choice

It is important to make every effort to ensure, with due regard to human rights and fundamental freedoms, that future as well as present generations enjoy full freedom of choice as to their political, economic and social systems and are able to preserve their cultural and religious diversity.

Article 3— Maintenance and perpetuation of humankind

The present generations should strive to ensure the maintenance and perpetuation of humankind with due respect for the dignity of human person. Consequently, the nature and form of human life must not be undermined in any way whatsoever.

Article 4— Preservation of life on Earth

The present generations have the responsibility to bequeath to future generations an Earth which will not one day be irreversibly damaged by human activity. Each generation inheriting the Earth temporarily should take care to use natural resources reasonably and ensure that life is not prejudiced by harmful modifications of the ecosystems and that scientific and technological progress in all fields does not harm life on Earth.

Article 5— Protection of the environment

1. In order to ensure that future generations benefit from the richness of the Earth's ecosystems, the present generations should strive for sustainable development and preserve living conditions, particularly the quality and integrity of the environment.

2. The present generations should ensure that future generations are not exposed to pollution which may endanger their health or their existence itself.
3. The present generations should preserve for future generations natural resources, necessary for sustaining human life and for its development.
4. The present generations should take into account possible consequences for future generations of major projects before these are carried out.

Article 6— Human genome and biodiversity

The human genome, in full respect of the dignity of the human person and human rights, must be protected and biodiversity safeguarded. Scientific and technological progress should not in any way impair or compromise the preservation of the human and other species.

Article 7— Cultural diversity and cultural heritage

With due respect for human rights and fundamental freedoms, the present generations should take care to preserve the cultural diversity of humankind. The present generations have the responsibility to identify, protect and safeguard the tangible and intangible cultural heritage and to transmit this common heritage to future generations.

Article 8— Common heritage of humankind

The present generations may use the common heritage of humankind, as defined in international law, provided that this does not entail compromising it irreversibly.

Article 9— Peace

1. The present generations should ensure that both they and future generations learn to live together in peace, security, respect for international law, human rights and fundamental freedoms.
2. The present generations should spare future generations the scourge of war. To that end, they should avoid exposing future generations to the harmful consequences of armed conflicts as well as all other forms of aggression and use of weapons, contrary to humanitarian principles.

Article 10— Development and education

1. The present generations should ensure the conditions of equitable, sustainable and universal socio-economic development of future generations, both in its individual and collective dimensions, in particular through a fair and prudent use of available resources for the purpose of combating poverty.
2. Education is an important instrument for the development of human persons and societies. It should be used to foster peace, justice, understanding, tolerance and equality for the benefit of present and future generations.

Article 11— Non-discrimination

The present generations should refrain from taking any action or measure which would have the effect of leading to or perpetuating any form of discrimination for future generations.

Article 12— Implementation

Sates, the United Nations system, other intergovernmental and non-governmental organizations, individuals, public and private bodies should assume their full responsibilities in promoting, in particular through education, training and information, respect for the ideals laid down in this Declaration, and encourage by all appropriate means their full recognition and effective application.

2

THE STATE IN A CHANGING WORLD : WORLD DEVELOPMENT REPORT, 1997

The last fifty years have shown clearly both the benefits and the limitations of state action, especially in the promotion of development. Governments have helped to deliver substantial improvements in education and health and reductions in social inequality. But government actions have also led to some very poor outcomes. And even where governments have done a good job in the past, many worry that they will not be able to adapt to the demands of a globalizing world economy.

The new worries and questions about the state's role are many and various, but four recent developments have given them particular impetus:

* The collapse of command-and-control economies in the former Soviet Union and Central of Eastern Europe
* The fiscal crisis of the welfare state in most of the established industrial countries
* The important role of the state in the "miracle" economies of East Asia
* The collapse of states and the explosion in humanitarian emergencies in several parts of the world.

The determining factor behind these contrasting developments is the effectiveness of the state.

What makes for an effective state differs enormously across countries at different stages of development. What works in the Netherlands or New Zealand, say, may not work in Nepal. Even among countries at the same level of income, differences in size, ethnic makeup, culture, and political systems make every state unique.

RETHINKING THE STATE—THE WORLD OVER

The world is changing, and with it our ideas about the state's role in economic and social development.

In a few countries things have worked out more or less as the technocrats expected. But in many countries outcomes were very different. Corruption became endemic. Development falered, and poverry endured.

The clamor for greater government effectiveness has reached crisis proportions in many developing countries where the state has failed to deliver even such fundamental public goods as property rights, roads, and basic health and education. There a vicious circle has taken hold: people and businesses respond to deteriorating public services by avoiding taxation, which leads to further deterioration in services. In the former Soviet Union and

Central and Eastern Europe it was the state's long-term failure to deliver on its promises that led finally, to its overthrow. But the collapse of central planning has created problems of its own. In the resulting vacuum, citizens are sometimes deprived of basic public goods such as law and order. At the limit, as in Afghanistan, Liberia, and Somalia, the state has sometimes crumbled entirely, leaving individuals and international agencies trying desperately to pick up the pieces.

A TWO-PART STRATEGY

Getting societies to accept a redefinition of the state's responsibilities will be one part of the solution. This will include strategic selection of the collective actions that state will try to promote, coupled with greater efforts to take the burden off the state by involving citizens and communities in the delivery of core collective goods.

But reducing or diluting the state's role cannot be the end of the reform story. Even with more selectivity and greater reliance on the citizenry and on private firms, meeting a broad range of collective needs more effectively will still mean making the state's central institutions work better. For human welfare to be advanced, the state's capability—*defined as the ability to undertake and promote collective actions efficiently*—must be increased.

This basic message translates into a two-part strategy to make every state a more credible, effective partner in its country's development:

- *Matching the state's role to its capability is the first element* in this strategy. Where state capability is weak, how the state intervenes—and where—should be carefully assessed. Many states try to do too much with few resources and little capability, and often do more harm than good. A sharper focus on the fundamentals would improve effectiveness. But here it is a matter not just of choosing what to do and what not to do-but of how to do it as well.
- But capability is not destiny. Therefore the second element of the strategy is to *raise state capability by reinvigorating public institutions.* This means designing effective rules and restraints, to check arbitrary state actions and combat entrenched corruption. It means subjecting state institutions to greater competition, to increase their efficiency. It means increasing the performance of state institutions, improving pay and incentives. And it means making the state more responsive to people's needs, bringing government closer to the people through broader participation and decentralization. Thus, the Report not only directs attention to refocusing the state's role, but also shows how countries might begin a process of rebuilding the state's capability.

MATCHING ROLE TO CAPABILITY

Matching role to capability is not a simple message of dismantling the state. In some areas much greater focus is badly needed to improve effectiveness: choosing what to do and what not to do is critical. But this also involves choosing how to do things—how to deliver basic services, provide infrastructure, regulate the economy—and not just whether to do them at all. The choices here are many and must be tailored to the circumstances of each country.

The First Job of States: Getting the Fundamentals Right

Fundamental rights Five fundamental tasks lie at the core of every government's mission, without which sustainable, shared, poverty reducing development is impossible:

- Establishing a foundation of law
- Maintaining a nondistortionary policy environment, including macro-economic stability
- Investing in basic social services and infrastructure
- Protecting the vulnerable
- Protecting the environment.

Although the importance of these fundamentals has long been widely accepted, some new insights are emerging as to the appropriate mix of market and government activities in achieving them. Most important, we now see that markets and governments are complementary: the state is essential for putting in place the appropriate institutional foundations for markets. And government's credibility—the predictability of its rules and policies and the consistency with which they are applied—can be as important for attracting private investment as the content of those rules and policies.

A survey, specially commissioned for this Report, of domestic entrepreneurs (formal and informal) in sixty-nine countries confirms what was already known anecdotally: that many countries lack the basic institutional foundations for market development. High levels of crime and personal violence and an unpredictable judiciary combine to produce what this Report defines as the "lawlessness syndrome." Weak and arbitrary state institutions often compound the problem with unpredictable, inconsistent behavior. Far from assisting the growth of markets, such actions squander the state's credibility and hurt market development.

To make development stable and sustainable, the state has to keep its eye on the social fundamentals. Lawlessness is often related to a sense of marginalization: indeed, breaking the law can seem the only way for the marginalized to get their voices heard. Public policies can ensure that growth is shared and that it contributes to reducing poverty and inequality, but only if governments put the social fundamentals high on their list of priorities.

Too often, policies and programs divert resources and services from the people who need them most. The political clout of the more affluent in society sometimes leads governments to spend many times more on rich and middle-class students in universities than on basic education for the majority and scholarships for the less well off. In many regions poverty and inequality are often biased against ethnic minorities or women, or disfavored geographic areas. Marginalized from public discussion and excluded from the broader economy and society, such groups are fertile ground for violence and instability, as many parts of the world are increasingly learning.

Public policies and programs must aim not merely to deliver growth but to ensure that the benefits of market-led growth are shared, particularly through investments in basic education and health. They must also ensure that people are protected against material and personal insecurity. Where poverty and economic marginalization stem from ethnic and social differences, policies must be carefully crafted to manage these differences, as Malaysia and Mauritius have done.

Government regulation is not the only answer to pollution. An expanding tool-kit of innovative and flexible incentives is now available to get polluters to clean up their act. Although there is no substitute for meaningful regulatory frameworks and information about the environment, these new tools, which rely on persuasion, social pressure, and market forces to help push for improved environmental performance, can often succeed where regulation cannot. Countries are using some of these tools, with promising results, in four areas:

- Harnessing the power of public opinion
- Making regulation more flexible
- Applying self-regulatory mechanisms
- Choosing effective market-based instruments.

Going Beyond the Basics: The State need not be the Sole Provider

There is a growing recognition that in many countries monopoly public providers of infrastructure, social services, and other goods and services are unlikely to do a good job. At the same time, technological and organizational innovations have created new opportunities for competitive, private providers in activities hitherto confined to the public sector. To take advantage of these new opportunities—and better allocate scarce public capability—governments are beginning to separate the financing of infrastructure and services from its delivery, and to unbundle the competitive segments of utility markets from the monopoly segments. Reformers are also moving to separate programs of social insurance, designed to address the problems of health and employment insecurity for all, from programs of social assistance, intended to help only the poorest in society.

Coping with Household Insecurity

It is now well established that the state can help households cope with certain risks to their economic security: it can insure against destitution in old age through pensions, against devastating illness through health insurance, and against job loss through unemployment insurance. But the idea that the state alone must carry this burden is changing. Even in many industrial countries the welfare state is being reformed. Emerging economies from Brazil to China will be unable to afford even pared-down versions of the European system, especially with their rapidly aging populations. Innovative solutions that involve businesses, labor, households, and community groups are needed to achieve greater security at lower cost. This is especially important for those developing countries not yet locked into costly solutions.

Effective Regulation

Well-designed regulatory systems can help societies influence market outcomes for public ends. Regulation can help protect consumers, workers, and the environment. It can foster competition and innovation while constraining the abuse of monopoly power. Thanks to regulatory reforms initiated in the early 1980s, Chile's telecommunications industry has enjoyed sustained private investment, increasing service quality and competition, and declining prices. By contrast, until some recent reform initiatives, dysfunctional regulation led the Philippine telecommunications industry—long privately owned—to under invest. The result was poor and often high-priced service, imposing a high cost on citizens and other firms. Making the best use of the new options emerging for private provision of infrastructure and social services will also rely, often, on a good regulatory framework.

Industrial Policy

When markets are underdeveloped, the state can sometimes reduce coordination problems and gaps in information and encourage market development. Many of today's oldest industrial economies used various mechanisms to spur the growth of markets in their early stages of development. More recently, Japan, the Republic of Korea, and other countries in East Asia used a variety of mechanisms for market enhancement, in addition to securing the economic, social, and institutional fundamentals. Sometimes these interventions were quite elaborate: the highly strategic use of subsidies, for example. Other times they were less intrusive, taking the form of export promotion and special infrastructure incentives. But the ability to choose wisely among these interventions and use them effectively is critical; ill-considered trade, credit, and industrial policies can and have cost countries dearly. Many developing countries pursued ill-thought-out activist industrial policies, with poor results. Countries that have pursued an activist industrial policy successfully could not have done so without strong institutional capability.

Managing Privatization

Carefully designed regulations and other active government initiatives can enhance the growth of markets. But in many countries this can take time, as private initiative is held hostage to a legacy of antagonistic state-market relations. And poorly performing state enterprises are often a big drain on the state's finances. Privatization provides an obvious solution. In general it is easier to sell off state assets once a supportive environment for private sector development is in place. Economies such as China, Korea and Taiwan (China) have therefore opted not to give top priority to privatization, but to allow the private sector to develop around the state sector. This option, however, may not be available where the fiscal burden is very high, and where the presence of poorly performing state enterprises impedes much-needed overall restructuring of the economy.

Experience has shown that the way privatization is managed is terribly important to the end result. The key factors are transparency of process, winning the acquiescence of employees, generating broad-based ownership, and instituting the appropriate regulatory reform. Where privatization has been managed carefully, it is already showing positive results: in Chile, for example, and the Czech Republic. Its importance in the strategy to foster markets may vary, but for many developing countries seeking to scale back an overextended state, privatization must be kept on the front burner. A carefully managed privatization process brings very positive economic and fiscal benefits.

Knowing the state's limits

The key to predictable and consistent implementation of policy is a good fit between the state's institutional capabilities and its actions. In well-developed states, administrative capability is normally strong, and institutionalised checks and balances restrain arbitrary action, even as they provide government organizations the flexibility to pursue their mandates. By contrast, states with weaker institutions may need to err on the side of less flexibility and more restraint. This can be done in two ways.

- Through self-restricting rules, which precisely specify the content of policy and lock it into mechanisms that are costly to reverse. Regional common-currency arrangements, such as the CFA currency zone in francophone Africa or quasi currency boards as in Argentina, are examples of such mechanisms in the field of monetary policy. "Take-or-pay" contracts with independent power producers serve a similar function in utilities regulation.
- Through working in partnership with firms and citizens. In industrial policy, for example, states can foster private-to-private collaboration. In financial regulation they can give bankers an incentive to operate prudently. And in environmental regulation they can use the spread of information to encourage "bottom-up" citizen initiatives.

Countries in transition face a special challenge: not only are roles changing as a result of the adoption of market-based systems; so are capabilities. Some transition countries retain inherent capabilities in the form of qualified people and usable equipment, but they are not organized to perform in their new roles. Sometimes islands of excellence are found in countries where overall effectiveness has suffered. The task of improving effectiveness here is in some ways easier and in some ways more difficult: easier because capability does not start from a low base, more difficult because rebuilding capability means changing attitudes. Reform is not a matter of simply assigning people new responsibilities.

REINVIGORATING STATE INSTITUTIONS

Acknowledging the state's existing, possibly meager capabilities does not mean accepting them for all time. The second key task of state reform is to reinvigorate the state's institutional capability, *by providing incentives for public officials to perform better while keeping arbitrary action in check.*

Countries struggle to build the institutions for an effective public sector. One reason the task is so difficult is political. Strong interests may develop, for example, to maintain an inequitable and inefficient *status quo*, whereas those who lose out from this arrangement may be unable to exert effective pressure for change.

But the problem of continued ineffectiveness, or of corruption, is not entirely political. Often politicians and other public officials have strong incentives and a sincere interest in improving public sector performance. But managing a public bureaucracy is a complex business that does not lend itself to clear, unambiguous solutions. In fact, building institutions for an effective public sector requires addressing a host of underlying behavioral factors that distort incentives and ultimately lead to poor outcomes. Three basic incentive mechanisms can be used, in a variety of settings, to combat these deeper problems and improve capability.

- Effective rules and restraints
- Greater competitive pressure
- Increased citizen voice and partnership.

Effective Rules and Restraints

Over the long term, building accountability generally calls for formal mechanisms of restraint, anchored in core state institutions. Power can be divided, whether among the judicial, legislative, and executive branches of government or among central, provincial, and local authorities. The broader the separation of powers, the greater the number of veto points that can check arbitrary state action. But multiple veto points are a double-edged sword: they can make it as hard to change the harmful rules as the beneficial ones.

In many developing countries legislative and judicial oversight of the executive is weak. The setting of goals and the links to the policies needed to achieve them are sometimes diffuse, legislatures suffer from limited information and capability, and judicial independence is compromised. An independent judiciary is vital to ensure that the legislative and executive authorities remain fully accountable under the law, and to interpret and enforce the terms of a constitution. Writing laws is the easy part; they need to be enforced if a country is to enjoy the benefits of a credible rule of law. These institutions of restraint take time to establish themselves, but international commitment mechanisms such as international adjudication, or guarantees from international agencies, can serve as a short-term substitute.

A major thrust of any effective strategy to reinvigorate the public sector will be to reduce the opportunities for corruption by cutting back on discretionary authority. Policies that lower controls on foreign trade, remove entry barriers for private industry, and privatize state firms in a way that ensures competition—all of these will fight corruption. Such reforms should not be half-hearted: reforms that open opportunities for private entry into closed sectors of the economy, but leave that entry to the discretion of public officials rather than establish open and competitive processes, also create enormous scope for corruption. Formal checks and balances can also help reduce official corruption, but they are seldom enough. Reforming the civil service, restraining political patronage, and improving civil service pay have also been shown to reduce corruption by giving public officials more incentive to play by the rules.

Where corruption is deeply entrenched, more dramatic efforts will be needed to uproot it. These efforts should be focused on better monitoring of official action—both by formal institutions and by individual citizens—and punishment of wrongdoing in the courts. In Hong Kong (China, as of July 1, 1997), an independent commission against corruption is one successful example of such an approach. Likewise, recent reforms in Uganda have incorporated several elements of the anticorruption strategy outlined here, with some encouraging results. The same mechanisms could be applied around the globe: corruption, despite claims to the contrary, is not culture specific. Reducing it will require a multipronged approach, which must include the private sector and civil society more broadly. The briber has as much responsibility as the bribed; effective penalties on domestic and international business must be part of the solution.

Subjecting the State to more Competition

Governments can improve their capability and effectiveness by introducing much greater competition in a variety of areas: in hiring and promotion, in policy making, and in the way services are delivered.

Boosting Competition within the Civil Service

Whether making policy, delivering services, or administering contracts, a capable, motivated staff is the lifeblood of an effective state. Civil servants can be motivated to perform effectively through a combination of mechanisms to encourage internal competition:

- A recruitment system based on merit, not favoritism
- A merit-based internal promotion system
- Adequate compensation.

Starting in the nineteenth century, all of today's established industrial countries used these principles to build modern professional bureaucracies. More recently these principles have been applied in many countries in East Asia, which have transformed weak, corrupt, patronage based bureaucracies into reasonably well functioning systems. But many developing countries do not even need to look overseas or to history for role models: they exist at home. Central banks, for example, often continue to work effectively and retain their competence even when all other institutions have declined. These agencies work well for all the reasons listed above. They are less subject to political interference. They have limited but clear objectives. They are given adequate resources and training. And their staff are usually better paid than their counterparts in other parts of government.

Cross-country evidence reveals that bureaucracies with more competitive, merit-based recruitment and promotion practices and better pay are more capable. In several countries (Kenya, the Philippines) political appointments run quite deep, whereas countries such as Korea have benefited from reliance on highly competitive recruitment and a promotion system that explicitly rewards merit. Ongoing reforms in the Philippines are examining these issues in an effort to improve bureaucratic capability. By and large, countries in which broader checks and balances are weak need to rely more heavily on more transparent and competitive systems. The experience of certain high performing East Asian economies also shows that meritocracy and long-term career rewards help build an esprit de corps, or a shared commitment to collective goals. This reduces the transactions costs of enforcing internal constraints and builds internal partnerships and loyalty.

In many countries civil servants' wages have eroded as a result of expanding public employment at lower skill levels and fiscal constraints on the total wage bill. The result has been a significant compression of the salary structure and highly uncompetitive pay for senior officials, making it difficult to recruit and retain capable staff. Some countries, such as Uganda, are undertaking far-reaching reforms to reduce overstaffing dramatically, increase average pay, and decompress the salary structure. But in many countries these problems have yet to be addressed.

More competition in the provision of public goods and services

In many developing countries services are delivered badly or not at all. Politicians often intervene in the day-to-day operations of public agencies, and managers have limited flexibility. There is limited accountability for results. And in many countries the public sector has assumed a monopoly in delivery, eliminating pressures for better performance.

Building an effective public sector in these circumstances will mean opening up core government institutions, to improve incentives in areas that the public sector has long monopolized. Dozens of countries throughout the Americas, Europe, and Asia have capitalized on changes in technology and introduced competition in telecommunications and electric power generation. This has resulted in lower unit costs and a rapid expansion of service. Competition is also being enhanced by contracting out services through competitive bids and auctions. This is a significant trend in industrial countries (the United Kingdom, Victoria State in Australia), but such mechanisms are also being used to improve efficiency in developing countries (for example, that of road maintenance in Brazil). Faced with weak administrative capacity, some countries (Bolivia, Uganda) are also contracting out the delivery of social services to nongovernmental organizations.

There is a growing trend to set up focused, performance-based public agencies with more clarity of purpose and greater managerial accountability for outputs or outcomes. New Zealand provides the most dramatic example among the high-income countries. It broke up its conglomerate ministries into focused business units, headed by chief executives on fixed-term, output-based contracts with the authority to hire and fire and to bargain collectively

Singapore has long followed a broadly similar approach with its performance-based statutory boards. Other developing countries are following suit, with Jamaica, for example, establishing executive agencies along the lines of the British model.

But countries with inadequate controls and weak capacity need to proceed with caution. For these countries, giving public managers more flexibility will merely increase arbitrariness and corruption with no commensurate improvement in performance. And writing and enforcing contracts, particularly for complex outputs, require specialized skills that are scarce in many developing countries. These countries need first to strengthen rule-based compliance and financial accountability (as Argentina and Bolivia have done) within the public sector, provide greater clarity of purpose and task, and introduce performance measurement (as in Colombia, Mexico, and Uganda). As output measurement and ex post controls on inputs are strengthened, agencies can be provided more flexibility in exchange for their greater accountability for results.

Bringing the State Closer to People

Governments are more effective which they listen to businesses and citizens and work in partnership with them in deciding and implementing policy. Where governments lack mechanisms to listen, they are not responsive to people's interests, especially those of minorities and the poor, who usually strain to get their voices heard in the corridors of power. And even the best-intentioned government is unlikely to meet collective needs efficiently if it does not know what many of those needs are.

Giving People A Voice

Partnership involves bringing the voice of the poor and of marginalized groups into the very center of the policy making process. In many countries, voice is distributed as unequally as income. Greater information and transparency are vital for informed public debate and for increasing popular trust and confidence in the state—whether in discussing expenditure priorities, designing social assistance programs, or managing forests and other resources. Client surveys (in India, Nicaragua, and Tanzania) and citizen charters (in Malaysia) are providing new options for making voices heard.

The best-established mechanism for giving citizens voice is the ballot box. In 1974 only thirty—nine countries—one in every four worldwide—were independent democracies. Today, 117 countries—nearly two of every three—use open elections to choose their leaders. But periodic voting does not always mean the state is more responsive. Other mechanisms are needed to ensure that the concerns of minorities and the poor are reflected in public policies. Getting genuine intermediary organizations represented on policy making councils is an important first step in articulating citizen interests in public policy making. Even more effective in local and provincial government, these organizations have recently become very active in developing countries—especially where the state has performed poorly and where such organizations are not suppressed.

Broadening Participation

Evidence is mounting that government programs work better when they seek the participation of potential users, and when they tap the community's reservoir of social capital rather than work against it. The benefits show up in smoother implementation, greater sustainability, and better feedback to government agencies. Higher returns from water-borne sanitation systems in Recife, Brazil; housing schemes for the poor in Port Elizabeth, South Africa; forest management efforts in Gujarat State, India; and health care in Khartoum, Sudan, are all testament to the power of partnership—the participation of local people. This is in contrast with top-down approaches, which often fail.

In successful countries policy making has been embedded in consultative processes, which provide civil society, labour unions, and private firms opportunities for input and oversight. In East Asia public-private deliberation councils-such as Korea's monthly .export promotion meetings, Thailand's National Joint Public and Private Consultative Committee, and the Malaysian Business Council-have provided mechanisms for feedback, information sharing and coordination.

Devolving Power, Carefully

The typical developing country has a more centralized government than the typical industrial country. But with some significant exceptions, the past thirty years have seen a small shift in public spending power in developing countries from the national to lower levels. The industrial economies have seen an opposite trend, with spending power moving to the center. Neither of these observations, of course, takes into account the decentralization implicit in recent market reforms, which have clearly reduced the direct power and resources of central government in a broad range of countries.

Decentralization is bringing many benefits in China, India, much of Latin America, and many other parts of the world. It can improve the quality of government and the representation of local business and citizens' interests. And competition among provinces, cities, and localities can spur the development of more-effective policies and programs. But there are three big pitfalls to watch out for:

- *Rising inequality.* The gap between regions can widen—an issue of considerable concern in China, Russia, and Brazil. Labor mobility provides a partial solution, but it in seldom easy, especially in ethnically diverse countries where migrants are not always welcome.
- *Macro-economic instability.* Governments can lose control of Macro-economic policy if local and regional fiscal indiscipline leads to frequent bailouts from the center, as occurred in Brazil.
- *Risk of local capture.* A serious danger is that of local governments falling under the sway of special interests, leading to misuse of resources and of the coercive power of the state

These dangers show, once again, how central government will always play a vital role in sustaining development. The challenge is to find the right division of labor between the center and the other tiers of government.

Strategic Options for Reform

Building a more responsive state requires working on mechanisms that increase openness and transparency, increase incentives for participation in public affairs, and where appropriate, lessen the distance between government and the citizens and communities it is intended to serve. This yields four broad imperatives for policy makers:

- Where appropriate, ensure broad-based public discussion of key policy directions and priorities. At a minimum this includes making available information in the public interest and establishing consultative mechanisms—such as deliberation councils and citizen committees—to gather the views and make known the preferences of affected groups.
- Encourage, where feasible, the direct participation of users and other beneficiaries in the design, implementation, and monitoring of local public goods and services.
- Where decentralization is considered desirable, adopt a carefully staged and/or sectoral approach in priority areas. Introduce strong monitoring mechanisms and make sure sound intergovernmental rules are in place to restrain arbitrary action at the central and the local level.
- At the local level, focus on mechanisms—and horizontal incentives in government's relations with the rest of the community—that build accountability and competition.

Of course, a strategy of more openness and greater decentralization has its dangers. The more numerous the opportunities for participation, the greater the demands that will be made on the state. This can increase the risk of capture by vocal interest groups, or of gridlock. Bringing government closer to some people must not result in taking it even further away from others. Equally, without clear-cut rules to impose restraints on different tiers of government, and incentives to encourage local accountability, the crisis of governance that afflicts many centralized governments will simply be passed down to lower levels. But there are some safe ways to start the ball rolling, including the use of communication and consensus building to render reform intelligible to citizens and firms and enhance its chances of success.

BEYOND NATIONAL BORDERS: FACILITATING GLOBAL COLLECTIVE ACTION

Globalization is a threat to weak or capriciously governed states. But it also opens the way for effective, disciplined states to foster development and economic well-being, and it sharpens the need for effective international cooperation in pursuit of global collective action.

Embracing external competition

The state still defines the policies and rules for those within its jurisdiction, but global events and international agreements are increasingly affecting its choices. People are now more mobile, more educated, and better informed about conditions elsewhere. And involvement in the global economy tightens constraints on arbitrary state action, reduces the state's ability to tax capital, and brings much closer financial market scrutiny of monetary and fiscal policies.

"Globalization" is not yet global—it has yet to touch a large chunk of the world economy. Roughly half of the developing world's people have been left out of the much-discussed rise in the volume of international trade and capital flows since the early 1980s. Governments' hesitance to open up to the world economy is partly understandable. Joining the global economy, like devolving power from the center, carries risks as well as opportunities. For example, it can make countries more vulnerable to external price shocks or to large, destabilizing shifts in capital flows. This makes the state's role all the more critical, both in handling such shocks and in helping people and firms grasp the opportunities of the global marketplace. But the difficulties should not be exaggerated, particularly when laid against the risks of being left out of the globalization process altogether.

The cost of not opening up will be a widening gap in living standards between those countries that have integrated and those that remain outside. For lagging countries the route to higher incomes will lie in pursuing sound domestic policies and building the capability of the state. Integration gives powerful support to such policies—and increases the benefits from them—but it cannot substitute for them. In that sense, globalization begins at home. But multilateral institutions such as the World Trade Organization have an important role to play in providing countries with the incentive to make the leap.

Promoting global collective action

Global integration also gives rise to demands for states to cooperate to combat international threats such as global warming. Economic, cultural, and other differences between countries can make such cooperation difficult—even, at times, impossible. But stronger cooperation is clearly needed for at least five major concerns that transcend national borders:

- *Managing regional crises.* The threat of nuclear war between the superpowers has given way to a mushrooming of smaller conflicts, entailing costly problems of refugee relief and rehabilitation. No solid international framework exists for managing these conflicts or helping avoid them. A more integrated assessment of how state policies (and international assistance) help manage nascent conflict is needed in designing economic and social policy.
- *Promoting global economic stability.* Concern has been growing about the potentially destabilizing effects of large and rapid flows of portfolio capital, particularly when a crisis in one country can spill over into other markets. A variety of international mechanisms have been suggested to guard against such problems, and the International Monetary Fund has recently created a new facility to help members cope with sudden financial crises. But prudent and responsive economic policies at home will be countries' best protection. Growing international labor mobility is also raising a host of issues requiring international collective action.

- *Protecting the environment.* Urgent global environmental issues include climate change, loss of biodiversity, and protection of international waters. International collective action can help through better coordination, greater public awareness, more effective technological transfer, and better national and local practices. Progress has been slow, however, raising the worry that it will take a major environmental catastrophe to goad countries into concerted action.
- *Fostering basic research and the production of knowledge.* Now being revitalized to meet renewed challenges in food production, the Consultative Group on International Agricultural Research has shown how technology can be developed and disseminated through international collective action. Similar consultative mechanisms need to be developed to tackle other pressing research problems in the domains of environmental protection and health.
- *Making international development assistance more effective.* To become more effective, foreign aid needs to be tied more closely to the policies of the recipient countries. A high priority for aid agencies is to systematically channel resources to poor countries with good policies and a strong commitment to institutional reinvigoration.

REMOVING OBSTACLES TO STATE REFORM

The history of state reform in today's established industrial countries offers hope—and gives pause—to today's developing countries. Until the last century many of the problems that now appear to have reduced the effectiveness of the state in the developing world were in plain evidence in Europe, North America, and Japan. But the problems were addressed, and modern states with professional systems emerged. This gives us hope. But it also gives us pause, because institutional strengthening takes time. The reforms of the Meiji restoration, which launched Japan onto the path of development, took almost twenty-five years to take root. A more capable state can be built, but the process will be slow and will require immense political commitment. It is urgent to act now.

Over the past fifteen years many governments have responded to internal and external pressure by launching far-reaching reforms to improve their performance. Typically, changes in macroeconomic policy—dealing with exchange rates, fiscal policy, and trade policy—have come fastest. These reforms have political implications but do not require the overhaul of institutions. They can be undertaken quickly, often through decree, by a small group of competent technocrats. All it takes is the political decision to make the change.

But other state reforms, dealing with regulation, social services, finance, infrastructure, and public works, cannot be accomplished so rapidly because they involve changing institutional structures established for different purposes, to fit different rules of the game. This kind of institutional reform involves wrenching changes in the way government agencies think and act, and often a complete overhaul of long-established systems of patronage and corruption. But such change is absolutely essential if the capability of the state is ever to improve. The two together—good policies and more capable state institutions to implement them—produce much faster economic development.

Comprehensive reform along these lines will take a great deal of time and effort in many developing countries, and the agenda varies considerably from region to region. Reform will also encounter considerable political opposition. But reformers can make a good start by strengthening central agencies for strategic policy formulation, introducing more transparency and competition, hiving off activities and agencies with easily specified outputs, seeking more feedback from users about the delivery of services, and working with labor unions on programs that will enable workers to seek security in change rather than seek security against change.

When do reforms occur ?

Deep distributional conflicts and constraints embedded in state institutions are at the heart of the explanation for so many countries' failure to reform. But they are not immutable. Ultimately, change comes when the incentives to throw out the old policies and old institutional arrangements become stronger than the incentives to keep them. An economic crisis or an external threat, or the arrival of a new government with fewer vested interests in the old system, may provide the impetus for reform. But reform can be delayed if those in power stick with outdated policies because it is in their (or their allies') interest to do so. And the delay can sometimes be painfully long, as in Haiti under the Duvaliers, or Zaire today.

Neighbours, too, can be a powerful motivator for change. There is a clear domino effect at work in the wave of reform sweeping East Asia, Latin America, and much of Eastern Europe and the former Soviet Union. The threat of being left behind can goad countries to improve the functioning of their bureaucracies. But research has yet to explain why some countries respond to crises and others do not. Why, for example, does popular tolerance of inflation seem to be much lower in Asia than in parts of Latin America? And why can some countries endure a long period of economic decline before responding, while others take action much sooner?

Often the analysis of winners and losers yields a prediction of when—or at least whether—reforms will be undertaken. Reforms have little appeal if the winners cannot compensate the losers. Even when the potential gains are enough to allow for compensation, reform can be hard to achieve because the gains are spread over many people, whereas the losers, although smaller in number, are powerful and articulate. A further problem is that the benefits are often realized in the future, whereas the losses are immediate. Yet sometimes conditions have deteriorated so far that the winners far outnumber the losers. Then reform can produce immediate economic and political gains.

How can reforms be sustained ?

Reform-oriented political leaders and elites can speed reform by making decisions that widen people's options, articulate the benefits clearly, and ensure that policies are more inclusive. In recent years farsighted political leaders have transformed the options for their people through decisive reform. They were successful because they made the benefits of change clear to all, and built coalitions that gave greater voice to often-silent beneficiaries. They also succeeded—and this is crucial—because they spelled out a longer-term vision for their society, allowing people to see beyond the immediate pain of adjustment. Effective leaders give their people a sense of owning the reforms—a sense that reform is not something imposed from without.

Reforming the state requires cooperation from all g roups in society. Compensation of groups adversely affected by reform (which may not always be the poorest in society) can help secure their support. Although compensation may be costly in the short run, it will pay off in the long run. Deep-seated differences and mutual suspicions among groups can also delay reform. There are no quick fixes for removing age-old enmities, but social pacts, such as Spain's Moncloa Pacts and Benin's National Economic Conference, can help.

International agencies can encourage and help sustain reform in four ways. First, they can provide important technical advice on what to do and what not to do. This assistance is often invaluable, especially for smaller states that lack the resources to handle all the technical issues internally. But it must be complemented by local expertise, to adapt reforms to local conditions and institutions. The World Trade Organization plays a major role in trade reform, the World Health Organization on health issues, and the International Labour Organization on labour legislation and employment policy. Second, international agencies can provide a wealth of cross-country experience on a wide range of issues. Often staffed by people from all over the world, they can bring in experts from different backgrounds. Third, the financial assistance these agencies provide can help countries endure the early, painful period of reform until the benefits kick in. Fourth, they can provide a mechanism for countries to make external commitments, making it more difficult to backtrack on reforms. It the history of development assistance teaches anything, however, it is that external support can achieve little where the domestic will to reform is lacking.

GOOD GOVERNMENT IS NOT A LUXURY—IT IS A VITAL NECESSITY FOR DEVELOPMENT

The approach of the twenty-first century brings great promise of change and reason for hope. In a world of dizzying changes in markets, civil societies, and global forces, the state is under pressure to become more effective, but it is not yet adapting rapidly enough to keep pace. Not surprisingly, there is no unique model for change, and reforms will often come slowly because they involve a fundamental rethinking of the roles of institutions and the interactions between citizens and government. But the issues raised in this Report are now an integral part of the rethinking of the state in many parts of the world and are on the agenda of the international organizations that assist them.

People living with ineffective states have long suffered the consequences in terms of postponed growth and social development. But an even bigger cost may now threaten states that postpone reforms: political and social unrest and, in some cases, disintegration, exacting a tremendous toll on stability, productive capacity, and human life. The enormous cost of state collapse has naturally turned attention to prevention as a preferable and potentially less costly course of action-but there are no shortcuts. Once the spiral into collapse has occurred, there are no quick fixes.

Instances of state collapse are both extreme and unique, but they are growing. As the Report elaborates, no simple generalizations about their causes or effects can be made, nor, for that matter, are there any easy solutions to their reconstruction; each case brings its own challenges for countries, their neighbors, and the international system. The consequences, however, are almost uniformly borne by ordinary people, illustrating once again how fundamental an effective, responsive state is to the long-term health and wealth of society.

The quest for a more effective state even in the established industrial countries suggests that the returns to incremental improvements are high. This is especially true in countries where the effectiveness of the state is low. Over time, even the smallest increases in the capability of the state have been shown to make a vast difference to the quality of people's lives, not least because reforms tend to produce their own virtuous circle. Small improvements in the state's effectiveness lead to higher standards of living, in turn paving the way for more reforms and further development.

A tour of the world's economies in 1997 would turn up countless examples of these virtuous circles in action. But it would provide equally plentiful evidence of the reverse: countries and regions caught in vicious cycles of poverty and underdevelopment set in train by the chronic ineffectiveness of the state. Such cycles can all too easily lead to social violence, crime, corruption, and instability, all of which undermine the state's capacity to support development—or even to function at all. The crucial challenge facing states is to take those steps, both small and large, toward better government that set economies on the upward path, using the two-part framework suggested in this Report. Reform of state institutions is long, difficult, and politically sensitive. But if we now have a better sense of the size of the reform challenge, we are also much more aware of the costs of leaving things as they are.

3

TRANSNATIONAL COOPERATIONS, MARKET STRUCTURE : WORLD INVESTMENT REPORT, 1997

Foreign direct investment (FDI) continues to be a driving force of the globalization process that characterizes the modern world economy. The current boom in FDI flows, which has been accompanied by increasing. flows of foreign portfolio equity investments, underscores the increasingly important role played by transnational corporations (TNCs) in both developed and developing countries. This role has been facilitated by the liberalization of FDI policies that has taken place in many countries in recent years, as part of an overall movement towards more open and market-friendly policies.

GLOBAL AND REGIONAL TRENDS

The growing size and importance of international production

With an estimated $7 trillion in global sales in 1995—the value of goods and services produced by some 280,000 foreign affiliates—international production outweighs exports as the dominant mode of servicing foreign markets. The growth of global sales has exceeded that of exports of goods and services by a factor of 1.2 to 1.3 since 1987. But as far as developing countries are concerned, despite their growing involvement in international production—of the world's 45,000 parent firms, 7,900 firms were based in developing countries in the mid-1990s, compared to 3,800 in the late 1980s—exports continue to be the principal mode of delivering goods and services to foreign markets.

The gross product of foreign affiliates, a measure of their output, almost tripled between 1982 and 1994, and its share of world output rose slightly, from 5 per cent in 1982 to 6 per cent in 1994. In developing countries, the output of foreign affiliates has contributed (in 1994) more to gross domestic product than it has in developed countries: 9 per cent compared to 5 per cent.

The global FDI stock, a measure of the investment underlying international production, increased fourfold between 1982 and 1994; over the same period, it doubled as a percentage of world gross domestic product to 9 per cent. In 1996, the global FDI stock was valued at $3.2 trillion. Its rate of growth over the past decade (1986-1995) was more than twice that of gross fixed capital formation, indicating an increasing internationalization of national production systems. The worldwide assets of foreign affiliates, valued at $8.4 trillion in 1994, also increased more rapidly than world gross fixed capital formation.

The upward trend manifested in all of the indicators of international production, in absolute terms as well as in relation to various macro-economic indicators, suggests that international production is becoming a more significant element in the world economy. Its importance is apparent in the activities in which TNCs are involved. On the technology side, for example, an estimated 70 per cent of the global payments of royalties and fees constitute transactions between parent firms and their foreign affiliates.

Transnational corporations raise capital from a variety of sources at home and abroad: commercial banks, local and international equity markets, public organizations and their own corporate systems in the form of internally generated profits for reinvestment. Taking all these sources of finance into account, investment in foreign affiliates—the investment component of international production—was an estimated $1.4 trillion in 1996. Of this, only $350 billion, i.e., a quarter, were financed by FDI flows. This means therefore that the weight of international production is also considerably larger: expressed as a ratio of world gross fixed capital formation, about one-fifth was undertaken by foreign affiliates. (This measure does not capture additional investment controlled by TNCs via various non-equity measures, including corporate alliances.)

Returning to FDI flows themselves, the boom that began in 1995 continues, with inflows setting a new record of around $350 billion in 1996, a 10 per cent increase. Fifty-four countries on the inflow side and twenty countries on the outflow side set new records in 1996. Unlike the two previous investment booms in 1979-1981 and 1987-1990 (the first one being led by petroleum investments in oil producing countries, and the second one being concentrated in the developed world), the current boom is characterized by considerable developing-country participation on the inflow side, although it is driven primarily by investments originating in just two countries—the United States and the United Kingdom. There are signs that an even greater number of countries will take part in the present boom as it unfolds on the inward side (e.g., developing countries in Latin America), as well as on the outward side (e.g., France, Germany and Asian developing countries).

During 1995-1996, the share of developing countries in global inflows was 34 per cent. Although this is not much higher than the developing-country share during the investment boom at the beginning of the 1980s, qualitatively it reflects a wide variety of location-specific advantages enjoyed by developing countries over and above natural resources. The composition of the top developing-country recipients has also changed dramatically between these two investment booms, with oil producing countries now featuring far less prominently among the top recipients. Interestingly, the developing—country share of global inflows has been on the rise during the current boom, while during the 1987-1990 boom it declined. That decline went hand in hand with a boom in intradeveloped country mergers and acquisitions (M&As), at that time in response to heightened protectionist pressures in key developed countries. As in earlier FDI booms, the bulk of FDI flows goes to a limited number of developing countries.

Even in the current boom, cross-border M&As, especially in the United States and Western Europe, are playing an important role in boosting FDI, although this time there is no ensuing decline in the developing-country share of inflows. The value of such M&As increased by 16 per cent in 1996, to $275 billion. If majority-held transactions only are taken into account, the value of cross-border M&As in 1996 would be $163 billion, or 47 per cent of global FDI inflows (though the measured values are not strictly comparable).

Complementing the increases in M&As and FDI flows, the number of cross-border inter-firm agreements (equity and non-equity, other than strategic research-and-development (R&D) partnerships) has also increased. In 1995, nearly 4,600 such agreements were concluded, compared with about 1,760 in 1990. These agreements take place primarily between firms based in developed countries: United States firms participated in 80 per cent of them, European Union firms in 40 per cent and Japanese firms in 38 per cent. Recently, firms based in developing countries have also begun to conclude such agreements actively. The numbers of cross-border inter-firm agreements (other than strategic R&D partnerships) with developing-country firm participation has increased in absolute numbers, as well as a share of the world total (from 27 per cent during 1990-1992 to 35 per cent during 1993-1995). Although there was a decline in 1995, the number of strategic R&D partnerships (in core technologies, such as information technologies and biotechnology), has also been rising steadily since 1990. Again, developing-country firms assumed a bigger role in strategic partnerships (3 per cent in 1989 to 13 per cent in 1995), suggesting that these firms may have attained sufficient technological sophistication and capacity to make them worth having as partners.

Despite the growing number of small and medium-sized enterprises with investments abroad, a good part of FDI continues to be concentrated in the hands of a small number of companies. The largest 100 TNCs, ranked on the basis of the size of foreign assets, own $1.7 trillion assets in their foreign affiliates, controlling an estimated one-fifth of global foreign assets. In the United States, 25 TNCs are responsible for half of that country's outward stock, a share that has remained almost unchanged during the past four decades. For six out of nine developed countries for which such data are available, 25 TNCs account for more than a half of their respective countries' outward stocks.

For the first time, two developing-country TNCs, Daewoo Corporation (Republic of Korea) and Petroleos de Venezuela S.A. (Venezuela), have entered the list of the top 100 TNCs. Daewoo Corporation also tops the list of the 50 largest TNCs based in developing countries for the second year running, while Royal Dutch Shell (United Kingdom/Netherlands) continues to top the list of the largest 100 TNCs for the fifth consecutive year. With foreign sales amounting to $2 trillion and foreign employment close to 6 million persons in 1995, the largest 100 TNCs are prominent actors in international production. The top 50 TNCs based in developing countries, however, are catching up. While their foreign assets totalled only $79 billion in 1995, the increase in these assets between 1993 and 1995 was 280 per cent—compared with 30 per cent for the top 100 firms.

Both the top 100 TNCs worldwide and the top 50 developing-country TNCs are becoming more transnationalized, at a faster rate in the latter case. The food firms in the list of the top 50 developing-country TNCs exhibited the biggest increase in transnationality (measured on the basis of a combined index of the ratios of foreign assets, foreign sales and foreign employment in their respective totals)—from 16 per cent in 1993 to 37 per cent in 1995. On the whole, smaller firms tend to be more transnationalized than larger ones; for example, Solvay SA (Belgium) ranked seventy-fourth on the basis of the size of foreign assets, but ranked fifth on the basis of the transnationality index in the list of the top 100 TNCs. And Panamerican Beverages Inc. (Mexico) took the first place in the list of the top 50 developing-country firms on the basis of the transnationality index, as opposed to twenty-first on the basis of the value of foreign assets.

The Triad (European Union, United States and Japan) is home to 87 per cent of the top 100 TNCs and accounts for 88 per cent of their foreign assets. Likewise, China, the Republic of Korea, the Hong Kong Special Administrative Region of the People's Republic of China (hereinafter: Hong Kong, China) and Mexico are home to 56 per cent of the top 50 firms based in developing economies, and account for two-thirds of their foreign assets. Electronics is the most important industry as far as the largest TNCs are concerned, accounting for some 16 per cent of all firms' foreign assets in each of the two lists of top TNCs. Automotive and chemical firms also feature prominently in both lists, but more so in the list of the top 100 firms. Petroleum and mining firms, although few in number, tend to rank high in both lists.

The expansion of international production would not have been possible if it were not for the ongoing liberalization of FDI regimes. The trend towards greater liberalization was sustained again in 1996, with 98 changes in the direction of investment liberalization and promotion of a total number of 114 changes in investment regimes introduced during that year in 65 countries. Over the period 1991-1996, indeed, some 95 per cent of a total of 599 changes in the regulatory FDI regimes of countries were in the direction of liberalization. They mostly involved the opening of industries previously closed to FDI, the streamlining or abolition of approval procedures and the provision of incentives.

The desire of governments to facilitate FDI is also reflected in the dramatic increase in the number of bilateral investment treaties (BITs) for the protection and promotion of investment throughout the 1990s. As of 1 January 1997, there were 1,330 such treaties in the world, involving 162 countries, a threefold increase in half a decade. Around 180 such treaties were concluded in 1996 alone—one every second day.

The pattern of these treaties has changed considerably in recent years. While virtually all BITs used to have one developed country as a partner, and such countries took part in 83 per cent of all such treaties as of the end of the 1980s, by 1996 only 62 per cent of the world total involved developed countries. Indeed, countries in Central and Eastern Europe and developing countries have begun to conclude BITs among themselves. At the beginning of 1997, 16 per cent of all BITs were among developing countries, rising from 11 per cent at the end of the 1980s. In 1996 alone, nearly a third of all BITs were concluded between developing countries, led by China, Chile, Algeria and the Republic of Korea.

New ground is being broken at the regional and multilateral levels. Negotiations on an investment framework are taking place in the Organisation for Economic Co-operation and Development, with the conclusion of a free-standing Multilateral Agreement on Investment rescheduled for May 1998. In the framework of the discussions on a possible Free Trade Area of the Americas, a Working Group on Investment has been established, as well as a Working Group on Competition Policy. In the meantime, the Ministerial Meeting of the World Trade Organization in Singapore in December 1996 established two working groups to examine the relationship between trade and investment and between trade and competition policy. Independently of these developments, the ASEAN members are preparing to launch the ASEAN Investment Area. Cooperation among ASEAN members in the area of investment has already progressed with the signing of a protocol (in September 1996) updating the 1987 ASEAN Agreement for the Promotion and Protection of Investment.

The ongoing globalization of production begs the question of whether the upward trend in FDI flows witnessed to date will continue into the next century. A survey of foreign investors suggests that this may, indeed, be the case. More specifically, foreign sales are expected to increase as a proportion of total sales, especially for Japanese and United States' firms. Production by foreign affiliates is also expected to increase as a proportion of total production by TNCs, while home-country exports are expected to remain constant. Mergers and acquisitions, joint ventures and other equity and non-equity types of inter-firm agreements are expected to go hand in hand with the growth in FDI. Although smaller firms will be stepping up investments abroad, large firms will continue to account for the lion's share of outward investment. Corporate restructuring in developed countries, aimed at improving efficiency and modernization, is expected to continue, giving rise to efficiency-seeking investment. However, accessing markets will remain the principal motive for investing abroad: survey respondents placed twice as much weight on production for local markets than on labour-cost factors. Countries in developing Asia and, to a lesser extent, in Latin America and Central and Eastern Europe, are likely to be the main beneficiaries of the corporate restructuring. Investment at home generally will be given a lower priority than it has received until now. In contrast, investment in the same region will continue to be significant, while investment in more distant countries is likely to increase, thus broadening the geographical scope of international production. Foreign investors foresee dramatic increases in investments in infrastructure, distribution, non-financial services and automobiles, but slower growth in financial services and real estate. All in all, the growth of FDI is expected to remain brisk over the next five years, both in terms of absolute levels and as a proportion of corporate investment.

Developed countries' investments abroad reached an all-time high of $295 billion in 1996. The investment picture for developed countries is dominated by the United States, which, with $85 billion is by far the largest home country (by a margin of $31 billion over the United Kingdom, the second largest home country), as well as, with $85 billion, the largest recipient country (by a margin of $42 billion over China, the second largest recipient) in 1996. Around two-fifths of United States outflows go to the European Union and around 30 per cent to developing countries. Growing consumer markets have encouraged United States investments in the latter, while sluggish growth in the former has led to a decrease in its share of United State outflows. Investment flows into the United States—mostly in the form of M&As—were stimulated by its strong and sustained growth performance and potential for high profits.

Western Europe received $105 billion in inflows and invested $176 billion abroad in 1996. More European Union investment is now directed to non-European Union countries than in 1992, when the internal market was completed. These countries are investing increasingly outside Western Europe, mostly in North America, developing Asia and, to a lesser extent, Central and Eastern Europe. Nearly a half of—the European Union's investment outflows take the form of M&As. The share of European Union inflows accounted for by M&As, however, is considerably smaller because of regulatory and other barriers in existence in some countries (such as Italy and Germany) on this mode of investment. Japanese investment in the European Union is declining—to almost $2 billion in 1994, compared with nearly $7 billion at its peak in 1990.

Overall, however, the recovery of Japan's outward investment continues, with outflows reaching $23 billion in 1996, slightly over half their peak level of $41 billion during 1989-1991. (It should be noted that reinvested earnings, estimated at $14 billion in the manufacturing sector alone in 1994, are not included in these figures.) Japanese outflows are geared overwhelmingly towards developing Asia and the United States. But in Asia, China is no longer the favourite location and, in fact, its share of Japanese outflows declined in 1996. Brazil is beginning to receive Japanese investment, with Japanese outflows there (on the basis of notifications) tripling in 1996 over 1995. On the inward side, Japan remains a small FDI recipient, with inflows declining to $220 million in 1996.

Although developed countries received a record $208 billion in FDI flows in 1996, there has been a steady decline in their share of global inflows since 1989. That decline can be attributed partly to the increasing attractiveness of developing countries, especially those that are growing rapidly and have large domestic markets. Furthermore, some developed countries that are large outward investors are small investment recipients, especially in relation to the size of their economies; notable example are Germany, Italy and Japan. And as the rationalization of production through FDI in response to regional integration arrangements among developed countries (notably, the European Union) has reached a high level, firms are turning increasingly towards untapped markets found mostly in the developing world.

In light of the above, it is not surprising that developing countries received $129 billion of FDI inflows in 1996 and invested $51 billion abroad-both amounts are all-time highs. Their share of world inflows rose to 37 per cent in 1996 (from 30 per cent in 1995), while their share of outflows was 15 per cent in that year. With $42 billion, China was the largest developing-country recipient; the country's success can be attributed mostly to its large and growing domestic market, "soft landing" and macro-economic reforms, as well as to measures to promote investment in provinces other than those in the coastal areas.

Every developing region saw an increase in inflows. Even the 48 least developed countries experienced an increase in inflows of 56 per cent in 1996, to $1.6 billion. Cambodia was the largest recipient in this group of countries. In addition, and despite the small size of inflows (both in absolute values and as a share of all developing-country inflows), FDI is very important for many of these economies; inflows in as many as eight countries reached 10 per cent as a share of gross fixed capital formation in 1995.

Within the group of the least developed countries, there are significant disparities in performance as regards FDI. The Asian least developed countries are benefiting from the Asian industrializing economies' process of industrial restructuring in the framework of the "flying-geese" model, not only because the offer complementary locational advantages in the form of low-cost labour, but also because of their geographical proximity to them. More than four-fifths and nearly two-fifths, respectively, of cumulative investments received by Bangladesh and Myanmar over the period 1990-1994, for example, came from developing Asia. Since a similar "in-tandem" restructuring process is not taking place in Africa, the least developed countries in that continent do not have the same opportunity to benefit from the type of intra-regional FDI inflows that is the outcome of this process in Asia.

With $81 billion in inflows in 1996, South, East and South-East Asia received about two-thirds of the developing-country total in that year. The 25 per cent increase in these inflows over 1995 was also in sharp contrast with the large decline in the rate of growth of exports and, to a lesser extent, of the gross domestic product, in that year. China accounted for over two-fifths of the $16 billion increase in investment inflows in the region.

Next to China, Singapore was the second largest investment recipient, with inflows worth $9 billion, exceeding the combined inflows of the other newly industrializing economies (Hong Kong, China, Republic of Korea and Taiwan Province of China). Flows into Hong Kong, China, were $2.5 billion in 1996. Foreign investor confidence in Hong Kong, China, after its reversion to China on 1 July 1997 is strong, as indicated by a number of surveys of foreign (and local) companies. Indonesia, Malaysia, Philippines and Thailand together received some $17 billion in 1996, an increase of 43 per cent over 1995. Together, ASEAN members have, however, seen their share of the region's investment inflows decline, from 61 per cent during 1990-1991 to below 30 per cent during 1994-1996, attributed to domestic capacity constraints, infrastructure bottlenecks and, in particular, stiff competition from other economies. A 34 per cent increase in investment flows to India (to $2.5 billion) pushed total inflows to South Asia to $3.5 billion. Investment from other Asian economies in India, especially from the Republic of Korea, are outstripping those of some developed countries, such as the United States and the United Kingdom.

South, East and South-East Asia are emerging as important outward sources of FDI. Indeed, the region is the largest source of FDI in the developing world, with outflows increasing by 10 per cent in 1996, to $46 billion. Hong Kong, China is the single largest outward investor ($27 billion in 1996). Recently, the geographical scope of developing Asia's outward FDI has expanded to include non-traditional destinations, such as the European Union, Central and Eastern Europe and Africa. The extent to which Asian developing economies are transnationalized is reflected in the increasing ratios of investment outflows to gross fixed capital formation for the region as a whole, as well as for individual economies. That ratio, for example, is higher for Singapore (14 per cent) and Malaysia (11 %) than for Western Europe (10 %) and the United States (9 %).

Investment flows into Latin America and the Caribbean increased by 52 per cent in 1996, the highest increase of any developing region, to a record level of nearly $39 billion. Far-reaching changes in the region's FDI regimes—both at the national level and through the conclusion of bilateral investment treaties—have certainly contributed to this performance. Even during the turbulence in portfolio investment flows into that region in 1994 and 1995, FDI flows registered small but steady increases. Latin America and the Caribbean now account for 30 per cent of all developing country inflows. Investment inflows into Argentina tripled in 1996 to $4.3 billion, propelled by the country's membership in MERCOSUR (which contributed particularly to automobile investments), the liberalization of mining legislation and privatization schemes. But the most noteworthy performance has been that of Brazil. With nearly $10 billion, Brazil has surpassed Mexico (with around $8 billion) as the star performer in Latin America in 1996. (In the first four months of 1997, inflows were over $4 billion—two and a half times higher than inflows in the same period in 1996.) This represents a dramatic reversal: in 1992, with $2 billion, Brazil ranked third in the region (after both Mexico and Argentina). The upswing in Brazil's inflows is the outcome of large investments in automobiles (in the context of intra-regional production rationalization triggered by MERCOSUR) and the reactivation of its privatization programme. Foreign-investor confidence in Brazil (and in the region as a whole) is high: in a recent survey, company executives expressed more confidence in Latin America's prospects now than five years ago, placing Brazil, Mexico and Chile in top places.

The United States remains the foremost foreign investor in the region, with firms investing now more heavily in Brazil than in any other country there. Canada's investment in Latin America and the Caribbean is also Sizeable, but concentrated mostly in mining and exploration. Western Europe's investment in Latin America and the Caribbean (largely from Germany and Spain) is on the rise, and is mostly directed towards Brazil, Argentina and Mexico (in natural resources and services). Almost a half of Western Europe's investment into that region has come through privatization schemes, but in 1995 and 1996 greenfield investment has also been prevalent in automobile manufacturing. Japanese investment in Latin America remains small and highly concentrated in tax havens in the Caribbean. Intra-regional investment has increased substantially, with Chile, Brazil and Argentina being the principal source countries, and Argentina, Peru and Venezuela the principal destinations. Developing Asian countries continue to invest in export-related industries, although market-seeking investments spurred by the region's recent integration efforts are also on the rise.

Africa continues to receive small levels of investment flows (nearly $5 billion in 1996), an increase of only 5 per cent, the smallest of any developing region. On average, Africa's share of developing-country inflows has more than halved between 1986-1990 and 1991-1996—to 5 per cent in the latter period. Political unrest, armed conflict, low domestic investment levels and frequent changes in economic policies that affect business calculations of expected risks and returns have contributed to this relative decline.

However, Africa's investment performance looks less gloomy when put into perspective. In relation to the size of a number of economies, those investments can be fairly significant. For the region as a whole, the ratio of investment inflows to gross fixed capital formation was 5.4 per cent, compared with 5.5 per cent for Asia and 5.9 per cent for Western Europe during the first half of the 1990s. Putting the size of Africa's FDI stock in relation to the size of Africa's domestic market (GDP) yields a share of 10 per cent—compared with 14 per cent for Asia, 18 per cent for Latin America and the Caribbean and 13 per cent for Western Europe in 1995. While these figures suggest that the significance of the investment that Africa receives (without the benefit of large intra-regional investment) is certainly not negligible, they do not say anything about Africa's need for investment nor, for that matter, the continent's potential.

Prospects for increased flows to some parts of Africa are encouraging. Favourable growth performances, further investment and trade liberalization and privatization, regional cooperation agreements and the establishment of links with other regions are all likely to increase the region's attractiveness. In addition, South Africa could begin to play a significant role as a "growth pole", contributing to the region's economic development through FDI and trade. As regards the former, South Africa's contribution could be through the provision of investment capital, adding to capital formation in the recipient economies; the transfer of technology; the development of local human resources; and the opening up of its own market to the exports of foreign affiliates that have invested in neighbouring economies. Indeed, the question has arisen whether South African firms can induce the development of new industries, especially in manufacturing, in its neighlours by establishing an intra-regional division of labour in the framework of which production at home is upgraded to capital-and technology—intensive activities. In the "flying geese" process of industrial restructuring and upgrading, South Africa would play the lead role, similar to the role played by Japan in the context of Asia's development. At this point in time, however, it appears that the necessary conditions for this type of intra—regional restructuring to occur are still far from being met, including—to stay within the metaphor—because many of South Africa's neighbours are still in the "nest-building" stage.

After large disinvestments in West Asia in 1995 that resulted in negative inflows, particularly in Saudi Arabia and Yemen, inflows attained a level of nearly $2 billion in 1996. Excluding these two countries, investment flows into West Asia show a much more stable trend. In fact, the volatility of inflows to these two countries—albeit important ones—masks considerable improvements in the investment performance of other countries in the region in response to successful efforts to create business-friendly environments.

Over time, the share of West Asia in total developing country investment inflows has been declining—from 30 per cent during the first half of the 1980s to only 2 per cent during the first half of the 1990s. That shift reflects largely decreasing investment flows to oil producing economies (Saudi Arabia, Oman, Qatar and United Arab Emirates). While petroleum naturally remains the most popular industry in these economies in the non-oil producing countries (Jordan, Lebanon and Turkey) investments go mainly to manufacturing and services.

In 1996, FDI flows to Central and Eastern Europe experienced a decline—to $12 billion from $14 billion in 1995, partly reflecting declines in privatization-related investments in Hungary and the Czech Republic. As long as investment flows to that region depend to a large extent on the participation of foreign investors in privatization programmes, a certain degree of "lumpiness"—year-to-year volatility—is to be expected. The decline might also stem from other problems related to the transition to a market economy. Foreign investors, for example, might have overestimated the region's ability to absorb investments and might have temporarily shelved their plans for expansion. However, despite the decline, flows in 1996 were still more than twice as high as the annual average during 1992-1994. The estimated FDI stock in Central and Eastern Europe was $46 billion in 1996—almost comparable to the 1996 investment flows to China ($42 billion).

Investment flows to Central and Eastern Europe remain concentrated in the Czech Republic, Hungary and Poland, together accounting for some two-thirds of the region's inflows. Transnational corporations from Western Europe dominate the investment picture, followed by corporations from the United States and, more recently, the Asian newly industrializing economies. A small but growing share of inflows is attributed to corporations based in Central and Eastern Europe itself. This is also reflected in the fact that 16 per cent of the BITs concluded by Central and Eastern European countries has been with other countries in the same region.

Substantial flows of foreign portfolio equity investment to emerging markets is a recent phenomenon dating only from the early 1990s. The year 1993 was the watershed for such flows when their level trebled, to $45 billion, from the previous year. However, the level of these flows fell in the two subsequent years in response to the Mexican peso crisis—by 27 per cent and 2 per cent in 1994 and 1995, respectively—but recovered in 1996. The volume of new equity raised on international capital markets by emerging markets in that year increased by 34 per cent, reaching some $15 billion.

In principle, foreign portfolio equity investment and direct investment are quite distinct. By definition, foreign portfolio equity investment is distinguished from FDI by the degree of management control that foreign investors exercise in a company. Portfolio equity investors usually provide only financial capital without any involvement in a company's management, and typically have a shorter-term investment horizon than direct investors. The latter have a significant and long—lasting management interest in the company in which an investment is made. In general, the dividing line between the two types of investment is the threshold of a 10 per cent equity stake. In practice, however, the distinction between the two categories of investment is often less clear-cut and is subject to a number of qualifications.

The overriding motivation for investment by portfolio equity investors is their participation in earnings of local enterprises through capital gains and dividends. Transnational corporations tend to be more interested in accessing markets and resources and, more generally, in the contribution that an investment can make to the competitiveness of the transnational corporate system as a whole. The contrast in motives between TNCs and portfolio equity investors is not, however, always so stark. In the notable case of venture capital investment, the investment horizon tends to be somewhat longer than for foreign portfolio equity investment, and the existence of significant (and perhaps also long-term) management control is not unusual, although the foremost motivation is to share in the capital gains of the equity of a local enterprise when it is listed eventually on the stock exchange.

Two major factors lie behind the rise in foreign portfolio equity investment flows into emerging markets: the liberalization and globalization of financial markets and the concentration of substantial financial resources in the hands of institutional investors. Investments into emerging markets have been facilitated by the rapid provision of market information made possible by improvements in communications technology and the willingness of portfolio equity investors to bear greater risks in the expectation of reaping higher returns in these new and fast-growing markets. The higher returns have been made possible by the sustained superior growth performance of emerging markets in comparison to that of developed economies during the 1990s. Stock market capitalization in emerging markets has also grown much faster than that in developed countries. However, as in the case of FDI flows, portfolio equity investment flows have remained skewed towards a small group of mostly upper middle-income emerging markets, along with two large low-income countries with impressive growth performances and prospects. (Asia alone accounted for 53 per cent of net foreign portfolio equity investment flows to emerging markets in 1995.) This is not surprising. For many large institutional investors, it is more attractive to invest in more mature emerging markets that tend to have a relatively large market capitalization and provide high liquidity levels, relatively fast and reliable settlement systems and a generally more developed market infrastructure.

There is also a certain level of concentration when it comes to the origin of foreign portfolio equity investment flows. Over the period 1992-1994, it is estimated that more than 35 per cent of flows to emerging markets originated in the United States, 15 per cent in Japan and 11 per cent in the United Kingdom. In recent years, investors from Hong Kong and Singapore have also invested in emerging markets. For the United States, the most important scurce country, investment flows to emerging markets have followed the global trend, increasing substantially in 1993, decreasing in 1994 and 1995, and rising again in 1996, despite a clear upturn in stock-market returns in the United States.

In light of the vastly increased volume of foreign portfolio equity investment flows to emerging markets, the impact of these flows on host-country economies is likely to be significant. Although such investments can make an important contribution to the finarcing of equity capital of local companies, concerns have been expressed by host countries.particularly as regards the volatility of these flows and their effect on exchange rates. In order to address this issue, it is necessary to investigate the causes of that volatility and the availability of measures or mechanisms to reduce or withstand it.

FOREIGN DIRECT INVESTMENT, MARKET STRUCTURE AND COMPETITION POLICY

Functionng of Markets

As countries liberalize their FDI regimes and firms increase their investment activities across national borders, maintaining the proper functioning of markets assumes increasing importance. Freer flows of FDI mean a greater reliance on market forces to determine the volume and distribution of FDI and its economic impact. Countries, especially developing countries that are liberalizing rapidly, are therefore interested in ensuring that the reduction of regulatory barriers to FDI and the institution of standards of treatment are not accompanied by the emergence of private barriers to entry and anti-competitive behaviour of firms. Competition and competition policy in relation to FDI need, therefore, to be better understood. Part Two of WIR 97 focuses on the relationships between FDI, market structure and competition, and considers policy implications arising from these relationships, especially as they concern developing countries. The discussion of these issues rounds out, therefore, discussions in previous Reports, of FDI liberalization and related regulatory frameworks, including those relating to international investment arrangements.

The ultimate objective of FDI liberalization is to enhance economic growth and welfare in countries. Success in this respect depends not only on increasing FDI flows—and the capital, technology, managerial know—how and market access associated with them—but also on ensuring that the industries and markets in which TNCs participate operate efficiently. In market—based economies, the efficient functioning of markets depends on the contestility of markets—or the ease with which firms can enter and exit them—and the extent and nature of competition in markets. Foreign—direct-investment liberalization, by removing formal barriers to the entry of FDI, can increase the contestability of national markets and inject greater competition into them. However, because of the ownership-specific assets of TNCs, their transnational organizational structures and the relatively greater competitive strengths that they often have vis-a-vis domestic firms, FDI could also increase concentration, and TNCs could indulge, like dominant firms generally, in restrictive or anti-competitive practices. Government policy and practices aimed at attracting investments that grant exclusivity or allow firms, domestic or foreign, to erect informal impediments to the entry of other firms could contribute to the potential for such practices.

Competition Policies

Governments rely on several policy tools to ensure that their markets remain contestable and that competition in markets is maintained as far as possible, so that economic growth and welfare are not adversely affected by the inefficient allocation or use of resources. The tools of such policy include trade policy, FDI policy, regulatory policy with respect to domestic economic activity, and competition policy. While the first three comprise rules and regulations that serve several purposes and not only that of maintaining competition with a view to fostering efficiency, the last relates specifically to the rules and regulations—implemented by competition authorities—with respect to arrangements among firms/suppliers and the conduct of individual firms/suppliers, generally but not exclusively, in national markets. It is increasingly recognised that consistency and coherence between the different policies—some of which, as mentioned above, could serve competing objectives—are important. This is reflected in the fact that, in many developing countries, trade liberalization, FDI liberalization and domestic deregulation are currently taking place simultaneously. This ensures that the contestability and competition introduced by one set of policies are not undermined by another; but it also makes the pain of adjustment to competition, especially for hitherto protected domestic firms, a problem requiring attention and action by governments.

Even as barriers between national markets are reduced and producers can locate anywhere in the world (or in a region) to transact with buyers also located anywhere, the markets for many products remain national in scope. The include markets for products that can only be delivered through the presence of the producer at the location of the buyer—notably, services—and markets in countries that have significant restrictions on trade. The interaction of TNCs with the structure of these national markets, the process of competition and the performance of firms and industries within host countries all therefore continue to be of interest, especially for developing countries.

The opening up of economies to inward FDI can contribute directly towards increasing the contestability of—or potential competition in—host country markets. Sellers participating in these markets can now include not only domestic producers and (in the case of goods and tradeable services) exporters from other countries, but also TNCs from other countries that establish affiliates (as well as contractual arrangements with other firms) to produce in and for local markets. Furthermore, TNCs, with their ownership-specific or competitive advantages, are often better able than domestic firms to overcome some of the cost-related barriers to entry that limit the number of firms in an industry and the markets for its products. This potential for increasing competition by allowing FDI entry is particularly important for many service markets, in which competition through arm's length international trade is not possible or is limited.

Transnational corporations typically participate to a greater extent in industries that are more concentrated, at the national as well as the international level. This is largely due to that fact that industry concentration and the competitive advantages that enable firms to become transnational share common causes. However, inward FDI, when it takes place, can itself affect the concentration of producers in a host-country industry and, hence, of sellers in the market for its products. The nature of this effect depends, initially, upon whether or not the mode of entry is such as to add to the number of suppliers (and the quantity supplied) in a market and, subsequently, upon several factors related to the relative size, competitive strength and mode of competition of foreign affiliates and domestic and other firms competing in a market. In developed host countries, on balance, these factors are likely to be conducive towards reducing market concentration—or, at least, not to increase concentration.

In developing economies, the picture is more complex. Although the mode of entry of FDI into developing economies—generally, greenfield investment-is conducive to reducing concentration, market concentration has often been found to increase. Several factors may be involved: the disparity in size between foreign affiliates and domestic firms; the greater production efficiency or sales capability of foreign affiliates (which can lead to the exit of domestic enterprises that have yet to build up the necessary capabilities to withstand international competition, or to their merger with foreign firms); the use of modes of competition that are new to host country markets; the introduction of new products for which no other local producers or substitutes are available; and, most importantly in the case of tradeable goods and services, restrictions on international trade that give local producers protected markets. If there is a sizeable number of domestic firms that have accumulated some competitive strengths and/or the capabilities to learn from foreign firms, increased concentration is less likely. Similarly, the presence of imports can curb the possible dominance of foreign affiliates in a market. The increasing role of small and medium-sized TNCs and TNCs from developing countries, with sometimes smaller competitive advantages compared with those of large TNCs from developed countries, is also likely to contribute towards lessening the tendency towards greater concentration of host country markets in industries with substantial inward FDI.

The production efficiency of foreign affiliates is often higher than that of domestic firms in host developing countries. The implications of this for welfare in the host economy depend upon whether competition is maintained when FDI takes place, and markets work efficiently. If competition—between foreign affiliates themselves, between foreign affiliates and importers, and between foreign affiliates and domestic firms—is lacking, and foreign affiliates operate in highly concentrated markets with low contestability, the benefits to consumers from the entry of more efficient TNCs, in the form of lower prices, improved quality, increased variety, as well as innovation and the introduction of new products, may be limited. In addition, there may be scope for TNCs to engage in anticompetitive business practices that serve to keep new entrants out or result in inefficiencies and reduced consumer welfare.

In particular, if a host country market remains, or becomes, concentrated after the entry of TNCs, there may be a potential for TNCs to engage in business practices, including restrictive business practices, that could have anticompetitive consequences, especially in markets that are characterized by low contestability. The main types of anticompetitive behaviour include, as in the case of purely domestic firms, collusion among producers/sellers of the same product; monopolizing mergers and acquisitions; exclusionary vertical practices; and predatory behaviour. In the case of TNCs, these practices may sometimes be specifically related to, or facilitated by, the cross-border relationships and contacts that are specific to operating in more than one country.

Consumer welfare in host country markets may also be affected adversely if market-power inducements are granted by host country governments to TNCs in order to attract investments by the latter. These inducements include guaranteed exclusive rights of production and/or exclusive rights of sale of a product in the host country market, often supported by protection in the form of prohibitive tariff or non-tariff restrictions on trade. The granting of these inducements has direct anticompetitive effects, with adverse implications for efficiency and the benefits from FDI. Such inducements, like other incentives, are based on the objective of maximizing the long-term benefits (in the form of capital, technology, management know-how, and market access) that FDI is expected to bring; but, given the potential for adverse effects on the efficient functioning of markets, a careful assessment of costs and benefits is necessary if the granting of these inducements is to be justified.

In a liberalizing and globalizing world economy, TNCs operate increasingly in markets that are no longer national but regional or global in scope, with transactions between sellers and buyers of a given product from several different countries taking place across national boundaries. In various industries, TNCs take advantage of the widening scope of markets to restructure their operations and/or integrate their value-added activities internationally, either within their corporate systems or through inter-firms alliances and agreements, achieving efficiencies in production through functional specialization and economies of scale and scope.

The efficiency gains that some TNCs are able to reap through integrated international production enables them to lower prices, to introduce better quality products, or to introduce new products to capture a greater market share. This leads some industries (and markets) to become more concentrated at the regional or global level, a trend that affects all countries.

However, concentrated markets at the regional or global levels need not necessarily affect competition, industry performance or consumer welfare adversely. For one thing, such markets are, by definition, more contestable or open as regards entry (and exit) than segmented national markets, simply because sellers (and buyers) from a number of locations can participate in them. Furthermore, when integrated international production (including at the R&D stage of the value chain) for regional or global markets enables firms to overcome the high costs of, and reap the economies of scale and scope associated with innovation in industries with rapidly changing technology, it could actually enhance competition (through innovation), although the number of independent firms that perform a particular function may diminish. Consumers located in different national economies benefit when buying in those regional or global markets.

Particularly high degrees of concentration in regional and global markets would, of course, raise competition concerns. Business practices by regionally or globally dominant firms, including TNCs, could affect the continued contestability of the relevant markets and the sustainability of the benefits that the greater openness to FDI and trade is expected to bring.

In today's world economy, a number of factors facilitate the ease and speed with which TNCs can provide a supply response to a change in market conditions—signalled, for example, by a non-transitory price increase—through the establishment of new production facilities to enter a market. These factors are based on the reality that nearly all countries seek to attract FDI, many firms already have foreign affiliates in place, technological developments make the establishment of new affiliates relatively easy and competitive pressures often make the exploitation of new opportunities irresistible. More specifically, the supply response of many TNCs could be rapid, rivalling that of domestic producers and importers in a country because of the scanning capabilities of TNCs; their experience in trade and FDI; their access to resources within and outside their corporate systems, and access to markets; their ability to spread risks and enter into alliances to overcome entry barriers such as those of R&D; and their ability to draw upon existing affiliates for assistance. If supply response through FDI and non-equity arrangements by TNCs is relatively fast—with, say, not more than one to two years elapsing between the identification of an opportunity and the servicing of a market—it would be deserving of attention when considering the degree of competition in a given market. This is particularly important with respect to competition in markets for services, many of which cannot be traded across borders. All this suggests that the speed of the supply response through FDI must therefore be considered routinely—by competition authorities in developed and developing countries alike—when defining the relevant market for a product, or assessing the implications for competition of certain changes occurring in a market.

The possibility that new FDI will provide a viable supply response underlines the growing importance of FDI as a factor influencing contestability. Markets may not, however, always continue to remain contestable and competitive. This has several policy implications.

The liberalization of FDI regimes facilitates market entry and, therefore, can increase the contestability of markets. As the liberalization process advances, non-traditional barriers that may inhibit FDI are attracting the attention of policy makers. While some of these barriers are due to government measures (e.g., in the case of public monopolies), others—and these are receiving increasing attention—concern anticompetitive private business practices (or restrictive business practices). Some of the latter are normally prohibited per se (e.g., some horizontal cartels or vertical price fixing). The situation becomes more difficult when the practices concerned may have anticompetitive effects but are not considered illegal under the laws of the country in which they occur. While such practices do not necessarily discriminate between domestic and foreign firms, they may nevertheless constitute barriers to competition.

Furthermore, care must be taken that, in their eagerness to attract FDI, governments do not agree to market-power inducements which, by their very nature, restrict competition and reduce contestability. To avoid such situations, the trade-offs between the benefits associated with new FDI on the one hand, and the immediate costs of such inducements in terms of reducing economic welfare due to their anticompetitive effects, on the other hand, need to be identified as clearly as possible. Once a decision has been made that market-power inducements are required, another difficult task is to determine how much market power needs to be given away, for how long and for what range of activities, in order to attract a particular investment. A number of options exist that can be utilized to minimize negative effects:

- creating pre-entry competition (auctioning);
- circumscribing exclusivity in terms of time;
- circumscribing exclusivity through alternative sources of competition;
- ensuring fair and non-discriminatory access to essential facilities;
- breaking-up national monopolists into regional firms;
- periodically reviewing inducements by competition authorities; and
- regulating prices under certain circumstances.

In sum, the inherently anti-competitive nature of market-power inducements calls for their cautious scrutiny.

By 1997, some 60 countries worldwide had competition laws. Their main objective is to preserve and promote competition as a means of maximizing the efficient allocation of resources in an economy, resulting in the best possible choice of quality, the lowest prices and adequate supplies for consumers. Most competition laws deal with enterprise *behaviour* by prohibiting restrictive business practices such as competition-restricting horizontal agreements and abuses of dominant positions, as well as certain restrictive vertical distribution agreements. Moreover, an increasing number of competition laws deals with alterations in the *structure* of markets through the control of mergers and acquisitions, as well as joint ventures, with the aim of avoiding the creation of dominant positions or even oligopolies. Usually such cartel practices as price fixing, collusive tendering and market allocation are prohibited without need for market analysis, while distribution, joint ventures and M&As agreements are assessed in a market context and under a rule-of-reason standard in terms of efficiencies likely to be achieved and passed on to consumers.

Competition laws normally apply to all firms operating in given national territories, whether through domestic sales, imports, foreign affiliates or non-equity forms of FDI. (They may also, sometimes controversially, be applied when extra-territorial operations have an effect on those given territories.) They do not, in principle, discriminate between national and foreign firms or between firms from different national origins. In this manner, competition law monitors the competitive behaviour of TNCs having effects in host countries, with a view to ensuring that these firms (like other firms) do not abuse market power. On a wider geographical scale, competition law is intended to prevent inefficiencies stemming from market-allocation agreements designed to lessen trade or investment.

Some of these agreements take the form of international market-allocation investment cartels that include promises not to invest in certain markets or not to compete when investing. By their very nature, such cartels directly restrict competition through FDI, typically to the detriment of host countries, and therefore require the attention of competition authorities.

Usually, however, the main interface between competition law and FDI occurs when foreign entry is accomplished by means of a significant merger, acquisition or joint venture. Indeed, countries are increasingly adopting merger-control regulations. Because M&As are dependent on current stock values and are difficult to unscramble once consummated, merger control of such transactions requires a carefully calibrated system of prior notification, rapid analysis, temporary injunctions and prompt decisions. Most countries use turnover or other thresholds to exempt transactions unlikely to have anticompetitive effects in order to minimize unnecessary interference and limit the number of cases screened by the competition authorities.

Most interventions by competition authorities occur in the case of horizontal M&As between competitors. Typical scenarios likely to raise competition issues are:

- The acquiring firm was exporting to a market before it acquired a competing firm in the market, or a foreign firm that already controls one firm in the market acquires another.
- A foreign firm uses FDI to set up a major plant in a market, another firm does the same, and then the two agree to merge (or one takes over the other), thereby eliminating local competition between their two affiliates.
- When a foreign firm, enters a market by means of a joint venture with a local firm, the issue arises as to whether the foreign firm would have been likely to have entered the market separately and competed with the local firm in the absence of the joint venture.
- The possibility that the acquiring firm will have an incentive to suppress rather than develop the competitive potential of the firm to be acquired.
- The merger of two foreign parent firms can sometimes create competition issues in countries other than the home or host countries of the merging firms, i.e., third countries.

- A parent firm acquires an enterprise abroad which, as an independent entity, is (or could be) a source of competition for the domestic market.
- Investments likely to lead to, or augment, worldwide dominant positions. Such cases typically arise in situations in which a transaction affects product markets in which firms compete at the regional or global level.

While the liberalization of FDI and trade regimes can be a means of promoting competition, the possibility of anticompetitive practices by firms requires the continuous attention of competition authorities. In fact, even in a national framework in which investment and "trade" are fully liberalized, the possibility of such practices provides one of the rationales for the existence of competition laws. Therefore, while an FDI entry may be unobjectionable from a competition point of view, or even beneficial in itself, it may raise competition issues in the longer term, depending on the behaviour of the firm.

For example, competition problems may arise because of restraints that are ancillary to the basic transaction, e.g., when tied purchasing is involved. Joint ventures are particularly susceptible to the combination of a pro-competitive basic transaction and ancillary restraints. Another example, which relates to secondary effects, concerns potential competition problems that can arise if a foreign investor assumes control of an essential facility; competition authorities may have to intervene to require dealing on reasonable terms. Moreover, as transfer pricing can be used for predatory purposes, competition authorities may have to monitor events in this area as well; given the nature of this practice, international cooperation is often required.

Finally, corporate non-equity alliances pose new challenges. Certain types of research-and-development alliances, in particular, are attracting increasing attention. Such alliances can have elements of cartelization and, as such, might be subject to competition-law scrutiny. Competition authorities may intervene as regards the structure of a research-and-development arrangement, particularly if parties envisage the joint exploitation of the results. At the same time, such arrangements can have important positive implications for an economy. Many countries therefore exempt certain technological alliances from competition regulations. Where this is not the case, a rule-of-reason standard on a case-by-case basis seems to be increasingly the prevailing approach in judicial reviews, to balance long-term efficiency gains against possible short-term anticompetitive effects.

While FDI liberalization can help to enhance the contestability of markets, it is not a sufficient condition: in so far as FDI liberalization creates more space for firms to pursue their interests in markets, competition laws become necessary to ensure that former statutory obstacles to contestability are not replaced by anticompetitive practices of firms, thus negating the benefits that could arise from liberalization. This need increases as liberalization becomes more widespread and extends to new areas.

If anything, this underlines that the principal dimensions of the FDI liberalization process (identified in the *World Investment Report 1994*) are, indeed, inextricably linked: the reduction of barriers to FDI and the establishment of positive standards of treatment for TNCs need to go hand in hand with the adoption of measures aimed at ensuring the proper functioning of markets, including, in particular, measures to control anticompetitive practices by firms.

This also underlines something else, namely, that the culture of FDI liberalization that has grown worldwide and has become pervasive, needs to be complemented by an equally worldwide and pervasive culture of competition (which, of course, needs to recognize competing objectives as well). Clearly formulated competition policies and their effective enforcement can contribute significantly to the growth of such a competition culture. In this respect, the trend towards adopting or strengthening competition laws suggests that a competition culture is, indeed, emerging in many parts of the world. However, for countries that are new to this practice, the transition to a more open, competition-oriented system cannot be achieved overnight and involves difficult political choices, the balancing of interests among many stakeholders and the resolving of a host of practical problems.

Moving from the plane of competition culture to the plane of policy, this means that competition policy should receive increased attention when it comes to the ideal mix of relevant policy instruments. This should also be the case because, as countries liberalize their investment regimes, they may become concerned that they are moving, for example, from a system of screening all take-overs by foreign firms of national firms to screening none; they may also see risks of foreign firms acquiring dominant positions. Therefore, there is a need to assess the competitive effects of foreign firms at the time of entry and after entry, and that function is increasingly assumed, where appropriate, by competition authorities. Competition policy thus has a major role to play in the process of liberalization, notably by ensuring that markets are kept as open as possible to new entrants, and that firms do not frustrate this by engaging in anticompetitive practices. In this manner, the vigorous enforcement of competition law can provide reassurance that FDI liberalization will not leave governments powerless against anticompetitive transactions or subsequent problems.

When formulating their competition policies, countries need, of course, to keep in mind that competition policy is not a substitute for FDI policy and trade policy, but rather that all three are mutually supportive in the pursuit of efforts to ensure that markets function properly. Nevertheless, to the extent that contestability and competition considerations gain in importance in guiding policies, and the more liberal trade and FDI policies become—but, by themselves, do not always lead to contestable markets—competition policy emerges as *primus inter pares* among policy instruments used to maintain contestability and competition.

To make a difference, competition policy needs to be effectively implemented. This requires a strong competition law and an effective competition-enforcement agency, with broad powers to investigate enterprise behaviour and to analyse the competitive effects of concentrative forms of FDI and the competition implications of market-power inducements. Once the basic political decision has been made to adopt and enforce competition policy, the agency should be consulted in relevant contexts, and its enforcement decisions should not be subject to indiscriminate political intervention.

Still, it must be recognized that few countries have strong, well-functioning and well-funded competition authorities. And it may well take other countries many years to develop appropriate policies and the institutional set-up to implement them fairly and effectively. This means that, where contestability and competition are the objectives, many countries will need to continue to rely, for the foreseeable future, primarily on FDI and trade liberalization to meet these objectives in the context of closer integration into global markets.

Traditionally, competition laws, especially in developing countries, have focused mostly on protecting competition among domestic firms within the local market. When imports became important, they were included in competition analysis as well. As FDI has become more important than trade in terms of delivering goods and services to foreign markets, markets are increasingly regionalized or globalized, and national production systems are becoming more integrated through the activities of TNCs, attention now needs to expand to include the competition effect of FDI and corporate integrated international production systems, including corporate alliances. These developments have important policy implications :

- The regionalization and globalization of markets and their underlying production structures make it increasingly difficult to define and measure market concentration and to determine the emergence of dominant positions (and the possibilities of abuse of market power inherent in this) in terms of *individual national* markets alone.
- Closely related is that the efficiency gains that can be associated with corporate integrated international production systems (including alliances) need to be balanced against any anticompetitive effects of the relevant transactions for the markets supplied by these systems.
- When confronted with non-trivial and non-transitory price increases, competition authorities need to give more attention to a possible supply response through new FDI by foreign producers not yet servicing a market (in addition to supply responses by established domestic producers and imports). Competition authorities are only beginning to consider explicitly and systematically such new FDI as a normal possible source of supply response. The FDI supply response is particularly important because, in terms of its magnitude, world sales by foreign affiliates are larger than world imports. Perhaps more importantly, FDI is often the only international supply response possible in the services sector.

There are numerous reasons why—in an era of globalization—competition issues as they relate to FDI increasingly involve more than one country and, therefore, require international policy responses. Indeed, they are grounded in the very nature of the transnational character of the firms involved, and relate especially to such issues as access to information and the implementation of decisions.

However, a number of obstacles make international responses difficult. With respect to the *exchange of information,* the largest single obstacle is that of the confidentiality obligations of many competition authorities—which they need to have—regarding information submitted to them by various parties. Closer *competition-enforcement cooperation* is often impeded by basic substantive and procedural differences between the competition-law regimes of different countries; in fact, activities being investigated in one jurisdiction may have been encouraged by a government in another jurisdiction. Moreover, many governments simply may not see it in their country's interests to facilitate a foreign state's investigation of one or more of their companies.

Precisely because of such obstacles, issues relating to competition are increasingly being addressed at the international level, either in the form of separate arrangements relating to some aspects of competition policy or in the context of broader investment and trade arrangements :

Bilateral Cooperation among competition authorities is growing, although formal agreements are limited to a relatively small number of countries. Most of these efforts involve cooperation on the exchange of information. A number of bilateral agreements go further by establishing ground rules for notification of competition investigations, consultations and cooperation on competition-law enforcement, including commitments for comity (e.g., to take into account whether significant interests of any foreign sovereign would be affected).

Cooperation efforts at the regional level often take place in the context of regional integration schemes, which allow approaches and trade-offs that are more difficult to pursue in other settings. The most integrated in this respect is the European Union, in which the member countries have agreed to common competition rules and have a common competition authority. In the OECD, efforts to cooperate on restrictive business practices are not new, with recent recommendations strengthening previous provisions and setting out guiding principles for cooperation. Efforts are also being made within the context of other regional agreements, such as NAFTA, MERCOSUR and the Energy Charter Treaty.

At the *multilateral level*, the UNCTAD Set of Principles and Rules for the Control of Restrictive Business Practices is so far the only multilateral instrument covering all aspects of the control of restrictive business practices. Various WTO agreements also touch upon aspects of anticompetitive practices by firms, including in the context of the General Agreement on. Trade in Services, the Agreement on Trade-Related Aspects of Intellectual Property Rights and the Agreement on Trade-Related Investment Measures; the last of these Agreements provides for consideration to be given to whether the Agreement should be complemented with provisions on investment policy and competition policy.

Still, the question arises whether, to sustain the regionalization and globalization of markets and production structures, something more than expanded bilateral and regional cooperation is required. Indeed, recent international discussions reflect a growing recognition by the international community of the links between FDI policy, trade and competition policy. This is underlined in particular by the decision taken at the Ministerial Conference of the World Trade Organization in Singapore in December 1996 to establish one Working Group to examine the relationship between trade and investment, and another to study issues raised by members relating to the interaction between trade any competition policy, including anticompetitive practices, in order to identify and areas that may merit further consideration in the WTO framework. As furthermore stated in the Ministerial Declaration, these Working Groups are to draw upon each other's work if necessary and also to draw upon the work in UNCTAD and other appropriate intergovernmental fora.

Contestability

While FDI liberalization can increase competition in markets and thereby contribute to economic efficiency, growth, development and, ultimately, consumer welfare, there are limitations to competition. They arise in particular when markets tend naturally towards high level of concentration and when market outcomes conflict with other policy objectives.

In the first instance, limitations can arise from the fact that such natural factors as economies of scale, high sunk cost and high risk-related costs can make some markets, to a greater or lesser degree, difficult to contest (although technological developments can change the importance of some of these natural factors). One of the antidotes to these natural limits to contestability involves an increase in the size of the relevant market, especially through investment and trade liberalization. Where market enlargement is difficult to achieve, regulations can help to prevent abuses of dominant positions of market power.

Limitations also arise because government in all countries are often (if not always) faced with having to choose between competing objectives, and a number of these can conflict with the market outcomes that would be generated by reasonably competitive markets. Improving economic efficiency by making markets more competitive is subject to the same need to make choices. Competing objectives include safeguarding national security; protecting labour rights; safeguarding culture; promoting positive externalities; protecting property rights; avoiding negative externalities, protecting consumers; and promoting development.

For developing countries, of course, the promotion of development takes pride of place. Given the particular characteristics of developing countries — low income levels, skewed distribution of wealth, insufficient infrastructure, low levels of education, asymmetries in information, to mention but a few — the incidence of conflicts between market outcomes and competing objectives is often more frequent, especially when dynamic efficiency considerations are taken into account. Where such conflicts occur, their resolution may require creating a mix of policies that limit contestability for a given period of time and that include fade-out provisions, on the one hand, and measures to assist and encourage the building up of domestic capabilities, on the other hand. Indeed, the key issue is to help domestic firms to develop their potential, so that they can participate effectively in international competition and move up the value-added chain.

While limits to contestability may be needed to promote development, it is very difficult indeed to define general criteria on the basis of which such limits could be established. In any event, the main emphasis should remain on establishing, where possible, functioning markets. When limits are placed upon contestability, there is a need to achieve the right balance between efficiency and non-efficiency objectives in a dynamic context. Exceptions or exemptions to contestability and competition need to be tempered by the recognition that they often entail trade-offs with efficiency. Moreover, when governments choose to circumscribe competition, the means by which they do so should be the least damaging from an efficiency perspective; should be transparent; and should be subject to review in the light of changes in markets and the original rationale for such policies.

4

GLOBAL DIVERSE ISSUES

(i) HUMAN DEVELOPMENT REPORT—1996

The central message of Human Development Report 1996 is that there is no automatic link between economic growth and human development but when these links are forged with policy and determination, they can be mutually reinforcing and economic growth will effectively and rapidly improve human development. It provides both a mirror reflecting present patterns of global imbalance, and a telescope, showing the more positive prospects. In the past 15 years the world has become economically more polarised—both between countries and within countries. If present trends continue, economic disparities between industrial and developing nations will move from inequitable to inhuman.

Contrary to earlier theories, new theory and evidence suggest that growth and equity need not be contradictory goals. There is strong evidence from East Asia that heavy national investment in human development—spreading knowlidge and skills and meeting basic social needs—has been the prime mover for sustained economic growth over decades. Of course, policies must be tailored to national circumstances.

The gulf between the poor and the rich has been steadily widening. Of the $23 trillion global GDP in 1993, $18 trillion is in the industrial countries—only $5 trillion in the developing countries. (1 trillion = 10 raised to 12). The poorest 20 per cent of the world's people saw their share of global income decline from 2.3 per cent to 1.4 per cent in the past 30 years. Meanwhile, the share of the richest 20 per cent rose from 70 per cent to 85 per cent. That doubled the ratio of the shares of the richest and the poorest—from 30:1 to 61:1.

The assets of the world's 358 billionaires exceed the combined annual incomes of countries with 45 per cent of the world's people! The gap in per capita income between the industrial and developing worlds tripled, from $5700 in 1960 to $15,400 in 1993.

Economic growth is becoming lopsided and flawed in many countries. Determined efforts are needed to avoid growth that is jobless, ruthless, voiceless, rootless and futureless. Jobless growth—where the overall economy grows but does not expand the opportunities for employment. Ruthless growth—where the fruits of economic growth mostly benefit the rich, leaving millions of people struggling in ever deepening poverty. Voiceless growth—where growth in the economy has not been accompanied by an extension of democratic participation or empowerment. Rootless growth—which causes people's cultural identity to wither. There are about 10,000 distinct cultures, but many are being marginalised or eliminated. Futureless growth—where the present generation squanders resources needed by future generations. Rampant and uncontrolled economic growth in many countries is laying waste the forests, polluting rivers, destroying biodiversity and depleting natural resources.

UN agencies have estimated that to meet the basic social services needs in developing countries by the end of the decade would require an extra $30 billion to $40 billion a year—for basic education, health care and nutrition, low cost water supply, sanitation and reproductive health. The sum is huge but it is barely a quarter of what developing countries spend annually on their military services or to service their debt. And most of the funds could be mobilised through restructuring the existing budgets. In 1994 the military expenditure totalled about $778 billion, the industrial countries spending the lion's share (82%)

All these facts are revealing, but those who really matter—the ruling elite and the affluent sections—and who drain public finances through deep rooted and widespread corruption have to undergo a mutation in their mindset, which ultimately depends on right education, institutional, non formal, continuing lifelong education on ethical values. The judiciary and the media can certainly influence, but in the final analysis it is in the minds of the students that the seeds of this mutation have to be sown.

(ii) UNICEF REPORT ON STATE OF WORLD CHILDREN, 1997

Nearly every country in the world has notified the Convention on the Rights of the Child, which recognizes children's right to be protected from economic exploitation and from work that is hazardous or likely to interfere with their education or development. But UNICEF says many commitments still need to be put into action.

The report estimates that at least one-fourth of children in developing countries are working—some 250 million children aged five to 14 years old. UNICEF is calling for global action to tackle child labour and is demanding an immediate end to its most intolerable forms, such as prostitution and bonded labour. Carol Bellamy, Executive Director of UNICEF, describes these forms as "so grave an abuse of human rights that the world must come to regard them in the way it does slavery—as something unjustifiable under any circumstances."

Four Myths About Child Labour

UNICEF says one of the most persistent myths surrounding child labour is that it exists only in developing countries. There are child workers in all countries—rich and poor. In the United Kingdom, for example, between 15 to 26 per cent of 11-year olds are working. In the United States, a three-day sting operation in 1990 by the Department of Labour found more than 11,000 children working illegally.

Second, the report says it is a myth that child labour will never be eliminated until poverty disappears. It says child labour exists primarily because there are people willing to use children for profit—to exploit their poverty.

UNICEF says that while the effort to eliminate all forms of child labour must go hand-in-hand with measures to reduce extreme poverty. "The end of hazardous child labour does not have to—and must not—wait for the end of poverty."

A third myth—that child labour is mainly found in export industries—is also discounted by the report. In fact, only a small fraction of the world's child workers are employed in export-sector industries—probably less than 5%. Most children work on farms, plantations or in the home, far from the reach of labour inspectors and the media's scrutiny.

A fourth myth is that sanctions and boycotts are the only way to make headway against child labour. The report says this myth implies that the people and governments of developing countries have been ignoring the problem of child labour. In reality, governments, communities, organizations and individuals have been working to expose child labour abuses, develop local and national programmes, and promote consumer awareness at home and abroad.

UNICEF insists that any comprehensive attack on hazardous child labour must advance on several fronts and take into account the best interests of the child as a human being with a whole range of needs and rights, not simply as a child labourer. It must also aim to release children immediately from the most damaging situations, such as bonded labour and prostitution; rehabilitate those children who are released from work through the provision of adequate services and facilities, especially education; and protect working children who cannot immediately be released by making their life as safe and as conducive to development as possible.

National and International Changes Needed

National and international priorities must change to ensure that every child has access to relevant primary education. The report stresses the links between education and eradicating child labour and says education can liberate today's child labourers and prevent children from drifting into similar work in the future. "The longer and better the education," says the report, "the less likelihood that a child will be forced into damaging work." However, education must be of good quality. According to UNICEF, education is often underfunded, rigid and uninispiring. In 14 of the world's least developed countries, half the pupils have no textbooks. Classes are often huge, with 67 pupils per teacher in Bangladesh and nearly 90 per teacher in Equatorial Guinea. Around 30% of children in developing countries who enroll in primary school do not complete it. "Education has become part of the problem," says UNICEF. "It has to be reborn as part of the solution."

The report also calls on governments to allocate 20% of their budgets to education and basic social services, and it asks donor governments to do the same with their official development assistance. "It would cost," says the report, "an estimated US$6 billion a year, on top of what is already spent, to put every child in school by the year 2000. That may seem an enormous sum. Yet it is less than 1per cent of what the world spends every year on weapons."

Priorities for Urgent Action

The report calls for urgent action on several fronts, including: eliminating hazrdous and exploitative child labour; free and compulsory education for every child; stringent child labour laws and their vigorous enforcement in each country; registration of all children at birth; data collection and monitoring; and codes of conduct and procurement policies.

It says sanctions and boycotts have been used effectively to raise awareness about child labour in export industries and force some governments and business leaders to take vigorous action against it. However, different approaches are needed to reach the remaining 95 per cent of child labourers, whose work is often unseen and unreported. They include child prostitutes, form labourers, domestic servants and children working in local industries. In the Convention on the Rights of the Child governments are committed to establishing a minimum age for employment, regulations on terms and conditions of employment, and proper proper penalties to ensure that these labour laws are enforced. The report stresses these commitments must be put into action. "The lives of working children will not change unless the world backs its words with action," it says. "It is time morality prevailed. As we step into the next millennium, hazardous child labour must be left behind, consigned to history as completely as those other forms of slavery that it so closely resembles."

(iii) ILO WORLD EMPLOYMENT REPORT ON LABOUR MARKET CONDITIONS, 1996-97

The underlying causes of deteriorating labour market conditions are, among other things, lower growth rates in industrialized countries; the failure of many developing economies to recover from the 1980s economic crisis; and the progressive "eviction" from the work world of the long-term unemployed and the "casualization" of millions of informal sector workers.

At least 34 million people are unemployed in the world's wealthiest nations, the members of the Organization of Economic Co-operation and Development (OECD). In the European Union, unemployment rates in 1995 increased to an average of 11.3 per cent, with significant increases in France (11.8%) and Italy (11.5%). IN 1996 the trend continued with unemployment rates rising in Germary to 11.2 per cent and in Sweden to 8.3 per cent, among others. However, unemployment dipped in the United States from 5.4 per cent in 1994 to 4.9 per cent in 1996. Unemployment rates also declined in the United Kingdom from 9.4 per cent in 1994 to 7.8 per cent in 1996. But in both countries, the report warns, income disparities are widening.

Unemployment rates declined slightly in Central and Eastren European countries between 1994 and 1995, but they remained high at 11.6 per cent or more in Bulgaria, Hungary, Poland, Slovakia and Slovenia. Unemployment continued to increase in the Russian Federation and in some countries of the former Soviet Union.

In Latin America and other developing countries, up-to-date data on employment is rare. In Colombia, unemployment rose from 8 to 10.4 per cent between mid-1995 and 1996. In urban areas, unemployment between 1994 and 1995 increased in Argentina, Bolivia, Ecuador, Jamaica, Mexico, Uruguay and Venezuela; the rate was 10 per cent or more in Argentina, Uruguay and Venezuela.

Data on unemployment during the same period in other developing regions is available only for South Africa and the Republic of Korea. In South

Africa unemployment increased from 4.4% to 4.9%, and in Korea it declined from 2.4% to 2.2%. In many low-income countries in sub-Sahara Africa and parts of Asia, where data on unemployment does not exist, other indicators point to continuing underemployment and poverty; these indicators include the rate of economic growth and of industrialization.

Commitment to Employment Needed

The "priority requirement for reversing the prolonged deterioration in employment conditions is the restoration of high and sustained rates of economic growth," and "the concept of full employment, suitably updated, should remain as a principal objective of economic and social policy." Nothing short of a renewed international commitment to full employment is required to reverse the problem. "It is not just heartless but pernicious to assume that nothing can be done to remedy unemployment," says ILO Director-General Michel Hansenne. He questions the belief that "jobless growth" is the best that can be hoped for in an increasingly competitive economy, or that current rates of unemployment constitute a natural and inevitable outcome of market forces. "Current levels of unemployment," he says, "make no economic sense and are neither politically nor socially sustainable."

Recommendations for Developing Economies

Policy makers in the developing economies should aim for "a rate of growth of productive, modern-sector jobs that exceeds the rate of growth of the labour force and a reduction in the extent of under-employment in the rural and urban informal sectors of the economy." Economic reforms, where necessary, and called for to achieve macroeconomic stability and to generate an "environment conducive to high saving and investment and the efficient allocation of resources." This would permit developing countries to benefit fully from growing trade and investment flows in the international economy.

The Challenge to Transition Economies

Although many enterprises in the region have undertaken substantial restructuring, the formidable challenge remains of restructuring uncompetitive enterprises and adjusting enterprises structures to raise labour productivity. Given the high and potentially intolerable social tensions this is likely to generate, the ILO advises governments to choose "economic policies and labour-market institutions that are most likely to reduce unemployment," such as decreasing obstacles to new enterprise development and barriers to foreign investment.

Other practical problems include inadequate housing market flexibility and the difficulty of ensuring adequate social protection for workers affected by restructuring. An array of measures may need to be supplemented by temporary measures to contain the rise in unemployment. These measures include an improved institutional framework in which unions and employers' organizations can undertake effective collective bargaining.

Promoting Jobs in Industrialized Countries

Three fundamental preconditions are necessary for reaching full employment in industrialized countries. They are:

- increased economic growth rates via a combination of expansionary policies and measures to boost productivity, which means lower interest rates in an atmosphere of wage restraint and concerted efforts to overcome skills shortages;
- anti-inflation mechanisms, which could include improved coordination of wage bargaining procedures and a strengthened social pact; and
- improved labour-market policies, such as reforms of unemployment benefit systems and benefit-transfer programmes, subsidies for low-wage employment, and payroll tax deductions to encourage hiring of the long-term unemployed.

(iv) GENERAL ASSEMBLY RESOLUTIONS

Social Development

The GA adopted by consensus resolution 51/202 on implementation of the Outcome of the World Summit for Social Development. The five-part resolution covers : national action and itnernational cooperation for social development; mobilization of financial resources; involvement of civil society and other actors; the role of the United Nations system; and the GA special session in the year 2000 to review and appraise implementation of the Summit's outcome.

The preparatory process for the special session will begin when the Commission for Social Development, which has primary responsibility for monitoring follow-up to the Social Summit, will review summit implementation at its sessions in 1998 and 1999. In addition, the 52nd GA meeting in 1997 will establish a preparatory committee of the whole. The committee will hold an organizational session in 1998, and it will begin working on the substance of the review in 1999, with inputs from the Commission for Social Development, ECOSOC and others.

Resolution 51/202 reaffirms the need to ensure civil society and other actors are involved in planning, elaborating, implementing the evaluating social policies at the national level. It encourages NGOs to participate in the Commission for Social Development and in implementation of the summit "to the maximum extent possible. The resolution recognizes that implementation of the declaration and programme of action in developing countries, especially in Africa and least developed counties, will need additional financial resources and more effective development cooperation and assistance. It reiterates a call to governments to define time-bound goals and targets to reduce overall poverty and eradicate absolute poverty, expand employment and reduce unemployment, and enhance social integration.

Peace and Security

Resloution 51/136 on a Comprehensive Review of the whole Question of Peacekeeping Operations in All Their Aspects was adopted by 170 votes with none against and no abstentions. It endorses the proposals, recommendations and conclusions of the Special Committee on Peacekeeping Operations and mandates the committee to continue its efforts for a comprehensive rview of peace-keeping operations. However, the United States told the assembly it will not support future resolutions that cannot be carried out within the existing UN budget. The Special Committee on Peacekeeping Operations recommended to the GA that the UN explore ways to do more in the area of conflict prevention by promoting pacific solutions, such as negotiation, inquiry, mediation, conciliation, arbitration, and judicial settlement.

For the past three years, UN Member States have been grappling with questions concerning Security Council reform: how to achieve equitable representation on the council, how to increase its membership, and how to identify other measures to improve its efficiency and transparency. The council, which currently consists of 15 Member States, is responsible for maintaining international peace and security, including setting up UN peace-keeping operations, encouraging peaceful settlement of disputes, and providing a forum to address threats to international peace and security.

In a debate in the GA plenary from 29 October-1November 1996, governments reviewed progress of the Open-ended Working Group on the Question of Equitable Representation on and Increase in the Membership of the Security Council, which was established by the GA in 1993. The working group's report, which is contained in document A/50/47, covers its meetings and informal consultations from November 1995 to September 1996 and addresses issues such as: improvement in the council's working methods and its transparency; size and composition of the council; decision-making in the council, including the veto; amendments to the UN Charter; and periodic review of the council's composition and membership. An addendum to the report, document A/50/47 Add.1, contains papers submitted by governments, groups of governments and the working group's bureau. There is general agreement that the council needs to be more representative and reflect important changes in international relations. Some states that have risen to prominence are not members of the council, and some regions are under represented. The working group will continue meeting in 1997 and will submit a report including any agreed recommendations to the 51st GA before its last session in September. The working group is scheduled to meet from 10-21 March; from 28 April-9 May; and from 27 May-6 June.

Four out of five permanent members of the UN Security Council voted against resolution 51/193 on the Report of the Security Council. The resolution, which was adopted by a vote of 111 with four against and 41 abstentions, calls upon the council to include information on its consultations undertaken prior to its actions or deliberations, and on the process leading to action. It also calls on the council to highlight the extent to which it takes into account GA decisions and resolutions; report on decisions and recommendations of subsidiary organs, such as the sanctions committee; and update the GA regularly on the steps taken, or about to be taken, on improving its reporting. The resolution also requests the GA President to raise these questions in monthly informal meetings with the President of the Security Council, and it requests that the annual report of the Security Council be made available before the beginning of the GA's general debate. Under the UN charter, the Security Council submits annual, and when necessary, special reports to the General Assembly for its consideration. In the past, the General Assembly has debated the Security Council's annual report, but has limited its formal action to a one-line decision that says, "The General Assembly takes note of the report of the Security Council." However, with growing pressure for greater council transparency and accountability, a more substantive resolution on the report of the Security Council was put forward by Colombia on behalf of the Movement of Non-Aligned Countries. The balance of power and productivity between the Security Council and the General Assembly was a continuous subject of discussion and concern during the 51st session.

Resolution 51/208 on Assistance to Thrid States Affected by the Application of Sanctions requests the UN Secretary-General to develop a methodology to assess the adverse consequences of UN Security Council sanctions that are imposed on one country but affect the economies of neighbouring or uninvolved countries. The resolution recommends that the Security Council continue to increase the effectiveness and transparency of its sanctions committees. It also invites the UN system, international financial institutions, Member States and international and regional organisations to address directly the special economic problems of countries affected by the council's sanctions. The impact of sanctions was considered by the Special Committee on the Charter of the United Nations at its session in New York from 24 January-7 February 1997.

Disarmament and International Security

The GA First Committee (Disarmament and International Security) submitted 45 resolutions and two decisions on disarmament matters to the assembly. They focused on nuclear disarmament, the creation of nuclear weapon-free zones, bilateral disarmament negotiations, and the elimination of nuclear weapons. The work of the committee revealed disagreement about how to proceed on these issues: some states hailed the Comprehensive Test Ban Treaty as an historic achievement, while others said it had succeeded only in solidifying a dangerous and discriminatory nuclear weapons regime. There were also differences about the pace of nuclear disarmament. For example, draft resolutions submitted by the Non-Aligned Movement called for the elimination of nuclear weapons "within a time-bound framework," a concept several nuclear-weapons states opposed.

In resolution 51/38, the GA recommends guidelines for objective information on military matters as a means to increase transparency of military expenditures, and it requests states to report annually to the Secretary-General on their military expenditures for the latest fiscal year.

In a vote of 125 in favour with none against and 45 abstentions, the GA reaffirmed the need to reach early agreement on security arrangements for non-nuclear weapon states. It appealed to all states, particularly those with nuclear weapons, to work toward a binding international instrument. Resolution 51/43 also recommends that the Conference on Disarmament continue negotiations for effective international arrangements to protect non-nuclear weapon states from the use or threat of nuclear weapons.

Resolution 51/45J on Prohibition of the Dumping of Radioactive Wastes, adopted by consensus, requests the Conference on Disarmament to take radioactive wastes into account when negotiating a convention on the prohibition of radiological weapons.

Resolution 51/45A, adopted by a vote of 167 in favoura$ith none against and 2 abstentions (India and Israel), takes note of the decision of the states party to the Non-Proliferation Treaty (NPT) to hold the first Preparatory Committee Meeting of the Review Conference of the Parties to the Non-Proliferation Treaty at UN headquarters from 7—12 April 1997.

Resolution 51/45C calls for the preparatory committee to the 1999 Fourth Special Session of the General Assembly Devoted to Disarmament to be convened before the end of the assembly's 51st session, subject to consensus on objectives and agenda. The 1997 substantive session of the Disarmament Commission, which will meet from 21 April—13 May in New York, will take up this question.

The Assembly adopted resolution 51/45E on Environmental Norms in Disarmament and Arms Control Agreements by a vote of 137 in favour with four against (France, Israel, United Kingdom and United States) and 27 abstentions. The resolution asks the Conference on Disarmament to take radioactive wastes into account when negotiating for a convenion on prohibiting radiological weapons. It asks states to adopt measures to ensure that the application of scientific and technological progress to disarmament is "without detriment to the environment or to its effective contribution to attaining sustainable development." The resolution invites the Conference on Disarmament to take every necessary measure to include environmental norms and provisions when negotiating arms control and disarmament measures.

Resolution 51/45D on the Relationship between Disarmament and Development calls on states to devote resources made available by the implementation of disarmament and arms limitation agreements to economic and social development. It also asks states to submit proposals to the UN Secretary-General for implementing the action programme adopted at the 1987 International Conference on the Relationship between Disarmament and Development.

The Assembly adopted without a vote resolution 51/45F, which welcomes the Disarmament Commission guidelines for international arms transfers to curb the illicit transfer and use of conventional arms and invites states to enact national legislation to control the export and the import of arms.

Resolution 51/45H on Transparency in Armaments calls on states to provide data for the UN Register of Conventional Arms and to transmit their views on the development of transparency measures related to weapons of mass destruction.

In resolution 51/451, the GA encourages the Secretary-General to continue efforts to curb illicit traffic in-small arms by setting up national commissions on their proliferation in countries of the Sudano-Sahelian subregion, and by collecting weapons in the region with the support of the UN Regional

Centre for Peace and Disarmament in Africa and the Organisation of African Unity (OAU).

The General Assembly requested the Conference on Disarmament to consider formulating principles to serve as a framework for agreements on conventional arms control at the regional and subregional levels in resolution 51/45Q. It also adopted by a vote of 170 in favour, with none against and India abstaining, resolution 51/45K calling on states to conclude agreements for nuclear non-proliferation, disarmament and confidence-building measures at the regional and subregional levels. The resolution stresses the need for sustained efforts within the framework of the Confernece on Disarmament and under the umbrella of the UN to make progress on the entire range of disarmament issues.

Resolution 51/45M, on the Advisory Opinion on the International Court of Justice on the Legality of the Treaty on Use of Nuclear Weapons, expresses "its appreciation to the International Court of Justice for responding to the request made by the General Assembly at its forty-ninth session (and) underlines the unanimous conclusion of the Court that there exists an obligation to pursue in good faith and bring to a conclusion negotiations leading to nuclear disarmament in all its aspects under strict and effective international control." The resolution calls on "all states to fulfil that obligation immediately by commencing multilateral negotiations in 1997 leading to an early conclusion of a nuclear weapons convention prohibiting the development, production, deployment, stockpiling, transfer, threat or use of nuclear weapons and providing for their elimination." It requests the Secretary-General to provide the necessary assistance to support implementation of the resolution.

Resolution 51/45O urges nuclear-weapon states to stop improving, developing, producing and stockpiling nuclear warheads and their delivery systems, and to undertake "a phased programme of progressive and balanced deep reductions of nuclear weapons. . . with a view to the total elimination of those weapons within a time-bound framework." Resolution 51/45G on Nuclear Disarmament with a view to the Elimination of Nuclear Weapons calls on nuclear-weapon states to reduce nuclear weapons globally, and urges states not party to the Non-Proliferation Treaty to accede to it. The resolution also calls on all states party to the NPT to work for a strengthened review process at the 1997 preparatory committee for the next review conference, to be held in the year 2000.

The General Assembly welcomed the prospective entry into force in April 1997 of the Convention on the Prohibition of the Development, Production, Stockpiling and Use of Chemical Weapons and on Their Destruction. In resolution 51/45T, it calls on states to sign and/or ratify the convention, and it emphasizes the importance of possessors of chemical weapons or production facilities, particularly the US and Russian Federation, to be among the original parties to the convention.

By a vote of 155 in favour with none against and 10 abstentions, the GA adopted resolution 51/45S, which urges states to pursue an effective international agreement to ban and use, production and transfer of anti-personnel landmines. The resolution calls on states to accede to the Convention on Certain

Conventional Weapons and its amended Protocol II. (See N*GLS Roundup* on Landmines.)

In Resolution 51/54, the General Assembly called on all signatory states to ratify the Biological Weapons Convention and for all states to become parties to the convention. The resolution also requests the Secretary-General to continue assisting the depository governments of the Convention on the Prohibition of the Development, Production and Stockpiling of Bacteriological (Biological) and Toxin Weapons and on Their Destruction.

The assembly did not take action on amending the Treaty Banning Nuclear Weapons Tests in the Atmosphere, in Outer Space and Under Water, or on the Report of the Implementation of the Comprehensive Nuclear Test-Ban Treaty.

Transnational Crime, Drugs and Terrorism

Resolution 51/210 on Measures to Eliminate International Terrorism strongly condemns all acts, methods and practices of terrorism as criminal and unjustifiable regardless of political, philosophical, ideological, racial, ethnic, religious or other considerations to justify them. It calls on states to accelerate research and development of methods to detect explosives and other harmful substances, and it notes the need to find means consistent with national law to prevent the use of electronic or wire communications systems and net works by terrorist organisations. The resolution asks states to investigate the abuse of organisations or groups by terrorists using them as a cover for their own activities. It also asks states to recommend that relevant security offícals undertake consultations to: improve the capacity of governments to prevent, investigate and respond to terrorist attacks on public facilities, particularly on public transport; develop mutual legal assistance precedures to facilitate investigations and evidence collection, as well as cooperation between law enforcement agencies to detect and prevent terrorist acts; and employ domestic measures to prevent and counteract the financing of terrorist organizations. The resolution establishes an ad hoc committee to elaborate an international convention for the suppression of terrorist bombings, and a subsequent international convention for the suppression of acts of nuclear terrorism. The committee meets in New York from 24 February—7 March and from 22 September—3 October 1997.

The assembly asks states to submit their views on elaborating an international convention against transnational organized crime in resolution 51/120. It asks states do this at least two months in advance of the sixth session of the Commission on Crime Prevention and Criminal Justice, to be held from 28 April—9 May 1997 in Vienna.

The GA, acting on the report of the Economic and Social Council, adopted resolution 51/191 containing the UN Declaration Against Corruption and Bribery in International Commercial Transactions. In the declaration, states pledge to deny tax deductions for bribes paid by private or public corporations or individuals to any public official or elected representative of another country. States pledge to criminalize bribery of foreign public officials in an effective and coordinated manner and encourage the development of business codes, standards and best practices that prohibit corruption. bribery and related illicit practices in international commercial transactions. The resolution invites other bodies of the UN system, including UNCTAD, to promote the objectives of the resolution and the proposed declaration. It also asks Member States and competent international, regional and non-governmental organisations to provide information to the Secretary-General to assist in the preparation of a progress report on implementation of the resolution. The report will be submitted to the General Assembly in 1998.

The GA adopted five resolutions on crime prevention and criminal justice. Resolution 51/59 on Action Against Corruption includes in its annex an International Code of Conduct for Public Officials. The code defines the roles and responsibilities of public officials and includes provisions on conflicts of interest, disclosure of assets, acceptance of gifts, disclosure of confidential information and political activity. The resolution recommends that states use the code as a tool to guide anti-corruption efforts.

Enhanced bilateral and multilateral cooperation to fight criminal organizations responsible for "smuggling aliens" by sea was the subject of resolution 51/62. It requests the Commission on Crime Prevention and Criminal Justice to address the question at its 1997 session in Vienna.

Resolution 51/60 contains the UN Declaration on Crime and Public Security, which urges states to combat serious transnational crime, smuggling, terrorism, and money laundering, and work to eradicate organized crime trafficking in illicit drugs, arms and people. Under the declaration, states will also promote regional and global enforcement and cooperation to apprehend and prosecute persons guilty of serious transnational crimes.

A seven-part resolution on International Action to Combat Drug Abuse and Illicit Production and Trafficking :

* reaffirms the fight against drugs must be carried out in full conformity with the purposes and principles enshrined in the Charter of the United Nations and international law;
* reaffirms the importance of the Global Programme of Action, which addressed international cooperation against drugs, adopted at the 17th special session of the General Assembly in 1990.

Refugees and Humanitarian Affairs

Resolution 51/194 on Strengthening of the Coordination of Emergency Humanitarian Assistance of the United Nations addresses the process of improving the UN's ability to respond quickly and in a coordinated fashion to complex humanitarian emergencies and natural disasters. It emphasizes the importance of a smooth transition from relief to rehabilitation and requests the Secretary-General to make proposals to ECOSOC at its June/July session for clearer identification of priority needs and for the formulation of a coherent humanitarian strategy. The assembly resolution encourages members of the Inter-Agency Standing Committee to cooperate closely with each other, and with the Bretton Woods Institutions and the regional development banks, to ensure that relief, rehabilitation, reconstruction and long-term development is addressed in a more effective manner. The resolution invites UN agencies, funds and programmes, as well as NGO's to participate in and support the Relief Web, an Internet home page established by the Department for Humanitarian Affairs (DHA).

A series of six resolutions on refugees and displaced persons addresses issues including resettlement in the Great Lakes Region of Africa, the burden on asylum countries with limited resources, and assistance to unaccompanied refugee minors. Resolution 51/73 advises the Office of the United Nations High Commissioner for Refugees (UNHCR) to incorporate policies aimed at preventing refugee family separation and urges the international community to support UNHCR's search for durable solutions to refugee problems, including voluntary repatriation, integration and resettlement. Resolution 51/71 on Assistance to Refugees, Returnees and Displaced Persons in Africa calls on the Secretary-General, UNHCR and intergovernmental, regional and non-governmental organizations to increase the capacity to coordinate and deliver humanitarian emergency assistance and disaster relief with states and others concerned. It also appeals to the international community to respond positively, in the spirit of burden-sharing, to third-country requests for help in resettling African refugees. The assembly expressed appreciation and support for African governments and local populations that continue to accept burdens imposed by increasing numbers of refugees, and it expressed concern about situations where the principle of asylum is jeopardized by the unlawful expulsion or the threat to life, physical security, integrity, dignity and well-being of refugees.

The General Assembly adopted seven resolutions of the activities of the United Nations Relief and Works Agency for Palestine Refugees in the Near East (UNRWA). Resolution 51/124 urges Member States to expedite aid and assistance for the development of the Palestinian people and the occupied territories. Resolution 51/125 requests the working group on the financing of UNRWA to continue its work for one year. Resolution 51/126 reaffirms the right of all persons displaced as a result of the June 1967 and subsequent hostilities to returen to their homes in the territories occupied by Isrel since 1967 to their Resolution 51/127 requests UNRWA to act as the recipient and trustee for special allocations for grants and scholarships to be awarded to qualified Palestine refugee candidates. Resolution 51/128 welcomes the transfer of UNRWA headquarters to Gaza and the signing of the headquarters agreement with the Palestinian Authority. Resolution 51/129 reaffirms the entitlement of Palestine Arab refugees to their property and income derived from it. Finally, resolution 51/130 requests the Secretary-General to take all measures to establish the *Al-Quds* University of Jerusalem. The overwhelming majority of Member States voted for these resolutions, while Israel voted against all of them and abstained on resolution 51/127.

(v) INFORMATION : GLOBAL INFOTECH AGREEMENT

Thirty-nine nations including India on March 26 signed a $500 billion blogal agreement to scrap tariffs in the booming information technology trade by the year 2000. The landmark information technology pact. which covers 217 tariff lines. will benefit customers. manufacturers and global trade. according to industry analysts and officials at the 130-member trade watch-dog. The information technology agreement will benefit customers, manufacturers and global trade, according to industry analysts and officials at the 130-member World Trade Organisation, the international trade watchdog. Poland and Panama, which had been expected to take part in the tariff-scrapping agreement, were not among the 39 countries for "operational reasons", according to WTO officials.

The accord, under which the first tariff cuts must take place in July, was shaped in December by ministers meeting in Singapore under WTO auspices. Tariffs are to be cut in four stages between 1997 and 2000 in five main product categories: computers. telecom products. semiconductors, semiconductor manufacturing equipment, software including diskettes and CD ROMs and scientific instruments. Developing countries like India have a longer time-frame to phase out tariff barriers. In the first phase which ends in 2000. India will eliminate import duties on 95 items. It will have to ensure zero duty on four products by 2003 and two others by 2004. The duties on the remaining 116 items will be eliminated only in 2005.

In end-February. India had offered to cut all its infotech import tariffs to zero by 2007. An extended deadline till 2007 had been sought for phasing out duties on certain telecommunications products on the grounds that the industry is at a nascent stage in India. However, this proposal was turned down by the other countries which were participating in pre-agreements talks. According to the final agreement, duties on infotech-related capital goods will be eliminated by 2000, while duties on computers, peripherals and telecom equipment such as switching and transmission apparatus will be brought to the zero level by 2005.

PART TWO

INDIA 1996-97

5

LAND AND ITS PEOPLE

India that is Bharat covering a land area 32,87,263 sq.km is the seventh largest and the second most populous country of the world. It stretches 3,214 km from North to South between the extreme latitudes and 2,933 km from East to West between the extreme longitudes. On this 2.4 per cent of earth's surface live 15 per cent (88 crore people) of world's population.

POPULATION

Over 160 million people are added annually to our population (President's Republic day Speech, 25th January 1989). Since 1881, the Census in India has been taken reqularly after ten years. According to 1991 Census, the total population of India (including the projected population of Jammu and Kashmir is 846,302,688. As compared 1981 census, it showed an increase of 23.85 per cent. According to 1991 Census, the growth of urban population in the country during the decade 1981-1991, slowed down by about ten per cent as compared to the earlier decade of 1971-1981. However, the number of cities and towns has been consistently increasing. The urban population at present in 25.72 per cent.

DENSITY

The average population of density of per km^2 in 1991 was 267. It varies considerably from State to State.

SEX RATIO

According to 1991 Census (Provisional) there are 43.7 crore males and 40.6 crore females; thus for every 1,000 males India has 929 females. Only Kerala has more women than men, i.e., 1,040 per 1,000 men. The lowest female ratio among the State is in Haryana i.e. 874 for 1,000 men and the lowest female ratio among the Union Territories is in Chandigarh where it is 733 per thousand.

LITERACY

According to 1991 Census, the literacy percentage is 52.21. Out of this 64.13 per cent of males and 39.29 per cent of females are literate.

MAJOR RELIGIONS AND PERSUASIONS

TABLE 5.1 : Major religions and persuasions, 1991 and 1981 (excluding Assam)

Religion Community	*Population*		*Percentage of Total Population*	
	1991	*1981*	*1991*	*1981*
Hindus	67,20,00,000	54,97,24,517	82.41	82.63
Muslims	952,00000	7,55,71,514	11.67	11.36
Christians	1,88,00,000	1,61,74,498	2.32	2.43
Sikhs	1,62,00,000	1,30,78,146	1.99	1.96
Buddhists	63,00,000	47,19,900	0.77	0.71
Jains	33,00,000	31,92,572	0.41	0.48
Other Persuasions	31,00,000	27,56,285	0.38	0.42
Religion not stated	4,00,000	60,217	0.05	0.01

LANGUAGES

The detailed data from the 1981 Census which were made available only in 1988, enumerate the main languages spoken in the household and not the mother tongue and groups related languages under a dominant language. By this count, 106 languages are separately recognised. Of these 94 are spoken by 10,000 or more people.

There were 1562 mother tongues, 10 writing system, and 76 languages as used in the school system out of 2000 codified languages.

Eighteen languages have been specified in the Eighth Schedule of the Constitution. These are: Assamese, Bengali, Gujarati, Hindi, Kannada, Kashmiri, Konkani, Malayalam, Manipuri, Marathi, Nepali, Oriya, Punjabi, Sanskrit, Sindhi, Tamil, Telugu and Urdu.

NATIONAL FLAG

The National Flag is horizontally tricolour with deep saffron *(Kesari)* at the top, white in the middle and dark green at the bottom in equal proportion. The ratio of the width of the flag to its length is two to three. In the centre of the white band is a wheel, in navy blue, which represents the *Charkha*. Its design is that of the wheel *(Chakra)* which appears on the abacus of the Sarnath Lion Capital of Ashoka. Its diameter approximates to the width of the white band and it has 24 spokes.

The design of the National flag was adopted by the Constituent Assembly of India on July 22, 1947. Its use and display are regulated by a code.

STATE EMBLEM

The State Emblem of India is an adaptation from the Sarnath Lion Capital of Ashoka as preserved in the Sarnath Museum. In the original, there are four lions, standing back to back, mounted on an abacus with a frieze carrying sculptures in high relief of an elephant, a galloping horse, a bull and a lion separated by intervening wheels (Chakras) over a bell-shaped lotus. Carved out of a single block of polished sandstone, the capital is crowned by the Wheel of the Law (Dharma Chakra).

In the State emblem adopted by the Government of India on January 26, 1950, only three lions are visible, the fourth being hidden from view. The wheel appears in relief in the centre of the abacus with a bull on the right and a horse on the left and the outlines of the other wheels in the extreme right and left. The bell-shaped lotus has been omitted. The words *Satyameva Jayate* from the *Mundaka Upanishad,* meaning *'Truth Alone Triumphs'* are inscribed below the abacus in Devanagari script.

NATIONAL ANTHEM

The song *Jana-gana-mana,* composed by Rabindranath Tagore (1861-1941) was adopted by the Constituent Assembly as the National Anthem of India on January 24, 1950. It was first sung on December 27, 1911 at the Calcutta session of the Indian National Congress. The complete song consists of five stanzas. The first stanza constitutes the full version of the National Anthem. It reads:

Jana-gana-mana-adhinayaka, jaya he
Bharata-bhagya-vidhata
Punjab-Sindhu-Gujarata-Maratha-
Dravida-Utkala-Banga
Vindhya-Himachala-Yamuna-Ganga
Uchchala-jaladhi-taranga.
Tava shubha name jage,
tava shubha asisa mage,
gahe tava jaya-gatha,
Jana-gana-mangala-dayaka jaya he
Bharata-bhagya-vidhata.
Jaya he, jaya he, jaya he,
Jaya Jaya Jaya, Jaya he!

Playing time of the full version of the National Anthem is approximately 25 seconds. A short version consisting of the first and last lines of the stanza (playing time approximately 20 seconds) is also played on certain occasions.
The following is Tagore's English rendering of this stanza:

Thou art the ruler of the minds of all people,
dispenser of India's destiny.
Thy name rouses the hearts of Punjab, Sind, Gujarat and Maratha
Of the Dravida and Orissa and Bengal;
It echoes in the hills of the Vindhyas and Himalayas,
mingles in the music of Jamuna and Ganges

and is chanted by the waves of the Indian Sea.
They pray for thy blessings and sing thy praise.
The saving of all people waits in thy hand,
thou dispenser of India's destiny.
Victory, victory, victory of thee.

NATIONAL SONG

The song *Vande Mataram,* composed by Bankimchandra Chatterji (1838-1894), was a source of inspiration to the people in their struggle for freedom. It has an equal status with *Jana-gana-mana.* The first political occasion on which it was sung was the 1896 session of the Indian National Congress. The following is the text of its stanza :

Vande Mataram !
Sujalam, suphalam, malayaja shitalam,
Shasyashyamalam, Mataram !
Shubhrajyotsna pulakitayaminim,
Phullakusumita drumadala shobhinim,
Suhasinim sumadhura bhashinim,
Sukhadam, Varadam, Mataram!

The English translation of the stanza rendered by Sri Aurobindo (1872-1950) in prose is:

I bow to thee, Mother,
richly-watered, richly-fruited,
cool with the winds of the south,
dark with the crops of the harvests,
the Mother!
Her nights rejoicing in the glory of the moonlight,
her lands clothed beautifully with her trees in flowering bloom,
sweet of laughter, sweet of speech,
the Mother, giver of boons, giver of bliss.

NATIONAL CALENDAR

A uniform National Calendar based on the *Saka Era* with *Chaitra* as its first month and a normal year of 365 days was adopted from March 22, 1957 (along with the Gregorian calendar) for the following official purposes in particular :

(i) Gazette of India
(ii) News broadcast by All India Radio and T.V.
(iii) Calendars issued by the government of India, and
(iv) Government communications addressed to members of the public.

The dates of the National Calendar have a permanent correspondence with the dates of the Gregorian calendar; *Chaitra 1* falling on March 22 normally and on March 21 in a leap year.

Chaitra 1 of *Saka Era* is the New Year Day. *Saka Era* was established in A.D. 78 by Emperor Kanishka of the Saka dynasty, who ruled in the North and North-Western India in the first century of the Christian era. The day, which has been chosen to become the first day of the New Year, is vemal equinox when the day and the night are of equal duration throughout the world. *Saka* calendar is based on *Solar Chaitra* and not on *Lunar Chaitra*. *Chaitra Shukla Partipada*

1. As published in *Sri Aurobindo Birth Centenary Library,* Popular edition, 1912, vol. 8. which is celebrated as New Year Day in many parts of the country, is called differently. It is *Gudi Padwa* in Maharashtra and *Yugadi* in Karnataka based on lunar calendar, etc. April 13, *Baisakhi* in Punjab, Pongal on April 14 in Tamil Nadu and *Palia Baisakhi* in West Bengal are based on solar calendar. In solar calendar this discrepancy of 22 or 23 days (between March 22 and April 13/14) has been caused by an astronomical phenomenon called the precession of the equinoxes.

NATIONAL ANIMAL

The majestic tiger *[Panthera tigris* (Linnaeus)], the national animal of India for its rich colour, illusive design and formidable power, has always been held in high esteem in India. Among the carnivores, the tiger is very georgeous and attractive with roaring voice as symbol of power. Out of eight races of the species known the world over, the Indian race is the Royal Bengal Tiger. The Royal Bengal Tiger is found throughout the country except the North-Western region and also in Nepal, Bhutan and Bangladesh. As shrinkage of habitat in India dwindled its population to only 1,827 in 1972, the Project Tiger was launched on April 1'st 1973. Since then there is a gradual increase in its population. The tiger population 4,430 of the country according to 1989 census was 4,339. So far 19 tiger reserves have been established covering over 29,716 sq km forest area.

NATIONAL BIRD

The Indian peacock *[Pavo cristatus* (Linnaeus)], the national bird of India, is one of the most beautiful birds, particularly the males having the glistering blue neck and breast, fanshaped crest and long magnificent tail. The courtship dance of the male by fanning out the tail before the female is most spectacular. From time immemorial, this bird has found a profound place in Indian literature, folkore and legends.

The Indian peafowl, as the peacock is called, is widely found in the country in south and east of Indus river, Jammu and Kashmir, east Assam, south of Mizoram and the whole of Indian peninsula. It is fully protected under the Indian Wild Life (Protection) Act, 1972.

(Source : India 1993).

PRESIDENTS OF INDIA

January 26, 1950 — May 13, 1962	Rajendra Prasad
May 13, 1962 — May 13, 1967	S. Radhakrishnan
May 13,1967 — May 3, 1969	Zakir Husain
May 3,1969 — July 20, 1969	V.V. Giri (Acting)

July 20, 1969 — August 21, 1969	M. Hidayatullah (Acting)
August 24, 1969 — August 24, 1974	V.V.Giri
August 24, 1974 — February, 11, 1977	Fakhruddin Ali Ahmed
February 11, 1977 — July 25, 1977	B.D.Jatti (Acting)
July 25, 1977 — July 25, 1982	N.Sanjeeva Reddy
July 25, 1982 — July 25, 1987	Zail Singh
July 25, 1987 — July 25, 1992	R.Venkataraman
July 25, 1992 —	S.D.Sharma

VICE PRESIDENTS OF INDIA

1952-1962	S.Radhakrishnan
1962-1967	Zakir Husain
1967-1969	V.V.Giri
1969-1974	G.S.Pathak
1974-1979	B.D.Jatti
1979-1984	M.Hidayatullah
1984-1987	R.Venkataraman
1987-1992	S.D.Sharma
1993-	K.R.Narayanan

PRIME MINISTERS OF INDIA

August 15, 1947 — May 27, 1964	Jawaharlal Nehru
May 27, 1964 — June 9, 1964	Guljari Lal Nanda (Acting)
June 9, 1964 — January 11, 1966	Lal Bahadur Shastri
January 11, 1966 — January 24, 1966	Guljari Lal Nanda (Acting)
January 24, 1966 — March 24, 1977	Indira Gandhi
March 24, 1977 — July 28, 1979	Morarji Desai
July 28, 1979 — January 14, 1980	Charan Singh
January 14, 1980 — October 31, 1984	Indira Gandhi
October 31, 1984 — December 1, 1989	Rajiv Gandhi
December 2, 1989 — November 10, 1990	V.P.Singh
November 10, 1990 — June 21, 1991	Chandra Shekhar
June 21, 1991 — May 16, 1996	P.V.Narasimha Rao
May 16, 1996 — June 1,	Atal Behari Vajpayee
June 1, 1996 —	H. D. Deve Gowda

SPEAKERS OF THE LOK SABHA

1952-1956	G.V.Mavlankar
1965-1962	Ananthasayanam Ayyangar
1962-1967	S.Hukam Singh
1967-1969	N.Sanjeeva Reddy
1969-1975	G.S.Dhillon
1975-1977	B.R.Bhagat
March 1977 — July 1977	N.Sanjeeva Reddy
1977-1979	K.S.Hegde
1980-1989	Balram Jakhar
November 19, 1989 — June 1991	Rabi Ray

July 10, 1991 — May 22, 1996	Shivraj Patil
May 23, 1996 —	P. A. Sangma

IMPORTANT DAYS

National Youth Day	January 12
Army Day	January 15
Republic Day	January 26
International Customs Day	January 26
Martyrs' Day	January 30
National Science Day	February 28
International Women's Day*	March 8
World Consumers Rights Day	March15
World Disabled Day	March (Third Sunday of March)
International Day for the Elimination of Racial Discrimination	March 21
World Forestry Day	March 21
World Meteorological Day	March 23
National Maritime Day	April 5
World Health Day*	April 7
May Day (Worker's Day International Labour Day)	May 1
World Red Cross Day	May 8
World Telecommunication Day*	May 17
World Day for Cultural Development*	May 21
Commonwealth Day	May 24
World No-Tobacco Day*	May 31
World Environment Day*	June 5
International Day of Solidarity with the Struggling People of South Africa*	June 16
World Population Day*	July 11
Hiroshima Day	August 6
Quit India Day	August 9
Nagasaki Day	August 9
International Day of Solidarity with the Struggle of Women in South Africa*	August 9
Independence Day	August 15
Teacher's Day	September 5
International Literacy Day*	September 8
International Day of Peace	September (Third Tuesday of September)
World Tourism Day	September 27
International Day for the Elderly*	October 1
University Children's Day*	October (First Monday of October)
Mahatma Gandhi Birthday	October 2
World Habitat Day	October 5
Air Force Day	October 8

Universal Postal Union Day*	October 9
Day of Solidarity with South African Political Prisoners	October 11
Post Office Day	October 19
World Standard Day	October 14
World Food Day*	October 16
United Nations Day	October 24
World Development Information Day*	October 24
National Re-Dedication Day	October 31
Children's Day	November 14
National Integration Day	November 19
International Day of Solidarity with the Palestinian People*	November 29
World AIDS Day*	December 1
International Day of Disabled Persons*	December 3
Navy Day	December 4
International Volunteer Day for Economic and Social Development	December 5
Flag Day	December 7
Human Rights Day*	December 10
Kisan Day	December 23

* Proclaimed by UN System/UNESCO Associated Schools

6

INDIA SINCE INDEPENDENCE

ACHIEVEMENTS

Going back, India that is Bharat was the richest and the most prosperous country in the world. It was then known as the *'Golden Sparrow'*. The standard of living of the common man was reasonably high. Articles of everyday needs were available in plenty. A common man could get easily things like milk, butter, ghee and foodgrains. Literally speaking 'Rivers of milk flowed'. Indian handicrafts and industrial products were known for their excellence of design and quality all over the world. From the richness of this land and from the labour and wisdom of its people had sprung great wealth, great ideas, great skills and arts. Naturally, therefore, foreigners were tempted to come to India for learning. as well as loot and plunder.

The well-knit economic organization of the country received a serious setback with the advent of invaders and especially with the British rulers who were primarily concerned with the governance of the country, not its growth. They were greatly interested in draining out wealth from India. Industrial crafts, industries and agriculture, all suffered heavily. As a result, India became a poor country. People remained underfed, ill-housed and scantily dressed.

The statement 'A rich country inhabited by the poor people' seems paradoxical and strange. But it is still true to a considerable extent though since independence we have made a spectacular progress in different fields. The giant *irrigation dams* at *Bhakra, Hirakud* and *Nagarjunasagar*, the huge steel mills at *Bhilai, Bokaro, Rourkela* and *Durgapur;* the fertiliser factories at *Sindri* and *Nangal;* the 1000-tonne per day ammonia plant (said to be the largest in the world) at Tuticorin; the *aircraft factories at Bangalore, Hyderabad* and *Nasik;* the locomotive factory at Chittarajan; the atomic reactor at Trombay; the rocket launching station at Sriharikota; the ISRO's establishment like *Vikram Sarabhai Space Centre,* Trivandrum and Space Application Centre, Ahmedabad; launching of Indian Satellite *Bhaskara* and *Rohini;* three axis-stabilished Geostationary Communication Satellite; *APPLE (Ariahe Passenger Payload Experiment),* establishment of *Indian National Satellite System (INSAT);* participation of an Indian Cosmonaut in a joint Indo-Soviet Flight; nuclear explosion of Pokaran, etc., are the prized possessions of the Indian Nation.

November 21, 1988 marked the 25th anniversary of Indian Space Programme. The Silver Jubilee Year saw the launching of three major programmes; IRS-1A, ASLV-02 and INSAT-1A. Militarily we are among the first five countries in the world.

India is the sixth country to successfully detonate a nuclear device as part of its successful experiment for peace purposes.

We have the third largest reservoir of highly skilled scientific and technical manpower in the world.

India is the fifth nation to have its remote sensing satellite.

We have achieved self-sufficiency in foodgrains.

India is the third largest producer of books in English, next to the U.S.A and U.K.

The eradication of poverty problem of the masses became the first consideration of the government soon after we achieved independence. We decided to adopt the system of planned development for tackling our problem of poverty which was linked with rising prices, low production, unemployment and inequalities of income.

To frame a development plan for independent India, the *Planning Commission* was set up in March 1950, by a resolution of the Government of India. The aims of planning as defined by the resolution were, 'to promote a rapid rise in the standard of living of the people by efficient exploitation of the resources of the country, increasing production and offering opportunities to all for employment in the service of the community'.

The *First Five Year Plan* was initiated in April 1951. This covered the period 1951-1956. So far we have had eight Five Year Plans and Three Yearly Plans. The *Eighth Five-Year Plan,* covers the period 1992 to 1997.

The most important achievement of planning in the post-independence period is our self-sufficiency in foodgrains. Now we need not import foodgrains for domestic requirements as we did till a few years ago. The production was about 185 million tonnes in 1995-96 as against 51 million tonnes 1950-51. Production in 1996-97 in likely to be 191.2 million tonnes.

As a result of many multipurpose projects, area under irrigation increased from 226 lakh hectares in 1950 to 860 lakh hectares in 1990-91.

Our industry has many strengths: a wide range of products, a demonstrable ability to absorb and operate high technology, a large entrepreneurial capability and ample managerial and technical skills.

During the Plans, industrial production has made rapid strides, both in terms of quality and quantity. As per the index of *industrial production,* the growth rates achieved in the industrial sector as a whole were 8.6 per cent in 1984-85, 8.7 per cent in 1985-86, 9.1 per cent in 1986-87, 7.3 per cent in 1987-88, 8.7 in 1988-89, 8.6 in 1989 and 8.1 in 1990-91. However, there was setback in 1991-92. However, there has been a substantial upsurge in the growth of industrial production during 1995-96. The latest available index of industrial growth for October 1996 shows that overall production was 9.9 per cent.

In the year 1950-51, there were only two major units producing iron and steel. Now we have eleven relevant major steel plants. Steel production was about one million tonnes in 1950-51. He production of finished steel is likely to exceed 23.5 million tonnes during 1996-97.

Cotton textile industry holds the second place in the production of cloth in the world. At present there are about 700 textile mills in the country.

In 1951, we had 138 sugar mills in the country. This number increased to 351 in 1987. About half the mills are in the public sector.

The production of cement was 2.69 million tonnes in 1951. The production capacity is likely to reach 140 million tonnes by 2002 AD.

There has been a tremendous increase in power generation and in number of public undertakings. We had only 5 public enterprises in 1951.

The road network in the country has become very elaborate system of national highways, state and district roads, and rural roads totalling about 23 lakh kms. This is five and a half times the figure of 4 lakh km of roads in 1950-51. The volume of road transport has been growing at an average rate of 10 per cent. The share of road transport for trade traffic has increased from 11 per cent in 1951 to 60 per cent in 1995.

Prior to Independence, average life span of an Indian was 32 years. Today it has lengthened to 58 years.

Our Constitution can be described as a charter of freedom. It enshrines the supremacy of the will of the people and their resolve to secure for all citizens: justice, social, economic and political; Equity of status and opportunity, and to promote among them all Fraternity assuring the dignity of the individual and the unity of the nation. The will of the people is exercised through universal adult franchise and a parliamentary democracy. Election to Parliament and State legislature are open contests for all political parties, and independent candidated also enjoy full scope to express themsleves.

Notwithstanding various problems and the magnitude of the task of conducting elections, we have all *general elections* with significant success. Barring the period, March 1977 to July 15, 1979 and December 1989 to May 1991 when the Janata Party and National Front were in power at the Centre, the Congress had held the reigns of the Government since the first General Election in 1951-52.

Many political changes accompanied by government changes, especially in States have taken place in the country since Independence, through peaceful and constitutional means. Transfer of power from one party to another has taken place as a natural course and in an orderly manner.

Another historic step in the development of democracy in the country was the inauguration of *Panchayati Raj* in October 1950. The Panchayati Raj aims at giving full authority and responsibility to the village people and helping them play an active role in local development through the Panchayats. There are over 228,500 Village Panchayats in the country covering partially the entire population of India.

With the Panchayati Raj, we now have parliamentary democracy in operation from the Gram Sabha to the Lok Sabha.

We have got an estalished judicial system.

PROGRESS MADE AND TASKS AHEAD

Government continued to follow a multi-pronged strategy on Human Rights matters—strict enforcement of constitutional and legal safeguards, stern action against officials found guilty of human rights violations, providing necessary financial and administrative support to the National Human Rights Commission to enable it to discharge its functions effectively and promotion of human rights awareness both amongst the law enforcing agencies as well as common masses.

In order to strenghten the accountability of the executive of Parliament, 17 department-related standing committees of Parliament were constituted in April 1993 to make detailed examination of Bills, demands for grants, annual reports of the ministries and national basic long-term policy documents presented to the House. This will greatly facilitate the working of Parliament.

The country had its share of national calamities. However, the unprecedented scale of damage in the Maharashtra earthquake stands out among these. In all these instances, Government responded with commendable alertness and provided prompt relief. Governments of several other countries, the World Bank and other institutions promptly offered assistance. A massive reconstruction programme in the earthquake affected areas of Maharashtra was taken up at an outlay of Rs. 1,000 crore. Non-governmental organisations were appropriately associated with the reconstruction programme.

The economic reforms introduced in 1991 gained momentum and have been pursued consistently. The initial spurt of referms from 1991-92 to 1993-94 was very successful by all accounts. Economic growth jumped to 7.2 per cent in 1994-95. However, there was a marked slow down in the pace or reforms in 1995-96. Nevertheless GDP grew by 7.1 per cent in that year. In 1996-97 it is likely to be around 6.8 per cent. Still much more needs to be done. Government is aware that the reform is an irreversible and continuous process and needs to be implemented with determination and foresight, keeping the responses and circumstances in the country constantly in view. As a result of this approach, the progress of implementation has been steady and firm and based on a general consensus.

In drawing up the refrom package, stress has been laid by the Government on reforms in the financial sector. The financial institutions have necessarily to be restructured and strengthened to enable them to take on the new responsibility imposed by the expanded activity in the private sector. An important policy change was the unification of the exchange rate and the floating of the rupee in March 1993. As a result of this market based exchange rate the Rupee remained remarkably stable during 1993-94 and 1994-95. However, it came under stress in1995-96. In February 1996 Rupee touched a low of about Rs. 38 per US dollar. However, due to several measures taken by RBI it staged a recovery and in the range of 35-36.

Global investors have shown growing confidence in the Indian market. A number of changes have been made so far in 1996-97 in the areas of foreign investment. The Foreign Investment Council has been set up. The significant point of foreign investment is that the bulk of this, is proposed in sectors like power, oil refining, food processing, metallurgical industry, electrical equipment, chemicals, electronics and other priority areas. Total foreign investment (direct plus portfolio) during April-December 1996 surged to over US$ 4 billion.

Government continues to lay a great deal of emphasis on export promotion. The results of changes in the trade policy coupled with the floating of the exchange rate and the general liberalisation of the economy have yielded results and exports have shown good growth during the period of 1913 to 1995. According to Union Commerce Minister B.B. Ramaiah India's exports would achieve a growth rate of 18 per cent despite poor show in first half of 1996-97

Government attaches the highest priority to development of agriculture. The timely provision of adequate and reasonably priced inputs and the creation of a structure that provides for the timely announcement of prices which in turn promotes higher production so as to meet fully the domestic needs of the country as well as exports, are the major objectives of the Government. Agricultural crop production in 1996-97 is expected to show good recovery from the slower growth in 1995-96. The sharp decline in foodgrains production by 3.4 per cent in expected to be reversed by an increase of 3.3 per cent in 1996-97. Foodgrains production in 1996-97 is likely to be 191.2 million tonnes.

As part of the agriculture policy, States have been advised to remove all intra and inter-State restrictions on the movement of foodgrains.

It is Government determination that no vulnerable section of the population —be it women, children, minorities, Scheduled Caste, Scheduled Tribes or backward classes—should remain outside the main-stream of development. In all areas of development of the poor, resource allocations were considerably enhanced.

The Common Minimum programme underpins the strong commitment of the government to the development of the social sectors for achieving distributive justice. This commitment is reflected in the increase in the Central Government Plan and non-plan allocations for social services to a record high of 1.19 per cent of GDP in 1996-97 (BE). An additional amount of Rs. 2466 crore of central assistance to States and Union Territories' plans has also been allocated in 1996-97 budget for expenditure on basic minimum services.

The Government has also accorded high priority to poverty alleviation programmes. The Central plan allocations for social sectors and poverty alleviation programmes show highest growth of 85.6 per cent for education in 1996-97 over 1995-96 (BE). The outlay for elementary education has gone up by 247.8 per cent due to mid-day meal programme. The allocation for health was raised by 21.6 per cent and for rural development, encompassing the major programmes of poverty alleviation by 12. per cent in 1996-97 over 1995-96 (BE). The weaker sections, especially scheduled castes, scheduled tribes and women have been given importance in special programmes of poverty alleviation and employment as well as in several other programmes. The PDS has been streamlined recently in order to target the poorer sections of the population.

The working group on the Ninth Plan has projected a requirement of Rs.60,000 crore for rural development. The tentative target for the Ninth Plan under the self-employment Integrated Rural Development Programme (IRDP) is to cover 15 million families by 2001-02. However, the target has been nominally raised to benefit 15 lakh rural youth.

A large gap between the applications sponsored under the Prime Minister's Rozgar Yojana (PMRY) and the loans sanctioned has been identified as a major reason for the slow progress in the rate of employment growth. Efforts to speed up the employment growth under PMRY ad other employment generation programmes, especially in the Khadi and Village industries sector, will now be made.

Our relations with our neighbours continued to be cordial, and our interaction in various fields with Bangladesh, Bhutan, Maldives, Nepal and Sri Lanka recorded good progress. India and Bangladesh on December 12 ,1996 signed a historic 30-year treaty on sharing the Ganga waters, restoring specialties between the two countries. In the case of Pakistan, however, its continuing support for terrorism and subversion in Jummu and Kashmir and anti-Indian activities world-wide seriously hampered our efforts at normalising relations. The Prime Minister offered Pakistan a dialogue aimed at establishing good-neighbourly relations as enshrined in the Shimla Agreement. Bilateral talks have since taken place, but the stridency of Pakistan's anti-Indian statements has grown, adversely affecting efforts at improving bilateral ties. There are no quarrels between us and the people of Pakistan. We feel that for good relations between our countries the Government of Pakistan should give up its negative approach and reciprocate our desire to normalise India-Pakistan relations in accordance with the Shimla Agreement.

Our relations with China have improved markedly. The Prime Minister's visit to China in September 1993, and the signing of the agreement on the maintenance of peace and tranquillity along the line of actual control and China President Jiang Zemin's visit to India in November 1996 Chinese President called for joint efforts to explore ways and means of economic cooperation between the two countries have brought them to a new stage of development.

India values SAARC as an instrument of regional cooperation consistent with the objectives of its charter. SAARC has recorded progress in dealing with certain important issues of common interest such as poverty, terrorism, population growth, problems relating to the status of women, children, youth and drugs and psychotropic sustenances. We continue to pay an active role in SAARC with a view to promoting its socio-economic and other objectives in accordance with the SAARC charter.

Our interaction with the United States has traditionally ranged over a number of areas from education and science and technology to culture and sports. We have also cooperated in the UN on issues relating to disarmament such as the comprehensive test ban treaty. The response from the United States to our economic liberalisation policies has been very positive and the US investments in India were very substantial. We look forward to working with the United States towards mutual understanding, including on those issues on which such understanding needs enhancement. This will reflect the vibrant democratic and secular ideals of our two countries.

Relations with the Russian Federation,drawing upon rich traditions of our friendship of the past, continued with mutual understanding and cooperation. Despite certain difficulties the two countries face, cooperation in the political, economic, commercial and other areas was sought to be promoted by both sides. The goodwill and understanding that underpins our relations reinforce our joint efforts at identifying possibilities of further cooperation in various areas in today's changed context.

India was happy of the signing of the declaration of principles on interim self-government arrangements between Israel and the PLO in September 1993 as a notable step towards peace and stability in West Asia and the restoration of the legitimate rights of the Palestinian people. Israel President Ezer Weizman's visit to India in December. 1996 strengthened the relations between India and Israel.Four agreements were signed to intensify technical cooperation in science and technology

India continues to play an active role in shaping the global agenda on issues pertaining to political and security matters, economic and social development, human rights, environment and population.

CONCLUDING OBSERVATIONS

A large part of our population still remains backward. There is a wide gulf between the rich and the poor. *Unemployment* is on the increase. National integration is our urgent need. Erosion in the standard of values, in fact is the topmost blockade, which requires to be checked and a crusade for 'Clean Life, Clean Poltics and Clean Administration' is to be given first priority.

India is on the move. The tasks before us are very challenging and tremendous. But there is no causes for despair. By harnessing all our resources and working unitedly and sincerely, we can usher in an era of peace, progress and prosperity.

The 21st century beckons up holding fourth new hopes. We, the people of India, must march ahead as an integrated resurgent.

As *Gurudev Rabindranath Tagore* would advise, we must "hold the faith firm". surely "the day will dawn".

7

ECONOMY AND THE PLAN : AN OVERVIEW

INTRODUCTION

The Eighth Five Year Plan (1992-97) was launched immediately after the initiation of a set of stabilisation and structural adjustment measures, which were designed to combat the then prevailing crisis in the balance of payments (BoP) and resources position of the Government in 1991. The Plan took into account some of the changes that were expected to come about due to these reforms. The Plan also kept in view the poor performance of the economy in the base year (1991-92). The overall growth was estimated to be negligible during the base year. The annual inflation rate was ruling at double-digit level. On the balance of payments front, although there was some improvement in the foreign exchange reserves, exports were exceptionally sluggish. Given this performance of the economy in 1991-92, the Eighth Plan set down somewhat cautious macroeconomic targets. The plan aimed at an annual average growth rate of 5.6 per cent and an average industrial growth rate of about 7.5 per cent. These growth targets were planned to be achieved with relative price stability and a substantial improvement in the country's balance of payments. It was envisaged that the ratio of current account deficit will be maintained at about 1.6 per cent. The performance of the economy during the first four years of the Plan indicate that most macro-economic targets would be achieved by the end of the terminal year (1996-97).

GROWTH AND SECTORAL OUTPUT

In 1991-92, the base year of the Eighth Plan, and the first year of the economic reforms, GDP grew by less than 1 per cent as compared to an annual average growth at about 6 per cent during the Seventh Plan period. However, the economy soon absorbed the shock of the stabilisation measures and recovered within a year to record 5.1 per cent growth in 1992-93. The growth rate accelerated to 6.2 per cent in 1993-94 and over 7 per cent in the following two years. Thus, on an average, GDP has grown by 6.4 per cent during the first four years of the Eighth Plan. Despite some early indications of slowdown of industrial growth in 1996-97 (the last year of the Plan), GDP may still grow at over 6 per cent. Accordingly, the average growth of GDP during the Eighth Plan is expected to be a little over 6 per cent which is significantly higher than the Plan target of 5.6 per cent.

The growth performance of the economy reflects in good measure the successive good performance of the agricultural sector. After recording a decline of 2.3 per cent in 1991-92, agricultural GDP increased at an average growth rate of about 4.8 per cent per annum during the first three years of the Plan, before recording a marginal decline in 1995-96. Foodgrains production increased steadily from about 168 million tonnes in 1991-92 to about 191 million tonnes in 1994-95. Latest estimates suggest that the output of foodgrains during 1995-96 may be considerably lower at 185 million tonnes. However, following good monsoon during 1996, the production of foodgrains in likely to bounce back to its 1994-95 level or even exceed it. Overall, the growth of agricultural GDP during the Eighth Plan may be slightly above the targeted growth rate of 3.1 per cent.

On the industrial front, all the major segments witnessed severe recession during 1991-92. The index of industrial production grew by less than 1 per cent during 1991-92. The index of manufacturing production declined by about 1 per cent. GDP from industry, which had grown at about 7.5 per cent during the Seventh Plan period, registered a decline of 1.9 per cent in 1991-92. Since then its growth has picked up substantially to 4.3 per cent in 1992-93, 7.9 per cent in 1993-94, 9.9 per cent in 1994-95, and about 12.7 per cent in 1995-96. Thus the average growth of industrial GDP during the first four years of the Plan has been about 8.7 per cent. Despite indications of some slowdown in industrial production during 1996-97, industrial GDP may still grow at over 9 per cent in the terminal year of the Plan. Thus, the expected growth of industrial GDP at about 8.8 per cent per annum will be significantly higher than the Eighth Plan target of 7.5 per cent.

The performance of the service sector during the first four years of the Eighth Plan has been consistently good. Even during the height of recession during the base year of the Plan (1991-92), the service sector performed well by growing to about 5 per cent. The service sector, consisting of trade, transport, communication, finance, insurance and community and social services, has grown at an average of over 7 per cent during the first four years of the Plan. In the terminal year (1996-97) of the Plan, the service sector is expected to grow at over 7 per cent. Thus, the target of 6.2 per cent set for the service sector in the Eighth Plan is likely to be exceeded by a significant margin. However, the creation of new capacities in a number of sectors has fallen significantly short of the target during the Eighth Plan, primarily due to the slower pace of investment.

SAVINGS AND INVESTMENT

Gross domestic savings as a proportion of GDP averaged 23.2 per cent during 1992-93 to 1995-96. The savings rate which was relatively low, at 21.1 per cent in the first two years, staged a dramatic recovery in 1994-95. A record private corporate savings rate of 3.9 per cent and a substantial recovery of household savings rate at 19.2 per cent helped push the gross domestic savings rate to a new peak of 24.9 per cent in 1994-95. Quick estimates of the CSO indicate that savings rate has moved upwards to 25.5 per cent during 1995-96 despite decline of household financial savings rate by about 2 percentage points.

Gross domestic investment (adjusted for errors and omissions) as a proportion of GDP averaged 24.5 per cent during 1992-93 to 1995-96. The investment rate which was relatively low at 22.3 per cent during the first two years of Eighth Plan, received a boost in 1994-95. A relatively higher savings rate at 24.9 per cent and a current account deficit of about 1 per cent of GDP pushed the investment rate of 26 per cent in 1994-95. With the savings rate estimated to be around 25.5 per cent and the current account deficit estimated at about 1.7 per cent of GDP, the investment rate during 1995-96 may exceed 27 per cent of GDP.

FISCAL DEVELOPMENTS

The Eighth Plan document stated that a major aim of fiscal policy should be to roll back the fiscal deficit of the Centre and the States, taken together as a percentage of GDP, from an average of 10.6 per cent during the Seventh Plan and from about 11 per cent in 1990-91, to an average of about 7 per cent during the Eighth Plan period. This implicitly meant that the Centre's fiscal deficit would be required to be brought down to an average of 5 per cent, and that of the States to an average of about 2 per cent during the Eighth Plan period. Fiscal developments during the Eighth Plan period suggest that these targets, despite conscious efforts, would remain unfulfilled. The fiscal deficits of the States and the Centre during the full five year period is likely to remain at about 3 and 6 per cent of GDP, respectively.

Though on average the Centre's fiscal deficit at about 6 per cent of GDP during the Eighth Plan period appears high, it represents significant reduction from its level in 1990-91. Over the past six budgets, the fiscal deficit of the Centre has declined from 8.3 per cent in 1990-91 to a budgeted 5 per cent in 1996-97. More significantly, the primary deficit of the Centre has come down from 4.3 per cent in 1990-91 to only 0.2 per cent in 1996-97(BE). Unfortunately, interest payments as a percentage of GDP has increased continuously from 4 per cent in 1990-91 to 4.8 per cent in 1996-97 (BE). This has partly offset the efforts to reduce revenue deficit. Revenue deficit of the Central Government which was 3.5 per cent of GDP in 1990-91 has come down by only 1 percentage point in 1996-97(BE).

In effecting fiscal correction it is imperative in the Indian context to see that the Plan budget of the Government is not adversely affected. The Plan expenditure of the Centre, which consists of budgetary support for the Central Plan and Central assistance to the States and UT Plans, accounted for 5.3 per cent of GDP in 1990-91. Except in 1993-94, when the Plan expenditure constituted 5.4 per cent of GDP, this ratio has tended to decline over the years.

In the last two years of the Eighth Plan, the Plan expenditure has come down to about 4.4 per cent of GDP. Decline in Plan expenditure has adversely affected the budget support to the Central Plan, which has come down from 3.3 per cent of GDP in 1990-91 to 2.6 per cent in 1996-97 (BE). Though marginally, the Central assistance to States & UT Plans has also been adversely affected. This has happened in spite of significant reduction in non-plan expenditure, which has come down from 14.4 per cent of GDP in 1990-91 to 12.1 per cent in 1996-97 (BE).

Within the Plan budget, there has been a compositional change of expenditure. Expenditure on economic services (budget support) which accounted for 2.6 per cent of GDP in 1990-91 declined to 1.7 per cent in 1996-97 (BE). In contrast, expenditure on social services increased from 0.7 per cent of GDP in 1990-91 to over 0.9 per cent in 1996-97 (BE). Within economic services group, there has been some shift of expenditure away from conventional sectors such as energy, transport and communication and industry and minerals to agriculture, irrigation and rural development.

INFLATION

The Eighth Plan envisaged that there will be a reasonable degree of price stability. It was surmised that the planned fiscal adjustment would bring down the borrowing requirements of the Government, including the borrowings from the Reserve Bank of India, which would ensure that the annual growth of money supply is brought down from about 17 per cent in the recent past tc about 11 to 12 per cent during the Eighth Plan period. With income elasticity of demand for money estimated at about 1.5, and the economy planned to grow at about 5 to 6 per cent per year, it was anticipated that the projected monetary growth would enable the Government to contain the trend rate of inflation to about 5 per cent per year. In the event, none of the assumptions behind the anticipated inflation rate came true. As a consequence, average inflation rate as measured by the Wholesale Price Index (WPI) during the first four years of the plan exceeded 9 per cent. In the terminal year of the plan, the inflation rate is expected to be about 7 per cent. Thus, the average inflation rate during the Eighth Plan period would be a little less than 9 per cent, significantly higher than the projected 5 per cent.

Initially, following the stabilisation measures, the overall inflation rate on a point-to-point basis fell from 13.6 per cent in 1991-92 to 7 per cent in 1992-93. However, it accelerated to 10.8 per cent in 1993-94 and further by 10.4 per cent in 1994-95. The annual rate of inflation during 1995-96 had shown downward trend, recording a low of about 5 per cent since January, 1996. The average inflation rate during 1995-96 was higher at 7.8 per cent. Price rise continued to be subdued at about 5 per cent during the first half of 1996-97, and has shown signs of acceleration during the second half, due to hike in administered prices of petroleum products and coal.

BALANCE OF PAYMENTS

The current account deficit which was about $10 billion in 1990-91 has come down to about $5.5 billion in 1995-96. In some of the intervening years, it reached as low as $ 1.2 billion. As percentage of GDP, the current account deficit has declined from about 3.2 in 1990-91 to 1.7 in 1995-96. On average, during the first four years of the Eighth Plan, the current account—GDP ratio has been about 1.2 per cent and is likely to hover around 1.5 per cent for the full five year period, almost the same as projected in the Eighth Plan document.

Improvement in the current account deficit since 1990-91 has been brought about by improved trade balance as well as improved balance of the invisible account. Trade deficit (RBI data) as a percentage of GDP, which was 3.2 in 1990-91, had declined to about 1.6 in 1994-95, but increased significantly to about 2.7 in 1995-96. The improvement in trade deficit has been largely due to improved export performance. Exports as a percentage of GDP have successively increased from 6.2 in 1990-91 to about 10 in 1995-96. Net invisible balance, which was negative in 1990-91, improved significantly over the years to touch 1 per cent of GDP in 1995-96.

Despite widening of the current account deficit over the last three years, the foreign exchange reserves position has remained comfortable. India's foreign exchange reserves, comprising foreign currency assets, gold reserves and SDR balances, which stood at $9.2 billion in March, 1992 increased steadily to over $25 billion in March, 1995. It declined significantly to about $ 21.7 billion in March, 1996. By the end of June, 1996, however, there has been a modest build-up in the reserves to a level of $22.1 billion. The movement in the reserves closely reflected the developments in the current accound balance and the net capital inflows. The surge in capital inflows, especially in the form of foreign portfolio investment, helped build up substantial foreign exchange reserves since 1993-94

The exchange rate of the Rupee remained remarkably stable during 1993-94 and 1994-95 following introduction of the market based exchanged rate regime in March, 1993. The Rupee, however, came under stress in the second half of 1995-96. An indication of widening of the current account deficit and an ebbing of capital flows, and the pronounced appreciation of the US dollar against major currencies triggered off market expectations and resulted in depreciation of the Rupee from about Rs. 31.50 in April, 1995 to about Rs. 35.60 per US dollar in October, 1995. Following intervention by the RBI, the Rupee stabilised in the range of Rs. 34-36 until January, 1996. In February, 1996, the Rupee again suffered a bout of depreciation and touched a low of about Rs. 38 per U.S. dollar. Following a number of measures by the RBI in early February, 1996, the Rupee staged a strong recovery in March-April, 1996 and has since remained in the range of Rs. 35-36 per US dollar.

THE EIGHTH FIVE YEAR PLAN 1992-97

The current financial year, 1996-97 is the last year of the Eighth Five Year Plan (1992-97). The Eighth Plan commenced in April, 1992 against the backdrop of overall changes taking place in the world. These changes had profound impact on both the structure of international relations and the world economy.

Recognising the relevance of developmental planning in the changed scenario of globalisation of the economy, it was resolved that the Planning Commission would work on building a long-term strategic vision of the future with concentration on anticipating future trends and evolving integrated strategies for the achievement of higher possible level of development of the country in keeping with competitive international standards. The Eighth Plan document was endorsed by the National Development Council (NDC) in its forty-fourth meeting, held in May, 1992.

An attempt was made in the Eighth Plan to correct the fiscal imbalances from which the Sixth and Seventh Plan suffered. The non-inflationary manner to be adopted for funding of the Plan in order to avoid debt trap both internally and externally, called for a series of austerity measures which involved a reduction in Government's dissavings, higher resource mobilisation both by the Centre and the States and improvement in the performance of public sector units.

The Eighth Plan recognised the essential need to involve people in the process of development. The Plan envisaged substantial devolution of power to the people's organisations at the district, block and village levels. Special attention was paid to employment in the rural areas with the objective of eradicating poverty.

An average growth rate of 5.6 per cent per annum was proposed during the Plan period. The level of national investment was proposed at Rs. 7,98,000 crore.

EIGHTH PLAN (1992-97) PERFORMANCE

The overall public sector plan outlay during the Eighth Five Year Plan (1992-97) amounts to Rs. 4,34,100 crore at 1991-92 prices. The share of the Central Plan in this amount is Rs. 2,47,865 crore, or 57.1 per cent whereas the share of State Plans accounts for Rs. 1,79,985 crore, or 41.5 per cent. The plans of the Union Territories account for the remaining share of Rs. 6,250 crore, or 1.4 per cent of the overall Eighth Plan Public Sector outlay.

A review in real terms (i.e., after allowing for inflation and assuming that the revised estimates for 1994-95 and 1995-96 and budget estimates for 1996-97 would materialise), has shown that the Plan performance in financial terms during the Eighth Plan (1992-97) accounts for about 100 per cent of the approved Eighth Plan outlay in the Central Sector. The corresponding proportion works out to about 81 per cent and 116 per cent, for State Plans and UT Plans, respectively. Thus, in the case of Centre, the Plan expenditure during the

Eighth Plan period (1992-97) is likely to be as envisaged. While no shortfall in the case of UT Plans is expected, major shortfalls are likely occur in the Plan provision as well as expenditure of States vis-a-vis their Eighth Plan approved outlays.

ANNUAL PLANS 1992-97

For Annual Plan 1992-93, the first year of the Eighth Plan 1992-97, the actual expenditure for Centre, States and UTs amounts to Rs. 72852.44 crore which is less by Rs. 7919.52 crore (nearly 10%) than the approved outlay of Rs. 80771.96 crore. The shortfall in utilisation of outlays has been reflected both in the Central and States/UTs sectors.

The Annual Plan 1993-94 envisaged a total public sector outlay of Rs. 1,00,120.16 crore. The actual expenditure for Centre, States and UTs amounts to Rs. 88080.66 crore, which is lower by 12.03 per cent than the Budget Estimates for the Plan. The actual expenditure for Central Plan for 1993-94 amounting to Rs. 55215.88 crore, against the budget estimates of Rs. 63936.16 crore, represents an increase of 16.6 per cent in real terms over 1992-93, whereas in the case of States and UTs, the increase in actual expenditure in 1993-94 was only of the order of 4 per cent over 1992-93.

The Annual Plan 1994-95 envisaged a total public sector outlay of Rs. 1,12,197.12 crore in the budget estimates, which on revision came down to Rs. 1,06,204.25 crore. Thus, the revised estimates were lower by 5.3 per cent than the budget estimates for the Plan. While the Central Plan outlay, on revision was lower only marginally by 2.6 per cent the total outlay for States and UTs has come down by 9.9 per cent in the revised estimates.

The total public sector outlay for the Annual Plan 1995-96 was fixed at Rs. 1,28,589.98 crore which on revision came down by 6.7 per cent at Rs. 119954.33 crore. The shortfall in Centre was by 5.4 per cent, and in the State/ UT sector by 8.8 per cent.

During these four years, the shortfall in expenditure at the Central Sector was mainly due to inadequate mobilisation of Internal and Extra Budgetary Resources (IEBR) by the Public Sector undertakings and various Ministries/ Departments even after providing more budgetary support in the revised estimates. In the States sector, the reason for shortfall was lack of mobilising adequate resources due to deterioration in the balance of current revenues, erosion in the contribution of State Electricity Boards (SEBs) and State Road Transport Corporations (SRTCs), negative opening balances, mounting non-plan expenditure and shortfalls in the collection of small savings, etc.

The current year's Plan (1996-97) envisaged a total public sector outlay of Rs. 1,46,160.29 crore comprising Rs. 87086.17 crore for the Centre, Rs. 56,347.11 crore for the States and Rs. 2727.01 crore for the Union Territories. This represents an increase of about 10.4 per cent for the Centre and 18.5 per cent each in the case of States and the Union Territories over the Budget estimates of 1995-96.

TARGETS AND ACHIEVEMENTS

The average growth rate of GDP during the Eighth Plan is likely to exceed the envisaged target of 5.6 per cent. Much of this growth performance reflects the good performance of Agricultural and Industrial sectors. Though the service sector provided necessary support in achieving this growth rate, expansion of capacities in various infrastructural sub-sectors suffered setback due to lack of investments. Also, the performance in the social sector, including rural development, was not enough to meet the targets set for poverty alleviation.

Infrastructure

Sustained growth of the economy depends on adequate availability of basic infrastructural facilities, such as power, transport and communications, of adequate quality. The Eighth Plan has fallen significantly short not only of its targets but also of the Seventh Plan physical achievements, in these areas. This was primarily due to the slower pace of investment in these sectors. The investment needs in this sector were of a magnitude that were beyond the resources available to the Government. Keeping in view the importance of infrastructure sector for overall economic growth, as well as for attracting private investment to make good the deficiency in Public Sector investment caused by serious resource crunch, it is necessary to protect Plan outlays of certain crucial infrastructure sub-sectors in both Centre and State Plans.

Social Sector

The programmes of direct State intervention in poverty alleviation and development of the social sectors designed during the Seventh Plan continued in the Eighth Plan also with changes in their content and scope. However, the performance of social sectors like education, health and family welfare, women and child development, housing, water supply and urban development, which depend exclusively on budgetary support for financing their Plan outlays, have shown shortfalls in expenditure as compared to the Eighth Plan targets. Shortfall in making adequate allocations for social sectors during the operational Annual Plans of the Eighth Plan occurred due to severe budgetary constraints. It is imperative that the outlays in these sectors need be protected and proper utilisation of funds in the implementation of various schemes be ensured.

Employment and Regional Balance

The Eighth Plan envisaged an annual average growth rate of 2.6 per cent in employment, which was expected to generate 8 to 9 million jobs in the first half of the Plan and 9 to 10 million jobs in the second half. According to the 50th round of the NSS (1993-94), the growth rate of employment between 1987-88 and 1993-94 was 2.23 per cent, falling short of the target in the first half of the Eighth Plan. As a result, while open unemployment rates declined from 3.77

per cent in 1987-88 to 2.56 per cent in 1993-94, the rate of underemployment remained more or less constant at a little over 6 per cent. The States where the incidence of underemployment was over 10 per cent as per 1993-94 estimates are Goa, Kerala and Tamil Nadu. There is also evidence of deterioration of inter-regional disparities in per capita incomes. Some of the populous and less-developed States have experienced growth rates lower than the national average. In particular, the per capita State Domestic Product declined in Bihar from Rs. 1204 in 1990-91 to Rs. 1067 in 1994-95 at 1980-81 prices, while it stagnated in Uttar Pradesh, growing at less than 0.2 per cent per annum over the period.

RESOURCE MOBILISATION

The details given above clearly bring out the fact that the shortfalls in Plan expenditure in States sector have been bigger than in the Central sector. An important reason for shortfall in States, has been their inability to raise resources for financing their plans as per commitments made at the time of Annual Plan discussions. As a result, inspite of the increase in the share of States in total budgetary support to Public Sector Plan the share of the States in the total Public Sector Plan Outlay has come down.

It is, therefore, necessary to step up resource mobilisation efforts so as to protect the approved Plan outlays. In this regard, earnest efforts are required to improve the operational efficiency of State-level Public Enterprises, especially of the State Electricity Boards (SEBs) and State Road Transport Corporation (SRTCs) so as to derive efficiency gains from these enterprises and thereby provide the much-needed resources for financing the State Plan outlays.

In the Central sector also, there is need to ensure adequate flow of funds to infrastructure sub-sectors like power, ports etc. Also, it is necessary to improve the performance of the Central Public Sector Enterprises so as to minimise their dependence on budgetary support. Those sectors which have potential to raise their own investible resources should help increasing the share of capital expenditure in the total expenditure of the government and a substantial amount of budgetary resources, thus saved, could be invested in other priority areas, like poverty eradication and improving living standards of the people.

NINTH FIVE YEAR PLAN (1997-2002)

The Planning Commission prepared the Approach Paper to the Ninth Five Year Plan (1997-2002) based on the major policy direction given by the government in the form of "A Common Approach to Major Policy Matters and a Minimum Programme" and also taking into account the views of Chief Ministers of States, Parliamentarians, experts, specific socio-economic groups etc. The Approach Paper thus prepared has been deliberated upon in the meetings of full Planning Commission before the same was considered by the National

Development Council (NDC) in its meeting held on January 16. 1997. The Approach Paper to the Ninth Five Year Plan which has been approved unanimously in the above meeting of the NDC and would form the guiding document in the preparation of the Ninth Five Year Plan.

ANNUAL PLAN (1997-98)

Annual Plan 1997-98 is the first year of the Ninth Five Year Plan. The Secretary-level discussions for formulation of the Plan with various Central Ministries/Departments have been completed by the end of January, 1997. Though the Planning Commission has completed the assessment of States' Own Resources, outlays in respect of States/Union Territories are only being finalised since exercises in this regard are in progress.

8

NINTH FIVE YEAR PLAN (1997-2002)

NINTH PLAN GROWTH STRATEGY APPROVED

The accelerated growth strategy contained in the approach paper to the Ninth Plan got the Prime Minister's nod at a full-body meting of the Planning Commission held in New Delhi on November 29. The growth strategy envisages the 7 per cent growth in Gross Domestic Product to be accompanied by a 4 per cent growth in agricultural production, 14.5 per cent growth in exports, 15.0 per cent growth in imports and decline in unemployment rate from the existing level of 7.5 per cent to 5.5 per cent at the end of the plan period. Accordingly, the gross national investment during the plan period is estimated at Rs. 2,190,000 crore, of which the share of public sector investment is pegged at Rs. 760,000 crore. The Ninth Plan size is estimated to be in the order of Rs. 875,000 crore.

To meet the above-stated order of inve stment needs—that amounts to 28.6 per cent of the projected GDP during Ninth Plan—the approach paper has sought to raise gross domestic savings to 26.2 per cent of GDP. Since the scope for increase in private sector savings in limited, stringent measures would have to be initiated to raise public sector savings from the existing level of 2 per cent of GDP to 2.8 per cent of GDP. This would require effective fiscal consolidation so that the present trend of dis-savings at the Centre and the state government levels is reversed, the plan document argues. In addition to this, a current account deficit of 2.4 per cent of GDP can be permitted, the plan document states.

It said that the efforts on the resource mobilisation front should be complemented by initiatives on the expenditure front aimed at raising capital efficiency and better allocation. The incremental capital-output ratio will have to be brought down to 4.08 from the present level of 4.34 per cent. The Commission has also proposed that all the incremental investment be channelised into economic sectors with thrust on power, irrigation, mining, railways and communication while care is taken to maintain social sector with investment in real terms at the present level. The Commission's strategy also aimed at bringing down the share of current outlay component in the total public sector investment to 15 per cent. Endorsing the Commission's strategy to achieve a 7 per cent growth target for the Ninth Plan period, Prime Minister H.D. Deve Gowda asserted that social sector funding would not be "eroded in the bargain."

Identifying "growth with equity" as the main focus of the Plan, the Prime Minister told the Commission that high growth might require some difficult decisions. "In our concern for economic growth we must not ignore the concern for the poor and under-privileged and the need for massive investment in social sector", he added. Pointing out the huge shortfall in the Eighth Plan targets for social sector—the performance of which in some cases was even worse than the Seventh Plan—he said this must not be repeated in the Ninth Plan.The Prime Minister said sustained growth of economy depended on adequate availability of basic infrastructural facilities and noted that the Eighth Plan performance was not only significantly short of the expected outcome but in many crucial areas the achievement was below the levels registered during the Seventh Plan.

Investment Financing in Ninth Plan

(In Rs. thousand crore)

	Public Sector	*Private Sector*	*Household Sector*	*Total*
Cross investment	795	683	748	2190
	(10)	(8.9)	(9.7)	(28.6)
Financed by				
1. Own Savings	214	345	1447	2006
	(2.8)	(4.5)	(18.9)	(26.2)
2. Borrowings from				
Household Sector	498	201	–699	0
	(6.5)	(2.6)	(–9.1)	(0)
External Sector	47	137	0	184
	(0.6)	(1.8)	(0)	(2.4)

Note: Figures in brackets indicate percentage of GDP.

The Deputy Chairman of the Planning Commission, Prof. Madhu Dandavate, speaking on the occasion said that the Ninth Plan would focus on agriculture and rural development with special emphasis on "radical land reforms" for generating adequate productive employment and eradication of poverty. Prof. Dandavate expressed concern over the decline of the states' share in the total plan outlay and consequently agriculture, rural development, khadi and village industries, basic minimum services, health, education and electricity were most affected sectors. Stating that a fresh brief review of the Eighth Plan was made as a prelude to the Ninth Plan, he said it revealed concealed deficiencies like increase in casualisation with a corresponding fall in self-employment, both in rural and urban sectors. "In the Ninth Plan approach paper, the Planning Commission has accorded highest priority to generating adequate productive employment and eradication of poverty," he said while stressing on selective opening up of the economy for capital inflow in preferred sectors like infrastructure.

RS. 20 LAKH CRORE OUTLAY FOR NINTH PLAN

The Ninth Plan of the country would be of Rs. 20 lakh crore at 1996-97 base prices, registering an increase of 4 per cent of gross domestic product (GDP) as compared to the Eighth Plan. Disclosing this to newsmen in New Delhi on Dec. 16, Planning Commission Member Porf. S.R. Harshim said that about 40 per cent of the total Ninth Plan, Rs. 8 lakh crore would be, for the public sector. This would include Rs. 3.76 lakh crore as budgetary support, he said. He said that the GDP in the Ninth Plan would be around 28 per cent as against 24 per cent in the previous plan. The Ninth Plan would deviate from the previous plans and the emphasis would be on providing basic services, which include drinking water, primary health and primary education to all by 2001-02, when the plan would end. Prof. Hashim said that poverty elimination, generation of jobs, mid-day meal scheme, linking all villages with roads and improving communication facilities would also from the thrust areas of the new plan.

The recommendations of Chief Ministers made at a conference early this year had been kept in mind while chalking out the Ninth Plan, he said. Prof Hashim said that additional funds would be made available to states during the Ninth Plan to push forward the basic minimum services programmes in a time bound period. An additional Rs. 2,400 crore had been allocated to states over their 1996-97 plan, he added. The plan allocations for different states during the Ninth Plan are yet to be worked out, he said, adding that the amount would vary from state to state depending on the programme to be implemented. He said that in employment generation programmes the involvement of private sector in agricultural and small scale industries besides self employment schemes would be stressed. Supplementary services in the railways were also proposed to be opened to the private sector.

NDC ON NINTH PLAN, GROWTH RATE, TAX BASE

The National Development Council on January 16 reached a consensus on the 7 per cent accelerated growth scenario, as envisaged in the Ninth Plan approach document. A resolution to this effect was passed unanimously at the end of the council's day-long deliberations with a call from Prime Minister H.D. Deve Gowda for collective efforts by the Centre and the states to raise resources to the tune of Rs. 8,75,000 crore for implementing the Plan. Commending the Planning Commission's efforts to bring out the approach document in time, Mr. Gowda said that with the unanimous adoption of the document at the NDC meeting, work on formulating the Ninth Five Year Plan could now get into full swing. He expected the exercise to be completed by May this year.

Endorsing the approach document, the chief ministers of various states and heads of Union territories, however, said that a number of issues relating to devolution of financial resources and powers ramained unresolved and urged the Commission to look into them while formulating the Ninth Plan document. They demanded decentralisation of powers of the Central Government, review of the Gadgil-Mukherjee formula and transfer of the Centrally-sponsored schemes to the state list. They siad that the Centre must address these issues with right earnest to ensure co-operation of states to mobilise the resources required to achieve 7 per cent growth in the country's GDP.

The Prime Minister, in his capacity as the chairman of the council, assured the chief ministers that the commission would make best efforts to look into their demands and incorporate their suggestions on resource mobilisation. In the concluding remarks, Mr. Gowda further indicated that he would convene a meeting of all the chief ministers in early February to discuss various issues and suggestions thrown up at Thursday's meeting. He said that the Fifth Pay Commission would submit its report by the month-end and that the burden imposed by it would have to be shared by the Centre and the states. Hence, there was a further need for collective efforts at resource mobilisation, he stressed.

The Finance Minister P. Chidambaram has stated that the seven per cent growth target will require higher rates of investment, savings from both domestic and foreign sources and greater efficiency and productivity from the investments made. "All these require policy measures which involve hard political decisions that we must take in the interests of the country and the people particularly the poor." Speaking at the meeting in New Delhi on January 16, the Finance Minister said the approach paper has called for an increase in the economy's rate of investment from 25 per cent of GDP in the Eighth Plan to 28.6 per cent in the Ninth Plan. As public finances are limited, two-thirds of total investment will be done by the private sector both domestic and foreign. To achieve this it will be necessary to have investor-friendly policies of taxation, finance, foreign trade and payments, labour and use of land. Besides, it would be necessary to make massive investments in infrastructure without which it would not be possible to achieve the seven per cent growth target.

Citing the case of power, Mr. Chidambaram said the problem of power may reach crisis proportions in the next few years unless urgent action was taken by every State. "The financial, managerial and administrative structure of SEBs and their policies must be changed dramatically and urgently so that the electricity boards can raise tariffs to realistic levels, improve the quality of supply, contain power theft and become financially viable". The Finance Minister said the Central and State laws need to be changed to allow SEBs and private electricity companies to function autonomously subject to independent regulatory authorities.

Planning Commission, Deputy Chairman Madhu Dandavate on January 17 warned against "competitive populism" as a tool to win elections and said the NDC meeting had endorsed widening of the tax base to finance the Ninth Five Year Plan. Ruling out taxing the agriculture sector, Mr. Dandavate said "competitive populism is not going to help the development of the country" and said he was glad that the chief ministers had voiced unanimity on most of the issues. The thrust of the Ninth Plan would be sustained agricultural gowth of 4.5 per cent per annum to supplement the growth in the industry for achieving a 7 per cent real GDP growth during the Plan period, Mr. Dandavate told a Press conference in New Delhi. On a question on the electoral assurance of the Punjab Chief Minister to provide free power to small farmer. Mr. Dandavate said such a populism would be only to the peril of the economic growth and would make the target of curtailing Government dissaving even more difficult.

Advocating widening and deepening of the income tax base by way of devising methods like presumptive expenditure tax, Mr. Dandavate wanted monitoring of the income of the "fictitious agriculturists." He said most of the Chief Ministers stressed on decentralisation of resources and devolution of economic powers, with some demanding greater share in the tax resources. The Deputy Chairman expressed grave concern over the disparities between tax payers in India and some other countries. "While the tax payers in India constitute a mere 0.8 per cent of the population, Scandinavian countries like Danmark and Sweden have a tax base of 85 per cent of the population," he said. Noting that they were developed countries, Mr. Dandavate said the tax base disparities should be narrowed down. The chief ministers during the NDC meeting agreed on two ways for increasing tax revenues. One of the methods, he said, was to increase the tax exemption limit and the other was to provide rebate for savings. Quoting studies, Mr. Dandavate said for every Rs. 1,000 provided under tax exemption to an individual, the Government would lose Rs. 100 crore. He said providing incentives for savings would be anti-inflationary and would help in increasing the savings rate.

9

STATE OF INDIAN ECONOMY : GENERAL REVIEW

REVIEW OF DEVELOPMENTS

Macroeconomic Overview

1995-96 witnessed a very satisfactory growth rate in GDP of 7.1 per cent. The momentum of growth has been maintained in 1996-97, thus providing increasing evidence that the growth potential has improved as a result of the reforms Initiated in 1991. With the passing of election distractions, the pace of economic reform was also revived. Since June 1996, reform Initiatives have been introduced or strengthened in almost every critical infrastructure sub-sector. There have also been new policy measures in several areas such as Industrial delicensing, foreign investment, trade policy, financial sector and capital markets. With the growing participation of virtually the entire spectrum of political opinion in the reform process, there is a good prospect that a higher growth rate would become a permanent feature of the economy.

The initial spurt of reforms from 1991-92 to 1993-94 was very successful by all accounts, resulting in a jump in economic growth to 7.2 per cent in 1994-95 (in terms of GDP at factor cost). Since 1994-95, however, there was a marked slow down in the pace of reforms. Nevertheless, GDP grew by 7.1 per cent in 1995-96. The slackening of reforms preceding and during the election period may have been responsible for some loss of momentum, but this has been revived with a series of measures in recent months. Economic growth in 1996-97 is estimated by CSO to be around 6.8 per cent (GDP at factor cost). Thus, the Eighth Plan is likely to end with an average growth of 6.5 per cent per annum, 0.9 per cent point higher than the target rate of 5.6 per cent, and 0.5 per cent point higher than the actual achievement of the Seventh Plan (Tables 9.1 and 9.2). More important for the future is the fact that the average growth during the latest three years is 7 per cent, probably placing India among the top ten performers in the world during this period.

As the final year of the Eighth Plan draws to a close, a comparison of some salient dimensions of economic performance between the Eighth Plan period and its predecessor reveals the following :

- Overall economic growth has been faster;
- The manufacturing sector has grown almost 2 per cent points faster per year in the Eighth Plan period;

- Agriculture and allied sectors have grown at about 3.5 per cent per annum in both periods;
- Both exports and imports have grown significantly faster in the Eighth Plan period;
- The balance of payments has strengthened considerably, with trade and current account deficits declining as ratios of GDP, while exports and imports have grown rapidly both in value terms as well as in proportion to GDP;
- The Central Government's fiscal deficit as a proportion of GDP has declined significantly;
- The average rate of gross domestic savings has risen substantially from 20.6 per cent of GDP in the Seventh Plan period to 23.9 per cent in the first four years of the Eighth Plan;
- With the exception of telecommunications, the rate of growth of net output (value added) of infrastructure sectors has slowed; and
- The average rate of inflation has risen somewhat, though remaining below double digits.

Total gross domestic saving reached a new peak of 25.6 per cent of GDP in 1995-96, exceeding its previous peak of 24.9 per cent of GDP in 1994-95. (Table 9.3) This seems to vindicate the reform strategy of encouraging savings by expanding saving and investment opportunities, rather than giving special incentives. The rise in domestic saving in 1995-96 was primarily due to a rise in private saving to 23.7 per cent of GDP. This rise in private saving was smaller than the rise in private investment. As a result, the surplus of private saving over private investment was also smaller at 5.6 per cent of GDP in 1995-96, compared to 7.9 per cent of GDP in 1994-95. Within the private sector, the composition of household saving has also changed, with saving in the form of physical assets rising sharply from 7.7 per cent of GDP in 1994-95 to 10.7 per cent in 1995-96, and saving in the form of financial assets declining from 11.5 per cent to 8.8 per cent of GDP. The flow of saving into the organised/financial system declined from 17.2 per cent of GDP in 1994-95 to 14.9 per cent in 1995-96. The saving-investment gap of the public sector fell from 7 per cent of GDP in 1994-95 to 6.2 per cent of GDP in 1995-96.

Gross domestic Investment (adjusted), as a proportion of GDP at current prices, rose even faster than gross domestic saving in 1995-96 to a high of 27.4 per cent from 26 per cent in the previous year. Gross domestic investment in real terms, as a proportion of GDP at constant prices, reached a new peak of 27.1 per cent, exceeding the previous peak of 25.9 per cent in 1990-91 (Table 9.4). Gross fixed capital formation which is even more important for roductivity and growth, exceeded the 1994-95 peak of 21.9 per cent by substantial 2.2 percentage points, to reach a new peak of 24.1 per cent of GDP in 1995-96. This new record was due solely to a rise in private fixed investment from the previous record of 13.4 per cent of GDP in 1994-95 to a new record of 16.3 per cent of GDP. The contribution of real stock accumulation increased only

TABLE 9.1 : Key Indicators

	1993-94	1994-95P	1995-96P	1996-97P	1993-94	1994-95P	1995-96P	1996-97P
	Absolute Values				*Per cent change over previous period*			
Gross national product (Rs. thousand crore)								
At current prices	719.5	843.3	967.8Q	NA	16.2	17.2	14.8Q	NA
At 1980-81 prices	233.8	249.9	267.3Q	285.3 E	6.0	6.9	7.0Q	6.7 E
Gross domestic product (Rs.thousand crore)								
At current prices	731.9	858.3	985.8Q	NA	16.0	17.3	14.8Q	NA
At 1980-81 prices	238.9	256.1	274.2Q	292.9 E	6.0	7.2	7.1Q	6.8 E
Agricultural production(1)	157.3	165.0	164.3	169.2 A	3.8	4.9	-0.4	3.0 A
Foodgrains production (million tonnes)	184.3	191.5	185.0	191.2 A	2.7	3.9	-3.4	3.3 A
Industrial production(2)	232.0	253.7	283.3	291.2 (3)	6.0	9.4	11.7	9.8 (3)
Electricity generated (TWH)	323.5	351.0	380.1	291.5 (8)	7.4	8.5	8.3	3.5 (8)
Wholesale price index (4)	258.3	286.8	299.5	319.8 (5)	10.8	10.2	4.4	7.6 (5)
Consumer price index for industrial workers (6)	267.0	293.0	319.0	349.0 (7)	9.9	9.7	8.9	8.7 (7)
Money supply (M3) (Rs. thousand crore)	434.4	531.4	601.8	655.5 (10)	18.4	22.3	13.2	10.6 (11)

TABLE 9.1 : *(Contd.)*

	1993-94	*1994-95P*	*1995-96P*	*1996-97P*	*1993-94*	*1994-95P*	*1995-96P*	*1996-97P*
	Absolute Values				*Per cent change over previous period*			
Imports at current prices								
(Rs. crore)	73101	89971	122678	97111 (8)	15.3	23.1	36.4	12.8 (8)
(US $ million)	23306	28330	36678	27453 (8)	6.5	22.9	28.0	4.4 (8)
Export current prices								
(Rs. crore)	69751	82674	106353	85623 (8)	29.9	18.5	28.6	14.9 (8)
(US $ million)	22238	26330	31797	24205 (8)	20.0	18.4	20.8	6.4 (8)
Foreign currency assets								
(Rs. crore)	47287	66006	58446	71210 (9)	134.8	39.6	-11.5	21.8 (9)
(US $ million)	15068	20809	17044	19847 (9)	134.2	38.1	-18.1	16.4 (9)
Exchange rate								
(Rs/US $)+	31.37	31.40	33.45	35.42 (12)	7.7	0.1	6.1	5.6 (12)

Note : Gross national product and Gross domestic product figures are at factor cost.
A-Anticipated; P-Provisional; Q-Quick estimates; E-Advance estimates; NA: Not available

\+ Per cent change Indicates the rate of depreciation of the Rupee vis-a-vis the US dollar.

1. Index of agricultural production (principal crops) with base triennium ending 1981-82=100.
2. Index of Industrial production 1980-81=100.
3. April-October, 1996.
4. Index with base 1981-82=100.
5. As on January 11, 1997 for 1996-97 and for the last week of March for the earlier years.
6. Index with base 1982=100.
7. As in November, 1996 and in the last week of March for the earlier years.
8. April-December, 1996.
9. At the end of January, 1997 for 1996-97 and at the end of March for previous years.
10. As on January 17, 1997; end of financial year for previous years.
11. April 1, 1996 to January 17, 1997.
12. April-January, 1996-97.

TABLE 9.2 : Sectoral Real Growth Rates

(In per cent)

Industry	Average 7th Plan (1985-90)	Percentage change over the previous year					Average 8th Plan (1992-970
		1992-93	1993-94	1994-95 (P)	1995-96 (Q)	1996-97 (A)	
I. Agriculture and Allied Sectors	3.4	6.1	3.6	4.6	-0.1	3.7	3.6
II. Industry	7.5	4.2	6.8	9.4	11.6	8.7	8.1
1. Mining and quarrying	9.0	1.1	2.0	8.1	7.0	1.7	4.0
2. Manufacturing	7.7	4.2	8.5	10.2	13.6	10.6	9.4
3. Electricity, gas & water supply	9.5	8.4	7.1	8.6	9.1	4.2	7.5
4. Construction	5.2	3.4	1.3	6.9	5.3	4.6	4.3
Services	7.4	5.5	7.3	7.5	8.8	7.4	7.3
5. Trade, hotels, transport and Communication	7.1	6.3	7.5	10.0	13.3	9.4	9.3
6. Financing, insurance, real estates and business services	8.3	4.6	10.5	7.1	4.0	6.3	6.5
7. Community, social and personal services	7.3	5.0	3.9	3.8	6.2	4.9	4.7
Total Gross Domestic Product at Factor Cost	6.0	5.3	6.0	7.2	7.1	6.8	6.5

Note: P=Provisional; Q=Quick Estimates; A=Advance Estimates

TABLE 9.3 : Savings and Investment

	1985-90 7th Plan (Average)	*1990-91*	*1991-92*	*1992-93*	*1993-94*	*1994-95P*	*1995-96Q*	*1992-96 (Average)*
	(As per cent of GDP at current market prices)							
Gross Domestic Savings	20.6	24.3	22.8	22.1	23.1	24.9	25.6	23.9
Public	2.4	1.0	1.9	1.5	0.6	1.8	1.9	1.5
Private	18.3	23.3	20.9	20.5	22.5	23.1	23.7	22.5
Gross Domestic Investment*	23.1	27.7	23.4	24.0	23.6	26.0	27.4	25.3
Public	10.5	9.7	9.2	8.9	8.6	8.8	8.2	8.6
Private	13.1	15.5	13.5	15.1	13.1	15.2	18.1	15.4
Gross Domestic Investment*	23.1	27.7	23.4	24.0	23.6	26.0	27.4	25.3
GFCF	21.5	23.2	22.1	22.5	21.6	22.4	24.6	22.8
Change in Stocks	2.1	2.1	0.6	1.5	0.1	1.6	1.6	1.2
Saving-Investment Gap@	-2.5	-3.3	-0.5	-2.0	-0.6	-1.0	-1.8	-1.3
Public	-8.1	-8.7	-7.2	-7.4	-8.0	-7.0	-6.2	-7.1
Private	5.2	7.8	7.3	5.4	9.4	7.9	5.6	7.1

Note : (i) Gross Domestic Investment and Gross Domestic Capital Formation (GDCF)
(ii) Figures may not add up due to rounding off

* : adjusted for errors and emissions;

@ : refers to the difference between the rates of savings and Investment

GFCF : Gross Fixed Capital Formation;

P : Provisional estimates; Q:Quick estimates

Source : Central Statistical Organisation.

marginally from 1.8 per cent of GDP in 1994-95 to 1.9 per cent of GDP in 1995-96, and remained below the 2.4 per cent average of the Seventh Plan. Private sector investment appears to have responded vigorously to the policy of promoting competition, removing policy distortions and hurdles, and improving access to factors of production (e.g. technology, capital).

Estimates of savings and investment in 1996-97 are not yet available. Indicators are mixed. On the one hand, domestic capital goods production is buoyant and disbursement of financial institutions are significantly higher. On the other hand, capital goods imports have declined, non-oil imports are lower in the first nine months of the year, corporate demand for credit appears slack, and sanctions of financial institutions are substantially lower.

The economy in 1996-97 so far presents a mixed picture in other dimensions as well. Although overall economic growth remains high at 6.8 per cent, and agriculture has rebounded, the growth of manufacturing value added has slowed and the performance of key infrastructure sectors, especially power and crude oil, is weak. The annual rate of inflation (point to point) has risen back to average long-term levels and export growth has decelerated markedly in recent months. Despite the slowdown in exports, a combination of sluggish imports and reasonably buoyant inflows of invisibles and capital flows have led to a build-up of foreign exchange reserves by over $2.5 billion.

Production

Agricultural crop production in 1996-97 is expected to show good recovery from the slower growth in 1995-96. Growth is projected at 3 per cent after a fall of 0.4 per cent in 1995-96. The sharp decline in foodgrains production by 3.4 per cent, which was responsible for the slow growth in 1995-96, is expected to be reversed by an increase of 3.3 per cent in 1996-97. Foodgrains production is expected to recover to 191.2 million tonnes, only marginally lower than the level of production in 1994-95. This recovery is primarily due to coarse cereals, as well as an anticipated rise in wheat production which suffered a sharp setback in 1995-96.

As the agricultural year runs from July to June, the estimates for 1995-96 were only firmed up after the end of the financial year. A large downward revision (of 3 million tonnes) was made in the estimate of wheat production for 1995-96. The revision was unexpected and unexplained, because average rainfall in 1995-96 was quite normal. The revision, late in calendar year 1996, also created severe problems for the management of the food economy.

Commercial crop production has done extremely well in 1996-97 with oilseeds and cotton expected to reach record levels of 24.1 million tonnes and 14.3 million tonnes, respectively. The 9.2 per cent growth in cotton production has come on top of the 10.1 per cent growth last year. Jute and mesta have also shown a growth of 3.4 per cent this year. Sugarcane output is, however, unlikely to maintain the record level of 283 million tonnes attained in 1995-96.

Industrial production (as measured by the index of industrial production-IIP), grew by 9.8 per cent in the first seven months of 1996-97, 1.9 percentage points slower than the 11.7 per cent growth in the first seven months of 1995-96.

TABLE 9.4 : Real Gross Demestic Capital Formation

	1985-90 7th Plan (Average)	*1990-91*	*1991-92*	*1992-93*	*1993-94*	*1994-95P*	*1995-96Q*	*1992-96 (Average)*
			(As per cent of GDP at market prices, 1980-81 prices)					
GDCF*	21.8	25.9	21.6	22.4	22.7	25.6	27.1	24.4
Public	9.7	9.0	8.3	8.1	8.1	8.4	7.6	8.0
Private	12.6	14.7	12.7	14.3	12.7	15.3	18.4	15.2
GFCF	19.8	21.3	20.3	20.6	20.8	21.9	24.1	21.8
Public	9.5	8.6	8.7	7.7	7.8	8.5	7.8	8.0
Private	10.3	12.7	11.6	13.0	12.9	13.4	16.3	13.9
Change in stocks	2.4	2.4	0.7	1.7	0.0	1.8	1.9	1.4
Public	0.2	0.4	-0.4	0.4	0.2	-0.1	-0.2	0.1
Private	2.2	2.0	1.1	1.3	-0.2	1.9	2.1	1.3
			(Growth rate, per cent)					
GDCF*	11.5	18.1	-16.3	9.2	6.3	21.5	13.7	12.7
Public	3.4	4.6	-7.2	2.7	4.4	12.1	-2.5	4.2
Private	14.9	17.5	-13.3	18.7	-6.7	29.3	29.1	17.6
GFCF	8.6	9.9	-4.0	7.0	5.6	13.3	18.3	11.0
Public	3.7	4.8	2.0	-7.2	6.9	17.2	-1.5	3.9
Private	13.6	13.6	-8.1	17.5	4.8	11.0	30.9	16.1

Note : GDCF : Gross Domestic Capital Formation at 1980-81 prices; GFCF : Gross Fixed Capital Formation; Figures may not add up due to rounding off

* : adjusted for errors and omissions;

P : Provisional estimates, Q:Quick estimates

Source : Central Statistical Organisation

IIP growth of 11.7 per cent in 1995-96 was the highest growth rate in the past 25 years, and growth rate of 9.5 per cent to 10.5 per cent for 1996-97 as a whole would still be the second highest growth rate over this 25 year period. The good performance of industrial production in 1996-97 is due entirely to the manufacturing sector, which has maintained its high growth. During the first seven months of 1996-97, for the manufacturing sector, the rate of growth of 12.1 per cent is virtually the same as the 12.3 per cent growth in the first seven months of 1995-96 (based on the IIP for manufacturing). Even if the average growth for the whole of 1996-97 falls below the record breaking growth of 13.0 per cent during 1995-96, it could still be the second highest over the past fifteen years.

The slowing of industrial production is clearly attributable to the dramatic fall in the rate of growth of electricity production and a slowing of growth in the mining sector mainly because of the 10 per cent decline in crude oil production. During the first seven months of 1996-97, electricity production (as measured by the index) has grown by only 3.4 per cent compared to the 10.1 per cent growth in the corresponding period of 1995-96. It is somewhat surprising that manufacturing sector growth has been barely affected by the slow growth in electricity production. One possibility is that captive electricity generation, which is increasingly used as a back-up to public supply, has substituted for the lack of generation by electricity boards. The high growth of diesel imports, about 22 per cent by volume in the first seven month of 1996-97 (with total refinery throughput growing in the normal range of around 4 per cent), is consistent with this hypothesis. At present, electricity statistics incorporate little or no data on captive power generation.

Another noteworthy aspect of industrial growth this year is the acceleration in the rate of growth of capital goods production to 16.6 per cent in the first seven months of this year from 15 per cent in the first seven months of last year. This has off-set the decline in the rate of growth of consumer goods and basic goods. In contrast, capital goods imports have declined by 6 per cent in the first seven months of 1996-97. This shows the increased competitiveness of the domestic capital goods industry. In the initial stages of reforms, the capital goods sector was subjected to the fastest tariff reduction to ensure a quick recovery of private fixed investment. The sector appears to have adjusted rapidly. Subsequently, some of the tariff anomalies were removed gradually by reducing tariff rates on steel and other inputs closer to the 25 per cent rate on capital goods. This move to more uniform tariffs on manufactured goods has contributed to the growth of capital goods production, and will have a positive effect on employment generation.

The delicensing of investment in durables such as cars and white goods, and the decontrol of imports of parts for these goods, contributed to a boom in investment and production in this sector. The pick-up in growth rate in the production of consumer durables culminated in a phenomenal 37 per cent growth in 1995-96. Accelerated modernisation and development of this relatively backward sector required higher initial imports of capital goods, parts and components. The decline in the growth of consumer durables to 9.8 per cent in the first seven months of 1996-97, compared to 30.2 per cent in the first seven months of 1995-96, suggests that the pent-up demand in the domestic economy has been met. Further growth will depend on increased cost competitiveness, which requires fuller exploitation of the comparative advantage that India has in the production of (skilled and unskilled) labour intensive parts. It is possible that the slowing of non-oil imports is partly due to the maturing of the consumer durable industry.

A number of changes have been made so far in 1996-97 in the area of foreign investment. The Foreign Investment Promotion Council has been set up, the Foreign Investment Promotion Board (FIPB) streamlined and made more transparent, and the first ever guidelines have been announced by the Government for consideration of foreign direct investment proposals by the FIPB, which are not covered under the automatic route. The list of industries eligible for automatic approval of upto 51 per cent foreign equity has been expanded. Foreign Institutional Investors (FIIs) have been allowed to invest in unlisted companies and in corporate and government securities, and external commercial borrowing (ECB) guidelines have been liberalised and made more transparent.

Other industrial policy measures include the setting up of a Disinvestment Commission, delicensing of consumer electronics, changes in the sugar policy, enhancement of investment ceiling on plant and machinery of the small scale industries from Rs. 60 lakh/Rs. 75 lakh to Rs. 3 crore and of tiny units from Rs. 5 lakh to Rs. 25 lakh, and reduction of export obligation of non-SSI units producing reserved items from 75 per cent to 50 per cent. Another list of 9 industries eligible for automatic approval of upto 74 per cent foreign equity has been announced. State level industrial reforms also took a step forward with several states announcing comprehensive reform policies, including disinvestment in or privatisation of state public sector enterprises.

Since February 11, 1997 government has deregulated prices and distribution of D grade of non-coking coal, hard coke and soft coke, in addition to the existing decontrol of prices and distribution of coking coal and A, B and C grades of non-coking coal. The government has also allowed the Coal India Limited and the Singareni Collieries Company Limited to fix the prices of E, F and G grades of non-coking coal as per BICP escalation formula till January 1, 2000 and in relation to market prices after January 1, 2000. The Government has also decided to amond the Coal Mines (Nationalisation) Act, 1973 to allow any Indian company to mine coal and lignite not only for captive consumption but also for sale.

18. The overall performance of the core and infrastructure sectors during the first 8 months of 1996-97 (April-November) has been poor (Table 9.5). Six industries namely, electricity generation, coal, steel, crude oil, petroleum products and cement, with a combined weight of 28.8 per cent in the Index of Industrial Production (IIP), averaged a growth of 4.1 per cent in April-November, 1996, less than half the 8.9 per cent, in April-November, 1995. The deceleration in the growth rate of these infrastructure industries is mainly due to a decline in crude oil production and power generation. Hydro power generation declined by 7.7 per cent, and thermal power generation grew by only 6.4 per cent in April-November, 1996 as compared to 14.6 per cent in the April-March, 1995-

96. Coal, cement and refineries' throughput have grown faster in April-November, 1996-97 compared to the corresponding period of 1995-96. Growth of sectors such as railways, ports and telecommunication, which do not appear in the IIP, also slowed. The rate of growth of railways' revenue earning goods traffic decelerated marginally from 7 per cent during 1995-96 to 6.3 per cent for April-November 1996. Growth of cargo handled at major ports and new telephone connections provided decelerated more sharply to 4.7 per cent in April-November, 1996 (from 9.1 per cent in 1995-96) and 8.3 per cent in April-November, 1996 (from 23.3 per cent in 1995-96), respectively. The slower growth in cargo handled by ports is probably the result of a deceleration in the growth of external trade. The telecommunication slowdown, however suggests that the pace of implementation of telecommunication reform needs to be accelerated and its scope widened to include Department of Telecommunications as a service provider.

The past few Economic Surveys have emphasized the need to accelerate, widen and deepen reforms of the non-tradable infrastructure and energy sectors, to avert an impending mismatch between economic growth and provision of non-tradable services. Given the parlous financial state of many public utilities, particularly the State Electricity Boards, the possibility of crises worsens with each passing year. The new government has repeatedly stressed its firm determination to reform the infrastructure and energy sectors. In line with this commitment, a number of policy decisions have been taken and new initiatives launched. These include:

— To provide long-term finance for infrastructure, the Budget announced the establishment of an Infrastructure Development Finance Company (IDFC). The IDFC has since been incorporated under the Companies Act on 30.1.97 with an authorised share capital of Rs. 5,000 crore.

— A 5 year tax holiday for companies developing, maintaining and operating infrastructure facilities such as roads, bridges, new airports, ports and railway projects, was extended to cover water supply, sanitation and sewerage projects.

— After the National Highway Act was amended to enable private participation, projects involving Rs. 42 crore have been awarded on a Build-Operate and Transfer (BOT) basis. The capital base of the National Highways Authority of India has been increased by a provision of Rs. 200 crore, thereby providing greater leverage to borrowing from external funding agencies and other lenders.

— The provisions relating to foreign investment have been further liberalised to give automatic approval for foreign equity participation up to 74 per cent in key infrastructure sectors such as electricity generation and transmission, non-conventional energy generation and distribution, and construction and maintenance of roads, bridges, railbeds, ports, runways, pipelines and harbours. The automatic approval list for foreign equity upto 51 per cent has been expanded to include support services for land and water transport. This includes operation of highway bridges, toll roads and vehicular tunnels, operation and maintenance of piers, and loading and discharging of vessels.

TABLE 9.5 : Growth Rates of Core and Infrastructure Sectors

(Per cent p.a.)

Sectors	*Weight (IIP)*	*1990-91*	*1991-92*	*1992-93*	*1993-94*	*1994-95*	*1995-96*	*1995-96* (Apr-Nov.)*	*1996-97* (Apr-Nov.)*
Basic Infrastructure Sectors									
1. Electricity generation	11.4	7.8	8.5	5.0	7.4	8.5	8.3	9.9	3.4
(a) Thermal (Incl. nuclear)		5.1	11.1	8.1	9.5	6.1	14.6	16.6	6.4
(b) Hydro		15.2	1.4	-4.0	0.8	17.2	-12.1	-9.3	-7.7
2. Coal	6.6	5.4	8.3	3.9	3.3	3.2	6.4	6.3	9.4
3. Saleable steel	5.2	3.1	8.1	3.9	6.2	8.3	8.9	10.6	2.7
4. Crude oil	2.4	-3.1	-8.1	-11.2	0.3	19.3	9.0	11.6	-10.0
5. Refinery throughput	1.5	-0.3	-0.7	4.0	1.5	3.8	3.6	3.0	6.3
6. Cement	1.6	6.6	5.9	5.0	6.8	7.6	11.2	9.1	11.4
Over All	**28.8**	**5.0**	**6.4**	**3.1**	**5.3**	**7.8**	**7.7**	**8.9**	**4.1**
Other Infrastructure Sectors									
1. Cargo handled at major ports		3.0	3.3	5.7	7.6	10.0	9.1	11.2	4.7
2. New Telephone connections		14.7	51.5	34.2	24.5	44.0	23.3	32.5	8.3
3. Revenue earning goods traffic on railways		2.7	6.2	3.6	2.5	1.7	7.0	5.7	6.3

* Provisional

— Through an Ordinance, the Government has recently established a statutory Telecom Regulatory Authority of India (TRAI) which will separate the regulatory functions from policy formulation and operational functions. The Department of Telecommunications and financial institutions have also finalised an assignability agreement which will facilitate funding of cellular and basic telecom projects.

— Letters of intent have been given to basic telecom services in Karnataka and Madhya Pradesh. Cellular services are expanding rapidly beyond the four non-metro areas. The Government has announced that telecom will be treated as infrastructure and all fiscal benefits, like tax holiday and concessional duty on project imports, now being made available to the power sector will be extended to the telecom sector also.

— New guidelines have been published for private participation in ports for both leasing out of existing assets and construction and operation of new assets such as container terminals, cargo berths, warehousing, dry docking and ship repair. Private investment in ports will be on a BOT basis. It will include leasing out existing assets of ports and construction and operation of additional assets such as container terminals, cargo berths, warehousing, dry docking and ship repair. The concession period will be decided by the Port Trusts, up to a maximum period of thirty years. A contract for a private container terminal at JNPT, valued at Rs. 700 crore, has been awarded.

— An Independent Authority for regulating tariffs in major ports has been created through an Ordinance.

— New guidelines for private investment in the highway sector have been announced, procedures simplified, and environmental clearance and equity participation made easier. An Ordinance has been issued containing provisions for acquisition of land for development and maintenance of national highways. Once the Government declares that the land is required for a highway, it would be deemed vested in the Central Government and be non-justiceable. Only compensation can be settled through arbitration.

— A Common Minimum National Action Plan for Power was approved by the Centre and the States, in December 1996. As a part of this Plan, State Electricity Boards are to be urgently reformed and restructured to give them more autonomy, retail tariffs and wheeling charges are to be rationalised, and independent regulatory commissions are to be set up at the Central and State level. Private participation in distribution is to be encouraged. The Central Government has already issued an Ordinance allowing private entry into power transmission as an independent service. States have been given greater authority : they are now free to clear projects up to 250 MW. Renovation and modernisation schemes no longer need approval of the Central Electricity Authority.

— In principle approval has been given by the Government for a rail-based mass rapid transit system (MRTS) in Delhi. The cities of Bangalore, Hyderabad, Mumbai and Calcutta have proposed major improvements in their public transport systems through the introduction/augmentation of rail-based transit systems.
— A new policy for private investment in civil aviation has been announced and this includes allowing 40 per cent foreign equity in domestic airlines.

Money and Prices

The deceleration in inflation, initiated last year through a reduction in monetary growth, continued through the first quarter of 1996-97. As measured by the wholesale price index, the annual (point-to-point), inflation rate reached a trough of 4.5 per cent in May and June 1996. Since then the rate has crept up gradually to reach 7.5 per cent (provisional) in mid-January 1997. Despite the recent rising trend in the growth of the WPI, the average inflation for 1996-97 is expected to be at least one percentage point less than the average inflation in 1995-96. This is primarily due to continuing restraint on money supply growth, a reduction in the fiscal deficit (as a proportion of GDP) and the effect of competitive pressures on tradable goods consequent to the opening up of international trade in manufactures.

There was a complete change in the sectoral pattern of price changes during 1996-97. The annual rate of inflation accelerated sharply in the "fuel, power, light & lubricants" and "primary articles" groups, while decelerating in the "manufactures" group. The annual rate of price increase in the fuel power group went up to 17.4 per cent in January 1997, from 1.1 per cent a year ago, mainly because of the increase in the administered prices of oil and petroleum products forced upon the new government in mid-1996, thanks to the failure to correct petroleum prices for two and a half years. The rate of growth of primary prices also accelerated to 11.7 per cent by January 1997 from 2.6 per cent a year before, while the rate of growth of manufactured goods' prices declined to 3.6 per cent from 6.9 per cent in the previous year. As a result, primary goods' inflation contributed 50.4 per cent of the inflation in 1996-97 (up to January 11, 1997), while the "fuel, power, light & lubricants" group contributed 23.3 per cent.

The rise in primary goods' prices has been largely due to a rise in the prices of cereals, and fruits and vegetables. Among cereals, wheat was the main contributor to the price rise, and this was solely due to the lower production (3 million tonnes in 1995-96) and the consequent lower procurement (4 million tonnes) during April-June, 1996. After the new Government assumed office, a number of steps were taken to improve the supply position of food items. FCI continued its open market sales of wheat and rice through 1996-97, with a sale of 2.5 lakh tonnes of rice and 27 lakh tonnes of wheat by mid-January, 1997. FCI's monthly open market sales of wheat were stepped up to 6 lakh tonnes from December 1996. Wheat is also being imported to augment supplies through the Public Distribution System (PDS). The import duty on edible oils was reduced to 20 per cent, and STC imported 2 lakh tonnes of palmolein for PDS supply during 1996.

The rise in the international prices of crude and petroleum products during 1996-97 put further pressure on the import bill for petroleum and petroleum products. As administered price changes had been postponed, the effect of this external development (couple with higher imports necessitated by rising demand and falling domestic production) is channelled through the burgeoning deficit in the oil pool account. Though this deficit does not directly affect the gross fiscal deficit of the Central Government, it adds to the "quasi-fiscal deficit" of the public sector as a whole. And the cumulation of arrears due to domestic oil companies compromises their financial strength and operational effectiveness.

Money supply growth has been higher in 1996-97 so far than in 1995-96. Up to the fortnight ended January 17, 1997, broad money (M3) grew by 10.6 per cent as against 8.2 per cent growth in the corresponding period of 1995-96. The annual growth of M3 was 13.2 per cent on March 31, 1996, against the planned growth of 15.5 per cent, due to a somewhat tight monetary policy. This, along with the high real interest rates brought about by a sharp decline in inflation, gave rise to perceptions of a liquidity squeeze, and hence, a need to expand money supply in 1996-97. The growth rate of M3 was still only 15.7 per cent on January 17, 1997, a shade under the planned growth of 16 per cent. The gradual acceleration in money supply growth was not, however, due to any acceleration in reserve money growth. On the contrary, reserve money has declined by 2.9 per cent during 1996-97 (up to January 17, 1997) in contrast to the expansion of 14.0 per cent in the corresponding period of 1995-96. Annual growth of reserve money declined from 14.8 per cent on March 31, 1996 to 7.2 per cent on January 17, 1997.

The fall in reserve money growth is primarily due to a sharp reduction in refinance taken from the RBI by commercial and cooperative banks, because of easy liquidity conditions following the reduction in the Cash Reserve Ratio (CRR). Expansion of net RBI credit to Government at 3.3 per cent (Rs. 3987 crore) during FY 1996-97, was much smaller than the 14.7 per cent (Rs. 14961 crore) growth in the corresponding period of 1995-96. Reserve money has, therefore, fallen despite a rise in the net foreign exchange assets of the RBI by Rs. 11482 crore (a growth of 15.5 per cent), compared with the decline of Rs. 485 crore (-0.6 per cent) in 1995-96 (till January 1996). Despite the reduction in reserve money, the growth of money supply accelerated because of reductions in the CRR required to be maintained by the banks against their net demand and time liabilities. The average CRR was reduced from 14 per cent at the beginning of 1996-97 to 10 per cent in January 1997, in several phases.

The average effective Statutory Liquidity Ratio (SLR) of the scheduled commercial banks is estimated to have fallen from 28.2 per cent of their net demand and time liabilities in end-March 1996 to 27 per cent by end-December, 1996. The structure of net bank credit to government has also undergone a sharp change in 1996-97. The slower growth of RBI credit to government has been more than offset by an increase in "other banks" credit to government, which has grown by 18.7 per cent in 1996-97 till January 17, 1997. This compares with a growth rate of 11 per cent in the corresponding period of 1995-96.

In contrast, the growth of bank credit to the commercial sector at 5.3 per cent has been less than half of the 11.6 per cent in the comparable period of 1995-96. The growth of "other banks" credit to the commercial sector has also been lower at 5.6 per cent during the current financial year up to January 17, 1997, as against 11.9 per cent recorded in the last financial year up to January 19, 1996. While non-food credit of scheduled commercial banks has recently shown signs of a moderate pick-up, the overall growth so far (5.2 per cent) is about a third of the growth (15.2 per cent) registered in the corresponding period of 1995-96.

The easing of monetary policy during 1996-97 has been reflected in relatively low call money rates from the very beginning of 1996-97. The average call money rate declined from a high of 13.75 per cent at the beginning of the current financial year to a range of 5 to 11 per cent in September 1996, and ruled between 10 and 11 per cent in December 1996, before falling to low single digits in Januray 1997. The RBI resumed its repo auctions of government securities in November 1996 and internsified them with continuous operations in January 1997. The reversal of the 1995-96 excess demand for funds for investment in 1996-97 has led to a general softening of interest rates in 1996-97. The cut-off yields on 91-day treasury bills has come down from 12.4 per cent in the first week of July to around 7.5 per cent at the end of January 1997. Cut-off yields on 364-day treasury bills have also decilned from around 13 per cent at the end of June 1996 to 10.10 per cent at the end of January 1997. An increase in the rate of growth of deposits, coupled with the fall in demand for bank credit from large corporates, has also led to a reduction in bank interest rates, including the prime lending rates.

Fiscal Developments

The Budget for 1996-97 envisaged a reduction of the fiscal deficit by 0.8 per cent point of GDP from 5.8 per cent in 1995-96 (RE) to 5 per cent in 1996-97 (BE) (Table 9.6). The primary deficit is also budgeted to fall from 1.1 per cent of GDP to 0.2 per cent of GDP. The other dimension of fiscal adjustment is its quality, as reflected in the composition of fiscal adjustment. The revenue deficit is budgeted to fall to 2.5 per cent of GDP in 1996-97 (BE), from 3.0 per cent in 1995-96 (RE).

The reduction in the fiscal deficit has been attempted through an increase in revenues coupled with a reduction in expenditure. Revenue receipts (net) are budgeted to increase by 18.3 per cent during 1996-97. These receipts, as a proportion of GDP, are to edge up from 10 per cent in 1995-96 (RE) to 10.4 per cent in 1996-97 (BE). Despite a larger outgo on account of interest payments (Rs. 60000 crore), subsidies (Rs. 16320 crore) and provision for revision of salaries and pension benefits (Rs. 4000 crore), total revenue expenditure is budgeted to grow at a lower rate of 12.7 per cent compared with 17.5 per cent in 1995-96 (RE). This deceleration in the growth of revenue expenditure has led to a decline in the revenue expenditure to GDP ratio from 13.1 per cent in 1995-96 (RE) to 12.9 per cent in 1996-97 (BE). This favourable outcome on the expenditure side is largely on account of containment of non-interest non-plan expenditure growth at 9.3 per cent during 1996-97 (BE), about half the growth of 18.8 per cent in 1995-96 (RE). Consequently, non-interest revenue expenditure as a proportion of GDP is budgeted to fall to 8.1 per cent from 8.3 per cent in 1995-96 (RE). The revenue deficit is budgeted to fall by 0.5 per cent point of GDP.

A number of initiatives were outlined in the 1996-97 budget, signalling the Government's resolve to strengthen the infrastructure and social sectors. To provide long term finance for infrastructure sector, an infrastructure Development Finance Company (IDFC) has been set up. A budgetary allocation of Rs. 500 crore was made as Government's contribution. The budget also provided Rs. 200 crore to strengthen the capital base of the National Highway Authority. With a view to improve the living standards of the rural poor, an additional outlay of Rs. 2466 crore was provided as Central assistance for States' and Union Territories' Plans for certain basic minimum services. These cover a wide array of social programmes aimed at increasing the provision of safe drinking water, primary education, primary health centres, public housing, mid-day meals, and rural roads. Programmes for completing irrigation projects were augmented. Excise duty was reduced on a number of items of daily consumption and many mass consumption goods were exempted. The subsidy limit on small tractors, power tillers, sprinklers and drip irrigation equipment was enhanced, to reduce the cost of capital for the agricultural sector. A provision of Rs. 900 crore was made for matching loans from the Centre to the States for the timely completion of selected irrigation projects.

The 1996-97 budget also took some steps toward reform of the tax regime. On the import duty side, the basic duty rate on a number of items was reduced to 30 or 40 per cent. Progress was also made in unifying import duty rates on similar items, in order to avoid disputes arising out of misclassification and multiplicity of rates. On the excise front, the ambit of MODVAT was extended to cover textiles. This would help rationalisation of the rate structure and benefit the textile industry in general. A mandatory penalty for evasion of excise duty or misuse of MODVAT credit scheme on account of fraud, collusion etc., was also introduced.

On the direct taxes front, a mix of changes were made. The surcharge on corporate tax was reduced from 15 per cent to 7.5 per cent, bringing down the total company tax rate from 46 per cent to 43 per cent. This was off-set by the introduction of a Minimum Alternate Tax, to raise the effective corporate tax on corporations that do not pay taxes on corporate income because of numerous exemptions, but show high balance sheet profits. Companies engaged in the power and infrastructure sectors are outside its ambit. The scope of the five year tax holiday provision was extended to include enterprises in irrigation, water supply, sanitation and sewerage systems. The longterm capital gains tax for domestic companies was reduced to 20 per cent. The scope of the long term capital gains tax exemption was widened to include investment in shares issued by public companies in specified sectors.

As a follow-up to the Finance Minister's announcement in his budget speech, the setting up of a Tariff Commission has been approved by the Government.

TABLE 9.6 : Tax Revenue & Expenditure

	Seventh Plan (1985-90)	*1990-91 Actuals*	*1991-92 Actuals*	*1992-93 Actuals*	*1993-94 Actuals*	*1994-95 Actuals*	*1995-96 Revised Estimates*	*1996-97 Budget Estimates*	*Eighth Plan (1992-97)*
				(As per cent of GDP)					
1. Fiscal Deficit	8.2	8.3	5.9	5.7	7.4	6.1	5.8	5.0	6.0
2. Revenue Deficit	2.6	3.5	2.6	2.6	4.0	3.3	3.0	2.5	3.1
3. Budgetary Deficit	2.1	2.1	1.1	1.7	1.4	0.1	0.7	0.5	0.9
4. Primary Deficit	4.8	4.3	1.6	1.3	2.9	1.4	1.1	0.2	1.4
5. Gross Tax Revenue	11.2	10.8	10.9	10.6	9.4	9.7	10.0	10.6	10.0
(a) Direct Taxes of which	2.1	2.1	2.5	2.6	2.5	2.8	3.0	3.1	2.8
(i) Income Tax	1.0	1.0	1.1	1.1	1.1	1.3	1.4	1.4	1.3
(ii) Corporation Tax	1.1	1.0	1.3	1.3	1.2	1.4	1.5	1.6	1.4
(b) Indirect Taxes of which	9.1	8.7	8.5	8.0	6.8	6.9	7.1	7.4	7.2
(iii) Union Excise Duties	4.9	4.6	4.6	4.4	3.9	3.9	3.7	3.7	3.9
(iv) Customs	3.9	3.9	3.6	3.4	2.7	2.8	3.2	3.5	3.1
6. Total Expenditure of which	20.5	19.7	18.1	17.4	17.5	16.9	16.7	16.3	16.9
(i) Interest Payments	3.4	4.0	4.3	4.4	4.5	4.6	4.7	4.8	4.6
(ii) Major Subsidies	1.7	1.8	1.6	1.3	1.3	1.2	1.1	1.2	1.2
(iii) Defence	3.3	2.9	2.7	2.5	2.7	2.4	2.4	2.2	2.5
(iv) Other Non-Plan Expenditure	5.0	5.7	4.5	4.0	3.6	3.6	3.9	3.8	3.8
(v) Budget Support For Plan	7.1	5.3	5.0	5.2	5.4	5.0	4.4	4.4	4.9

Financial Developments

Decontrol of the banking system continued during 1996-97. The interest rate on term deposits of over one year was deregulated, as was the interest rate on non-resident external rupee deposits above two years. Selective credit controls on a number of commodities were eliminated from October 1996. The minimum maturity period of term deposits was reduced to 30 days, and the ceiling rate on term deposits of 30 days to one year was reduced to 10 per cent. A number of banks have reduced their prime lending rate (PLR) by 1 to 1-1/2 per cent points and announced a 2.5 to 4.5 per cent maximum margin over PLR. The rules for obligatory consortium lending were liberalised by the RBI in October 1996. The ground rules can now be framed by the participating banks themselves, without reference to the RBI. Competition in the banking sector has increased gradually as ten new private sector banks, out of the thirteen "in principle" approvals given so far, have started functioning. The RBI has issued guidelines for setting up of new local area private banks with jurisdiction over three contiguous districts. Two such banks have already been given "in principle" approval. Banks were allowed to fix their own foreign exchange aggregate gap limits, starting from April 1996. From October 1996, banks were permitted to provide foreign currency denominated loans based on their FCNR accounts, to be used for meeting either foreign currency or rupee requirements.

There has been a steady improvement in the capital adequacy of public sector banks over the last few years. The State Bank of India and its subsidiaries attained 8 per cent Capital to Risk weighted Assets Ratio (CRAR) by March 1996. Out of 19 nationalised banks, 11 reached the norm of 8 per cent CRAR, while 3 banks had a CRAR of 4 to 8 per cent. The Process of tightening norms of banking operations also continued. Recovery proceedings are being gradually streamlined, with six tribunals and one Appellate Tribunal functioning. Under the Banking Ombudsmen Scheme announced in June 1995 to expedite inexpensive resolution of customers' complaints, eleven ombudsmen are now functioning. Banks have opened 125 specialised branches for agricultural credit and 136 such branches for SSI credit.

Disbursements by Development Finance Institutions (DFI) grew by 16.6 per cent during April-December 1996, to Rs. 22257 crore, from Rs. 19088 crore during April-December 1995. This grwoth is only a little lower than the 17.4 per cent growth rate achieved in 1995-96. Sanctions by DFIs, however, declined by 30 per cent during April-December 1996, as a result of resource constraints, high interest rates and slowing of proposals for new projects from the corporate sector. To raise resources, most DFIs issued bonds during the year. They also began charging market based interest rates in the face of increasing competition for term loans by banks. Their interest rates increased in 1995-96 and in the first half of 1996-97, but declined subsequently. Minimum lending rates were reduced from 17 per cent to 16.5 per cent in October 1996.

Non-banking financial companies (NBFCs) have been brought under the regulatory puview of the RBI, through an Ordinance amending the RBI Act, 1934. To protect the interests of ordinary depositors, an NBFC has been defined to include a company whose "principal business is the receiving of deposits, under any scheme or arrangement or in any other manner, or lending any manner". All NBFCs will have to meet net worth and capital adequacy criteria. The RBI will also specify a conunting, income recognition and other norms under the law. Existing NBFCs will have a transitional period of three years to come up to the specified standards.

Steps were taken for development of the Government securities market. A number of primary dealers were set up and participated actively in the auctions. Their purchases through auctions were much higher than the minimum required under the agreement with the RBI, partly because of the commission given to them. The delivery-versus-payment system was extended to auction of treasury bills in February 1996 and to other public debt offices in May 1996. To encourage mutual fund schemes dedicated to Government securities and thus create a wider investor base, the RBI announced liquidity support to such funds in April 1996. The RBI will either purchase outright or engage in reverse repos, up to a maximum of 20 per cent of the mutual funds outstanding investment in government securities. The RBI issued guidelines to banks in June 1996 for retailing of Government securities to non-bank clients. The ratio of investments to be classified in current category by banks was raised from 40 per cent to 50 per cent for the year ending 1996-97, thus moving closer towards a fully "marked to market" system of valuation. The ratio is already 100 per cent for the new private sector banks. In January 1997, FIIs were alllowed to invest in government securities subject to ceilings.

An array of capital market reforms was introduced during 1996-97, encompassing primary and secondary markets, equity and debt, and foreign institution investment. Primary market reforms aimed at imparting greater flexibility in the issue process and strengthening the criteria for accessing the securities market. Reforms in the secondary market aimed at improving market transparency, integrity and trading infrastructure. Among the reforms undertaken were:

— Passing the Depositories Act, 1996 by Parliament, providing a legal framework for recording ownership details in book-entry form and facilitating dematerialisation of securities. The Depositories Related Laws (Amendment), 1997 issued through an Ordinance, will allow banks, mutual funds and IDBI to dematerialise their scrips.

— Formulation of SEBI (Depositories & Participants) Regulations, 1996, which allow SEBI to regulate establishment and functioning of depositories, and to protect investor interests.

— Tightening of entry norms for equity issue by companies, to improve quality.

— Giving up vetting of public issue offer documents by SEBI, to encourage self regulation. SEBI's comments (if any) to be sent within 21 days of filing.

— Debt issues not accompanied by an equity component permitted to be sold entirely by the book-building process.

— Issuers allowed to list debt securities on stock exchanges even if equity is not listed.

- — FIIs permitted to invest up to 10 per cent in the equity of any company, to invest in unlisted companies, to set up pure (100 per cent) debt funds, and to invest in government securities.
- — Eligibility criteria for registration as an FII were modified to allow endowment funds, university funds, foundations and charitable trusts/societies to register.
- — Stock lending scheme was introduced and this will not attract capital gains.
- — The SEBI (Mutual Funds) Regulations, 1993 were revised to provide for portfolio disclosure, standardisation of accounting policies, valuation norms for determining net asset value and pricing.
- — SEBI regulations on Venture Capital funds (VCF) were issued, allowing them to invest in unlisted companies, to finance turnaround companies, and to provide loans. These provide flexibility to VCFs so that high risk finance can be provided to the market.
- — Modified takeover code, based on the recommendations of the Bhagwati Committee, was approved. It requires a mandatory minimum public offer of 20 per cent purchase, when the threshold limit of 10 per cent equity holding is crossed. Those in "control" are permitted to purchase 2 per cent of shares per annum up to 51 per cent. To discourage frivolous attempts, acquirers will have to deposit a certain value of cash and assets in an escrow account. The escrow deposit would be higher for conditional public offers, unless the acquirer agrees to acquire a minimum of 20 per cent.
- — SEBI approved almost all the recommendations of the Dave Committee for improving the working of the Over The Counter Exchange of India (OTCEI).

The capital market remained subdued during 1996-97. The primary market was characterised by a reduction in the capital raised from Rs.14151 crore in April-December 1995 to Rs.10369 crore during April-December 1996. The secondary market saw low trading volumes and a downtrend in prices. Mutual funds and market intermediaries also suffered from lower volumes. Besides UTI, there are now 10 public sector mutual funds and 21 private sector mutual funds in operation. During April-December 1996, mutual funds, including UTI, raised Rs.2167 crore from different schemes. At the end of December 1996, 427 Foreign Institutional Investors (FIIs) were registered with SEBI. They have invested around US $2032 million in the securities market in 1996-97 till December, bringing the stock of FII investments to US $ 7235 million. Indian issuers also made Euro-issues (GDR's and FCCB's) of US $ 1301 million during the same period, an amount higher than that raised through Euro-issues in the whole of 1995-96.

Balance of Payments

The developments so far in 1996-97 in the balance of payments point to an easing of pressure on the current account and to buoyancy in capital inflows.

The deficit on trade account in 1996-97 is expected to be lower than in 1995-96, largely because of a sharp deceleration in the growth of non-petroleum (non-POL) Imports. This improvement in the trade deficit will be partly offset by an anticipated decline in invisible receipts, reflecting an increase in payments for factor services and some decline in private transfers. The current account deficit is expected to decline from 1.7 per cent of GDP in 1995-96 to less than 1.4 per cent of GDP in 1996-97. Net capital inflows in 1996-97 are expected to rise nearly three-fold over the previous year, largely because of buoyant inflows under non-resident deposits and foreign investment flows, including Euro-equities, and a sizable decline in repayments to the IMF. The easing of pressure on the current account and buoyant capital flows in 1996-97 resulted in a sizable build-up of foreign exchange reserves. The foreign currency assets of the RBI rose by over US $ 2.8 billion from about US $ 17.0 billion at end-March 1996 to US $ 19.8 billion at end-January 1997, providing cover for about 5.5 months of imports.

As per DGCI&S data, the trade deficit for April-December 1996 at US $ 3.3 billion was 8 per cent lower than in April-December 1995. During April-December 1996, imports recorded a growth rate of only 4.4 per cent, entirely due to a sharp 41 per cent increase in POL imports. Non- POL imports, on the other hand, showed a negative growth of 4.2 per cent during April-December 1996. Non-POL imports grew at an annual average into of 23 per cent during 1993-94 to 1995-96. The pattern of import growth suggests that the hump in imports, normally seen after a major trade and investment liberalisation is now behind us. The fall in non-oil imports may also partly reflect a slowdown of growth in investment and consumer durables' production.

There has also been a slowdown in the growth of exports in 1996-97. During April-December 1996, exports, in US dollar terms, grew only by 6.4 per cent as against the annual avarage growth rate of 19.7 per cent during the previous three years (1993-94 to 1995-96). The slow growth in exports during April-December 1996 is accounted for by large declines in exports of unmanufactured tobacco. tea, leather and leather manufactures, gems and jewellery, primary and semi-finished iron and steel, and a sharp decleration in the growth of exports of coffee, electronic goods, ready-made garments and handicrafts. Among the significant reasons for this decline are the slowdown in world treade growth in 1996 (by about 3 percentage points), inadequate avallability of non-tradeable infrastructure services, the fall in agriculture production, and large movements in cross-currency exchange rates. The impact of variations in the cross-currency rates is evident from the fact during the first nine months of 1996-97, exports valued in SDR terms grew by 12.7 per cent compared to only 6.4 per cent when valued in US dollar terms. The latest trend in the growth rates of exports seems to suggest that the initial impact of trade liberalisation in petering out and the trade flows are reverting to their normal trend determined by world demand and domestic activity. Despite the export slow down, self reliance, as measured by the coverage of imports by exports (DGCI&S), has risen to 66.2 for April-December 1996 from 86.7 during 1995-96.

Consistent with the liberal thrust of the 1992-97 EXIM Policy, the Government undertook a series of trade liberalization measures in 1996-97. These included shifting of a large number of items, including consumer goods, from the negative/restricted list to the list of items which can be imported under the export-linked, special import license (SIL) scheme. A large number of SIL items were also moved to the free (OGL) list.

In the capital account, foreign investment continued to dominate the capital flows. Total foreign investment (direct plus portfolio) during April-December 1996 surged to over US $ 4 billion, which is more than 50 per cent higher than in the corresponding period of 1995-96. This revival followed a modest decline in such investment flows from US $ 4.9 billion in 1994-95 to US $ 4.3 billion in 1995-96, mainly owing to a sharp fall in the issue of Euro-equities. Foreign direct investment flows were US $2.1 billion in 1995-96. During April-December 1996, FDI flows were US $1.7 billion, compared with US $1.5 billion in the corresponding period of 1995. Portfolio investment, comprising investment by FIIs and Euro-equities, doubled to over US $2.3 billion in the first nine months of 1996-97 from about US$1.1 billion in the corresponding period of 1995-96.

For the first time, detailed guidelines for the Foreign Investment Promotion Board were announced in January 1997. The list of industries eligible for automatic approval of foreign investments was expanded considerably. FII investments in securities of companies as 100 per cent debt funds have been allowed subject to certain guidelines; FIIs have also been allowed to invest in gilt-edged securities within the framework of the guidelines; and proprietory FII funds have been allowed to invest in the country. The guidelines for Euro-issues were liberalised in June 1996 so as to give the market a freer play in judging the quality of issues and the number of issues that can be floated in a year. The conditions relating to end-use of GDR proceeds have been relaxed significantly. Investment in the stock market and real estate is not, however, permitted out of GDR proceeds. Similarly, a number of changes were announced in June, 1996 in the external commercial borrowing (ECB) guidelines governing the maximum borrowing limits and end-use restrictions. In particular, exporters can raise ECB for meeting project-related rupee expenditure upto the equivalent of US $15 million, or the average annuale exports of the previous three years, whichever is lower. The maximum fimit under the US $ 1 million window has been enhanced to US $ 3 million, to help small and medium firms meet their working capital requirements. All infrastructure and greenfield projects have been permitted to avail of ECB to the extent of 35 per cent of total project cost, as appraised by a recognized financial institution or bank. Greater flexibility is allowed on merits to power projects. In January 1997, the ECB limit for the telecommunication sector was raised to 50 per cent of the total cost of the project.

The exchange rate of the rupee against the US dollar, which had depreciated to a monthly average of Rs. 3.63 in February 1996, recovered to Rs. 32.24 in April 1996. In the subsequent months, the rate moved in the narrow range of Rs. 35.01 to Rs. 35.87. The rupee-dollar rate remained steady although inflation in India was higher than in her major trading partners. This resulted in some appreciation of the rupee in real effective exchange rate terms.

Further measures were taken to simplify procedures related to the purchase of foreign exchange, so as to enhance current account convertibility. these included permission to Exchange Earner's Foreign Currency (EEFC) account holders to use these funds for business related current account transactions. Authorised Dealers (ADs) were allowed to export surplus currency to private money changers abroad, in addition to their own branches and correspondents. ADs were empowered to allow Indian resident families to remit US $ 5,000 per year to close relatives abroad, without reference to the RBI. Monetary ceillings on remittances for a wide range of purposes were also removed, so that ADs need not refer to the RBI.

India's external debt declined from US $ 99.0 billion at end-March 1995 to US $ 92.2 billion at end-March 1996. The downsizing of external debt resulted in a decline in the external debt-to-GDP ratio to 28.7 per cent in 1995-96. The share of concessional debt in the total remains stable at about 45.5 per cent. The share of short-term debt was 5.5 per cent at end-March 1996, and is low by international standards. The high component of concessional debt translates in to a present value (PV) of debt at US $ 70.7 billion at end-March 95. Debt service payments, as a per cent of current receipts, also declined from 27.5 per cent in 1994-95 to 25.7 per cent in 1995-96, and they are projected to decline further to about 25 per cent in 1996-97.

The India Development Bonds (IDB), issued in early 1992, fell due for redemption after five years in mid-January and mid-February,1997. Of the IDBs falling due, redemption of only about a half in net foreign currency terms continued to demonstrate the relative attractiveness of investments in India.

Social Sectors and the Poor

Rapid creation of productive employment opportunities is the best way of reducing poverty. The Economic Survey, 1995-96 reported Planning Commission estimates indicating a sharp increase in additional employment generated in the economy from 3 million in 1991-92 to over 7 million in 1994-95. These old estimates as well as the methodology for estimating employment are currently under review by the Planning Commission, and the employment estimates for 1995-96 have not yet been finalised. However, there is little doubt that the high growth of the last few years would have led to a rapid expansion of employment opportunities.

The estimated proportion of population below the poverty line is sensitive to the estimation procedure adopted. However, according to a variety of estimates, the decline in the proportion of population below the poverty line was between 2.9 and 8.7 percentage points in the six-year period ending in 1993-94. The appropriate methodology for estimation of poverty is also currently under review by the Planning Commission.

The Common Minimum Programme (CMP), underpins the strong commitment of the Government to the development of social sectors for achieving distributive justice. This commitment is reflected in the increase in Central Government Plan and non-Plan allocations for social services to a record high of 1.19 per cent of DP in 1996-97 (BE). This ratio was 0.96 per cent in 1995-96. An additional amount of Rs. 2466 crore of Central assistance to States' and Union Territories' plans has also been allocated in the 1996-97 budget for expenditure on basic minimum services.

The Government has also accorded high priority to poverty alleviation programmes. The Central Plan allocations for social sectors and poverty alleviation programmes show highest growth of 85.6 per cent for education in 1996-97 over 1995-96 (BE). The outlay for elementary education has gone up by 247.8 per cent, mainly because of the programme of nutritional support to primary school students. The alllocation for health was raised by 21.6 per cent and for rural development, encompassing the major programmes for poverty alleviation, by 12.1 per cent in 1996-97 over 1995-96 (BE).

The weaker sections especially scheduled castes/scheduled tribes and women have been given importance in special programmes of poverty alleviation and employment as well as in several other programmes. The PDS has been streamlined recently in order to target the poorer sections of the population.

ISSUES AND PRIORITIES

The Update to the Economic Survey 1995-96, published about seven months ago, had emphasised three key challenges for economic policy: how to control the fiscal deficit; how to provide adequate and reliable economic infrastructure services at a reasonable cost and with sustainable financing and pricing policies; and how to ensure broad-based employment-generating growth of agriculture, industry and other sectors, together with strengthened programmes for basic social services and anti-poverty programmes to ensure a rapid alleviation of poverty.

These challenges remain central to our concerns. It is essential to keep reducing the Centre's fiscal deficit to below four per cent of GDP as soon as possible in order to: reduce interest rates and free up resources to finance the high levels of investment, both public and private, envisaged in the Approach Paper to the Ninth Plan; to contain Central Government borrowing from the RBI and thus check the growth of inflationary potential and pressures; to moderate the growth of rapidly rising interest payments which preempt the resources available for spending of priority social and infrastructure needs; to facilitate orderly development of the market for long-term debt securities which is so essential for fostering the financing of infrastructure; and to reduce the risks associated with excessive government borrowing from external sources.

The path to fiscal deficit reduction is as well known in theory as it is difficult to limplement in practice. We must persevere with our programme of tax reforms which has helped to raise the ratio of revenues to GDP. We must seek higher non-tax revenues in the form of larger dividends from Government equity in public enterprises. We must reduce the growth of subsidies through better targetting and much more systematic application of user charges for Government services. The normally difficult task of expenditure management will be accentuated in the coming years by the challenge of accommodating the recommendations of the Fifth Central Pay Commission. Finally, Government must act expeditiously on the recommendations of the Disinvestment Commission.

The responsibility for fiscal consolidation and prudence does not rest with the Central Government alone. The states have to do their part in reducing their borrowing requirements through better design and implementation of their tax systems and through steps to curb low priority expenditures.

As described earlier, the Government has taken a wide array of initiatives to accelerate expansion of infrastructure services in power, telecommunications, roads, ports, civil aviation and irrigation. All these initiatives need to be followed through with vigour and dedication. We must quickly resolve the residual difficulties in the induction of private providers of basic and cellular telecom services. We must follow up on the experience with the recently announced guidelines for private projects in roads and ports to iron out any difficulties that may arise. We must resolve remaining ambiguities about our policy on civil aviation. We must urgently complete as many ongoing irrigation projects as possible to bring the benefits of assured water supply to millions of farmers. Above all, we must press ahead with the recently agreed Common Minimum National Action Plan for Power on a war footing.

The recurring power failures even in the capital city of Delhi this winter underline the critical nature of the power problem throughout the country. Because of unavailable, uncertain or erratic supplies from the public grid, the economy is paying a heavy price in the form of foregone production, lost exports of goods and services, frustrated investment intentions, recourse to high cost captive power generation, loss of international competitiveness, and barriers to the spread of information technology which is redefining the terms of production, technical progress and international specialisation throughout the world. The key elements of the Common Minimum National Action Plan for Power, which need to be pursued vigorously, include the establishment of Independent State Electricity Regulatory Commissions, the rationalisation of retail power tariffs, induction of private participation in electricity distribution and the restructuring and corporatisation of State Electricity Boards to run on commercial principles.

Power is only one, albeit critical, component of our energy economy. Today, the development of our petroleum sector is under a serious threat, with crude oil production having declined, oil imports rising sharply and the deficit on the Oil Pool Account increases each day and is expected to exceed Rs. 15,000 crore before the end of the financial year. Furthermore if we are to reap the benefits of increased investment and efficient production in all stages of the petroleum sector (ranging from exploration and development to refining and distribution), we must carry cut a phased dismantling of the existing administered price mechanism in this sector. The time for initiating this reform is already overdue.

A pick-up in the growth momentum of the economy will intensify the need for garnering increasing amounts of foreign savings to meel the investment requirements of the economy and to sustain the growth momentum itself. Foreign direct investment flows provide such savings without adding to the countrys external debt. As indicated in the Common Minimum Programme, Foreign direct investment should rise to US $10 billion per year from the current level of US $ 2 to 3 billion. We must learn from the pragmatic nationalism of China which received around US $ 40 billion of investment in 1996, and expects to attract more in 1997. We must also learn from the flexibility and speed of indonesia, which modified its policies rapidly in response to perceived competition from China and India, to double foreign investment inflows between 1994 and 1995. We must ensure that the regulations governing the inflow of foreign investment are transparent and attractive in comparison with what other Asian economies offer. A review of FERA is underway in this context.

Fifty years after achieving Independence, poverty, litcracy, disease and lack of minimum social services continue to affect hundreds of millions of our people. Experience from all over the world shows that rapid employment-generating growth is the most effective way of reducing poverty. Our policies and programmes must accord the highest priority to encouraging growth of sustainable and productive job opportunities in all sectors. In agriculture, income earning opportunities for farmers should be expanded by removing existing implements to domestic and international trade in agricultural products and removing controls on key agro-processing industries. At the same time, there have to be renewed efforts to strengthen rural infrastructure in the form of irrigation, rural roads, soil conservation, seed development, research and exstension, and rural credit systems. In many cases this may call for a review and redirection of existing programmes. Besides, it is imperative to find incremental resources for public investment in rural infrastructure. Such resources can be raised only partly through the budget. Without hurting the poor, the bulk of the resources would have to come from the larger and better-off farmers.

There is a tremendous scope for expanding productive employment in the construction and other service sectors, especially in the cities and towns. But to realise this potential, the Government must be prepared to remove impediments imposed by various laws and regulations, such as the Urban Land Celling Act.

For the vast majority of our people to benefit from extension of job opportunities stemming from rapid labour-intensive growth, there has to be a commensurate expansion and quality improvement in the basic social services such as primary education and primary health care. The experience of countries as diverse as China and Indonesia has demonstrated the critical requirement fc- priority attention to these basic services.

For those at the margins of a market driven economy, the effective provision of minimum social services and special programmes for employment and poverty alleviation fulfil an essential need. Over time these special programmes have proliferated, not always rationally. To maximise the beneficial impact of anti-poverty programmes, it would be desirable to seek ways of consolidation and rationalisation, and some attrition. The basic goal should be to enhance sustainable benefits to the poorest segments of the society, while reducing administrative duplication and wastage and minimising well-known "leakages".

Over the last 5 to 6 years the Indian economy has demonstrated enviable resilience and buoyancy as a result of wide ranging economic reforms and closer integration with the world economy. On the whole, those dimensions of of the economy have performed best where reform efforts have been most thorough and far-reaching. We must learn from this experience as we look ahead to meet the challenges of the future.

ADMINISTRATION OF THE FINANCES OF GOVERNMENT OF INDIA : MONETARY AND CREDIT, FINANCIAL, EXTERNAL SECTOR AND SOCIAL SECTOR DEVELOPMENTS

The economic reforms pursued since mid 1991 have helped in putting the Indian economy on a higher gowth path. Revised gross domestic product (GDP) estimates (at factor cost at 1980-81 prices) show an impressive increase in economic growth to 7.1 per cent in 1995-96 on top of a high gorwth of 7.2 per cent in 1994-95. Economic growth in 1996-97 is estimated by the Central Statistical Organisation to be around 6.8 per cent. Thus, the Eighth Plan is likely to end with an average growth of 6.5 per cent per annum which is significantly higher than the target rate of growth of 5.6 per cent.

Developments in Agriculture and Prices

The year 1996 was the ninth successive normal year and, the country-wide seasonal rainfall was 103 per cent of the long term average. 1996 monsoon arrived almost on time and covered the entire country by 30th June, two weeks earlier than the normal arrival date. By the end of monsoon season, 32 out of 35 meteorological sub-divisions and 81 per cent of the districts had received normal to excess rainfall. Foodgrain production in 1996-97 is likely to be 191.2 million tones as against 185 million tonnes in 1995-96. The expected wheat production in 1996-97 is 64.5 million tonnes as against 62.6 million tonnes in 1995-96. The total oilseeds production in 1996-97 may be of the order of 24.1 million tonnes. In 1995-96, the sugarcane production was 283 million tonnes and the likely production in 1996-97 would be around 273.6 million-tonnes. The production of cotton is expected to be around 143 lakh bales (of 170 kg each) as against 131 lakh bales produced last year. The production of Jute and Mesta in 1996-97 is likely to be around 9.2 million bales (of 180 kg each) as against 8.5 million bales in 1995-96.

During the current marketing season, wheat and rice procurement upto 27th January, 1997 was 8.2 million tonnes and 8.1 million tonnes respectively (as against 12.3 million tonnes and 6.3 million tonnes respectively during the corresponding period of last year).

For much of the current financal year 1996-97, the annual inflation rate remained at about 6 per cent despite the 18 per cent increase in the administered prices of petroleum products. Revision in prices of coal reinforced the uptrend and the escalation in the prices of foodgrains, especially wheat, sustained this undercurrent of inflationary uptrend towards the end of 1996 when the inflation rate crossed 7 per cent by mid December, 1996 and rose further to 7.7 per cent by end January, 1997. The undercurrent of inflationary rise is attributed largely to escalation in the prices of food articles especially foodgrains and vegetables. Among foodgrains, the major rise occurred in the prices of wheat which, by mid-January, increased by 32.9 per cent over its prices prevailed in the corresponding period last year. The increase was mainly due to short fall in production and lower procurement. Subsequently in order to meet the supply shortfall in wheat, Government contracted imports of up to 2 million tonnes of wheat.

Development in Industry and Infrastructure

The basic ingredients of the strategy for industrial reforms adopted by the government are abolition of restrictive policy such as licensing, a more level playing field between the public sector and the private sector and freer access to foreign investment and technology. The stringent conditions for entry of large units in ar-eas reserved for the small scale sector has been relaxed. Several procedural simplifications have been effected to give a boost to the process of liberalisation with full vigour. The new economic policies in the industrial sector, including providing a more competitive environment, inducing higher foreign investment and technology, restructuring PSUs are now bearing fruit and have contributed significantly in terms of industrial growth. There has been a substantial upsurge in the growth of industrial production during 1995-96. The latest available Index of Industrial Production (IIP) for October, 1996 shows that the overall industrial gorwth was 9.9 per cent supported by a growth rate of 11.0 per cent in manufacturing, -5.5 per cent in mining and 6.9 per cent in electricity generation. The cumulative growth of industrial production in April-October, 1996 was 9.8 per cent, aided by a growth rate of 12.1 per cent in manufacturing, 1.7 per cent in mining and 3.4 per cent in electricity. There are no major constraints to industrial growth and several surveys conducted by Industry associations and research institutions indicate a buoyant industrial scenario.

The performance of the capital goods sector has been quite impressive. The sector registered a growth of 16.6 per cent over April-October 1996 as compared to 15.0 per cent in April-October, 1995. The intermediate goods sector too, performed well showing a growth rate of 10.8 per cent, higher than 7.2 per cent in April-October 1995. Consumer goods registered a growth rate of 8.2 per cent in April-September, 1995. Basic goods, however, showed a growth rate of only 6.7 per cent. Over April-October 1996. food products, beverages and tobacco, paper products, chemicals, basic metals, electrical machinery and transport equipment industries performed particularly well, leading to the high growth for manufacturing sector. Negative performance were registered by jute textiles and other manufacturing industries during April-October, 1996.

Infrastructure

The provision and maintenance of adequate infrastructural facilities at reasonable cost are absolutely necessary if rapid economic growth is to be achieved and sustained. To achieve greater efficiency and accountability in these sectors it is necessary to introduce competition in the provision and operation of infrastructure services and to make them work on more accepted commercial principles. The overall performance of the infrastructure sector during the first nine months of the current financial year 1996-97 (April-December) has not been satisfactory. Seven critical infrastructure industries namely electricity, coal, steel, crude oil, refinery products, cement and fertilisers with a combained weight of about 31 per cent in the Index of Industrial Production (IIP) have achieved an average growth rate of 3.6 per cent in April-December, 1996 as compared with an average growth rate of 8.3 per cent in April-December, 1995. The deceleration in the growth rate of infrastructure industries is mainly due to a decline in crude oil production and hydro power generation. There was also a marked slowdown in thermal power generation. As infrastructure services have a basic role in providing the desired thrust to exports and in making Indian industries globally competitive, the ongoing economic reforms attach high priority to better utilisation of existing infrastructure assets and fresh development of infrastructure. Given the competing demands on limited resources available with the Government, the creation of quality infrastructure will need infusion of private capital, including foreign investment. To facilitate this the Government has formulated specific policy initiatives designed to render the infrastructure sector an attractive destination for investment. In October, 1994 the Ministry of Finance constituted an Expert Group an Commercialisation of Infrastructure Projects which submitted its report to the Finance Ministry on 22nd June, 1996.

Monetary and Credit Development

In the current financial year the growth of both narrow money and broad money has been faster than in 1995-96. Up to the fortnight ended January 17, 1997 broad money (M3) grew by 10.6 per cent as against 8.2 per cent growth in the corresponding period of 1995-96. There has been a step-up in the annualised growth of M3 from 13.2 per cent as on March 31, 1996 to 15.7 per cent as on January 17, 1997. Narrow money (M1) also recorded a higher growth of 5.4 per cent compared to 4.2 per cent growth in 1995-96 till January 19, 1996. The gradual acceleration in money supply growth was not, however, due to any acceleration of reserve money growth. On the contrary, reserve money has declined by 2.9 per cent during this financial year upto January 17, 1997 in contrast to the expansion of 4 per cent in corresponding period of the last financial year, while annual growth declined from 14.8 per cent as on March 31, 1996 to 7.2 per cent on January 17, 1997.

During the current financial year upto January 17, 1997 the expansion of net RBI credit to Government (NRCG) at 3.3 per cent (Rs. 3987 crore), was much smaller than its 14.7 per cent (Rs. 14961 crore) growth in the corresponding period of 1995-96. The contribution by net foreign exchange assets of RBI was higher by Rs. 11482 crore (15.5 per cent) as compared with the decline of Rs. 458 crore (-0.6 per cent) in 1995-96. Sharp reduction in refinance from RBI availed of by commercial banks because of significant improvement in their liquidity conditions following the CRR cuts and significantly lower growth in NRCG reduced the reserve money.

The structure of Net Bank credit to Government has undergone a sharp change this year. The slower growth of RBI credit to Government has been more than offset by an increase in "other banks" credit to Government. The growth of "other banks" credit to the commercial sector has correspondingly been weaker, at 5.6 per cent and less than one half of the 11.9 per cent in the comparable period of 1995-96. The growth of bank credit to commercial sector has been lower at 5.3 per cent during the current financial year up to January 17, 1997 as against 11.6 per cent recorded in the last financial year upto January 19, 1996.

While non-food credit has shown recent signs of a moderate pick-up, the overall growth so far is around one-third of the growth registered in the corresponding period of 1995-96. Given that the growth of deposits with the banking system has accelerated, the slowing down of credit growth despite a falling interest rate indicates mainly a lower off-take of credit by the corporate sector. This could be attributable to factors like (a) postponement of investment decisions because of later than usual presentation of Central Budget, (b) excess capacity in certain segments and (c) decline in export/import growth.

The easing of monetary policy has been reflected in call money rates which have been ruling easy from the very beginning of the current financial year. The average call money rate declined from the high of 13.75 per cent at the beginning of the current financial year to 5 and 10 per cent in October, 1996 and ruled between 6 and 12 per cent in December, 1996. The yield to maturity (YTM) on treasury bills has come down, on both 91-day and 364-day T-bills. The coupon rate on dated securities of Central Government has come down from 14.26 per cent in 1995-96 to 13.72 per cent on 4 year securities and from 14 per cent in 1995-96 to 13.85 per cent on 10 year securities in the current financial year.

Financial Development

There was a significant reduction of the Cash Reserve Ratio (CRR) required to be maintained by the banks against their net demand and time liabilities in the count financial year. The average CRR was reduced from 14 per cent to 13 per cent in two phases of 0.5 percentage point each, effective April 27 and May 11, 1996, and CRR on NRER deposits was brought down to zero. There was another phase of CRR reduction to 12 per cent effective July 6, 1996 on demand and time liabilities. CRR was further reduced by one percentage point in two phases of 0.5 percentage point each to 11 per cent effective from October 26, 1996 and November 9, 1996. Further one percentage point reduction was made in two phases of 0.5 percentage of points each from the fortnight beginning January 4 and 18, 1997 respectively.

The average SLR of the scheduled commercial banks is estimated to have fallen to 28.2 per cent of their total net demand and time liabilities (NDTL) in end-March 1996. Since the growth of aggregate deposits has been strong in this financial year, the average SLR on total outstanding NDTL should be close to 27 per cent by end-December 1996.

In 1995-96 the net profit of State Bank of India group at Rs. 793 crore was slightly less than the Rs. 846 crore in 1994-95. Out of the 19 nationalised banks seven banks suffered net loss out of which three had operating losses. The contraction of net profits of public sector banks in 1995-96 may be mainly attributed to the large depreciation on investments made by the banks in Government securities. However, this provision for depreciation on investments does not represent a loss but is only an "internal reserve" and hence does not involve any cash outgo.

There was a significant improvement in capital adequacy status of the public sector banks at the end of 1995-96. The State Bank of India and all its subsidiaries attained 8 per cent Capital to Risk Weighted Assets Ratio (CRAR) at March end, 1996 while in 1994-95 only SBI and one of its subsidiaries had this distinction. Out of 19 nationalised banks, 11 reached the norm of 8 per cent CRAR, and 3 banks had a CRAR of 4 to 8 per cent.

Under the Banking Ombudsmen Scheme announced in June 1995 to expedite inexpensive resolution of customers complaints, ten ombudsmen are now functioning.

The interest rate on NRE rupee deposits above two years was deregulated in order to bring them in alignment with domestic term deposits. Minimum maturity period of domestic term deposits was reduced to 30 days and interest rate on term deposits of over one year was deregulated. The ceiling rate on the term deposit of 30 days and upto one year was reduced to 10 per cent. A number of banks have reduced their Primary Lending Rate by 1 to 1-1/2 percentage points and announcing a 3 to 3.5 per cent margin over PLR.

Process of tightening norms of banking operations continued. From 1996-97 onwards banks will be required to classify small loans of Rs. 25,000 and above into the specified four asset categories and make appropriate provisioning for NPA's.

Six tribunals are functioning at Calcutta, New Delhi, Jaipur, Ahmedabad, Bangalore and Chennai and one appellate tribunal is at Mumbai. Ten new private sector banks have started functioning out of the thirteen "in principle" approval given thus far for setting up of new banks in the private sector. The RBI has issued guidelines for setting up of new local area private banks with jurisdictions over three contiguous districts as announced in 1996-97 Central budget and approval has been accorded to two local area private banks to be set up one each in Maharashtra and Karnataka. The rules for obligatory consortium were liberalised by RBI in October 1996. The ground rules of consortium arrangement, could be framed by the participating banks. This would also apply to existing consortiums.

The pursuance of the recommendations made by the Expert Group on Forex Markets, (Chairman: Shri O.P. Sodhani), banks were permitted from April 1996 to fix their own Aggregate Gap (arising out of maturity mismatches) Limits. They could do this depending on their foreign exchange operations, risk taking capacity, balance sheet size and other relevant parameters. In October 1996, banks were given permission to provide foreign currency denominated loans to their customers (who would bear foreign exchange risk) for meeting either foreign currency of rupee requirements, on the resource base of their FCNR Accounts.

In the context of the favourable price-supply situation, bank advances against a large number of price-sensitive essential commodities, which had been subject to selective credit controls up to October 21, 1996, were made exempt from such controls effective October 21, 1996.

During the current financial year scheduled commercial banks are required to attain 40 per cent ratio (to net bank credit) for priority sector advances. They have also been asked to attain the export credit norms of 12 per cent of net bank credit. Banks have opened 125 specialised branches for agricultural credit and 136 such branches for SSI credit.

During the first nine months of the current financial year (April-December 1996) the all India financial institutions disbursed Rs. 26813 crore as against Rs. 23187 crore disbursed in April-December 1995, implying an annual growth rate of 15.6 per cent. However, financial assistance sanctioned by them recorded a decline of 26 per cent. It appears that these institutions are mostly disbursing the pending sanctions of 1995-96.

Most of the development finance institutions raised resources during the year through issue of bonds. Their interest rates have also become more or less market-based in consonance with the on-going liberalisation in the financial sector. Their interest rates increased in 1995-96 and in first half of 1996-97, reflecting higher demand for funds on account of revival in real sector activities. Since October 1996, the minimum lending rate of DFIs, (excluding interest tax) has been reduced to 16.5 per cent from 17 per cent earlier.

The Depositories Bill was passed by Parliament in July, 1996 and in pursuance of this, the Depositories Act 1996 was published in the Gazette of India Extraordinary on 12th August, 1996. The main objective of the Act is to provide for regulation of depositories in securities and for related matters. Securities and Exchange Board of India (SEBI) granted registration to the first depository in the country namely, National Securities Depository Limited (NSDL) on 7.6.1996 for facilitating trading in securities and settlement of transactions in the Stock Exchanges in a dematerialised form and transfer of ownership of securities through an electronic book-entry system. NSDL has commenced operations and trading in a few selected scripts in a dematerialised form has started on the National Stock Exchange of India Limited with effect from 26th December, 1996.

The powers of the Government under the Securities Contracts (Regulation) Rules 1957 were transferred to SEBI by amending these Rules on 23rd December, 1996. The main objective of the amendments is to further strengthen the regulatory powers of SEBI over the securities markets. These powers cover, *inter alia,* matters relating to recognition of Stock Exchanges, qualifications for membership of a stock exchange, obligation of the Governing Body of an Exchange to take disciplinary action against a member, manner of enquiry in relation to the affairs of the Governing Body of a Stock Exchange, submission of Annual Report and requirements with respect to the listing of securities on Exchanges.

A Notification was issued on 13th June, 1996 under the provision of Section 16 of the Securities Contracts (Regulation) Act 1956 in order to permit certain Primary Dealers in Government securities market to undertake ready forward contracts in Treasury Bills of all maturities issued by the Government and in such dated securities of the Government as are approved by the RBI in consultation with the Government.

An Ordinance for amending the Depositories Act, 1996 was promulgated on 15th January, 1997 by the President. The Ordinance has amended the Depositories Act, 1996 and also made consequential amendments to the Companies Act, 1956, the Industrial Development Bank of India Act, 1964, the state Bank of India Act, 1955, the State Bank of India (subsidiary Banks) Act, 1959, the Banking Companies (Acquisition and Transfer of Undertakings) Act, 1970 and 1980 and the Indian Stamp Act, 1899. These legal changes will remove the existing impediments for companies and other statutory bodies in joining the depository mode and facilitate the smooth functioning of the depositories.

Policy relating to External Commercial Borrowings (ECB) was reviewed and certain modifications were made in the policy in order to improve transparency, simplify the procedures, and to provide easier access to external funds for the Indian industry. During July, 1996, the procedures for approval of liability management transactions by Indian Corporates for the specific purpose of hedging against interest rate or foreign exchange exposure were simplified. In order to streamline the procedures for external commercial borrowings, Government have decided to delegate the sanctioning powers for external commercial borrowings upto USD 3 million to the Reserve Bank of India (RBI) with effect from 15.12.1996.

External Sector Developments

The balance of payments situation in 1996-97 is characterized by easing of current account pressure and buoyant capital flows. Despite a slow down in export growth and some decline in net invisible receipts, the current account deficit, as a per cent of GDP, is expected to decline to about 1.4 per cent from 1.7 per cent estimated for 1995-96, mainly because of the sharp deceleration in the growth of non-POL imports. The improvement in the current account of balance of payments is reinforced by a sharp rise in net capital inflows, reflecting the upsurge in non-resident deposits and revival of funds raised abroad through Euro-equities. These developments in the current and capital accounts resulted in excess supply in the foreign exchange market enabling a substantial build up of foreign exchange reserves during the year. The foreign currency assets of the RBI rose by US$2.8

billion from US $17.0 billion at the end of March 1996 to US $19.8 billion on January 31, 1997. The current level of foreign currency assets lends cover to over 5.5 months of estimated imports in 1996-97. The year 1996-97 witnessed stability in foreign exchange market. The exchange rate of the rupee against the US dollar, which depreciated to Rs. 36. In February 1996, following volatility driven by speculation, recovered to Rs. 34.2 in April, 1996. In the subsequent months, the rate moved in the narrow range of Rs. 35.0 to Rs. 35.9. Taking into account the inflation differential between India and abroad, the rupee appreciated somewhat in real effective terms.

India's external debt declined by 6.88 billion from US $99.04 billion at the end of March 1995 to US $92.26 billion at the end of March, 1996. The down sizing of external debt resulted in further decline in external debt/GDP ratio to about 29 per cent in 1995-96. Despite a bunching of repayments arising from redemption of India Development Bonds, total debt service payments (comprising repayments of principal and interest payments) during 1996-97 will remain within manageable limit. In fact, the debt service payments, as a per cent of current receipts in the balance of payments, is expected to decline from about 26 per cent in 1995-96 to about 25 per cent in 1996-97.

Export performance has been quite robust in the past few years. According to the DGCI & S data, exports witnessed a growth rate of 18.4 per cent in 1994-95 and still higher growth of 20.9 per cent in 1995-96 in dollar terms. According to the data; for the period April-December, 1996, exports have grown by only 6.4 per cent against a high of 24.2 per cent in the corresponding period of last year. The decline in export performance in the recent months must be viewed in the backdrop of a steep decline in non-POL import growth from a high of 32.1 per cent during April-December 1995 to a negative 4.2 per cent during April-December 1996 which is a probable pointer towards general slowdown in industrial activity and a setback to economic dynamism as compared to last year. Domestic cyclical factors have no doubt played a role, given the rapid economic growth in the previous year. These factors appear to have been compounded by several external developments, including a fall in import demand by industrial countries, the effect on exports of large movements in the yen/dollar exchange rate, and a sharp drop in world semi-conductor prices.

The capital account of the balance of payments has undergone a major compositional change after 1992-93 with the non-debt creating foreign investment (direct and portfolio) emerging the dominant flows. The foreign investments, which surged in 1993-94 to US $4235 million, rose further to US $ 4895 million in 1994-95. In 1995-96, foreign investment flows declined to US $ 4347 million, mainly due to the sharp decline in issue of Euro-equities abroad. The market for Euro-equities improved in the current year. Foreign investment during April-December 1996 amounted to US $ 4.1 billion, registering a growth rate of about 55 per cent over the total flows in the corresponding period of last year.

The behaviour of foreign exchange market in 1996-97 so far has been orderly. The exchange rate of the rupee vis-a-vis the US dollar moved in the narrow range of Rs. 35.0 to Rs. 35.9 between May, 1996 and

January 1997. However, the rate of inflation in India which is significantly higher than the inflation rates in India's trade partner countries, has tended to offset the competitive advantage gained by the nominal depreciation. In 1996-97, the effect of the adverse inflation differential was reinforced by the nominal appreciation of the rupee against the Japanese Yen, Deutsche Mark and the French Franc, following the strengthening of the US dollar against these currencies in the international currency markets. As a result, the export weighted real effective exchange rate (REER) of the rupee, which takes into account the exchange rate of the rupee against the currencies of five major trading partners of India and the inflation differentials between India and these countries, stands appreciated in November 1996 by about 8.1 per cent compared with the REER for the financial year 1993-94.

India subscribed w.e.f. 1.1.97 to the Special Data Dissemination Standards (SDDS) established by the International Monetary Fund (IMF). This requires provision of comprehensive, timely accessible and reliable economic and financial statistics in a world of increasing economic and financial integration. Now Indian data and dissemination practices—its metadata will be displayed on an electronic bulletin board of IMF. This is expected to help India better access to international capital market.

Insurance Sector Development

During the financial year 1995-96, the Life Insurance Corporation of India (LIC) secured total new business (sum assured) of Rs. 52,071.53 crore under 110.34 lakh policies as compared to Rs. 55,468.82 crore sum assured under 108.88 lakh policies in 1994-95. New business under Group Insurance Scheme (including Group Gratuity) was of the order of Rs. 62718.50 crore covering 227.24 lakh lives. The total rural new business procured by the corporation during 1995-96 works out to be 41per cent of its total new business in terms of sum assured and 47.7per cent in terms of the policies issued. The total business in force (individual assurance) as on 31st March, 1996 was Rs. 2,95,758 crore under 709.60 lakh policies as compared with Rs. 2,54,572 crore under 655.29 lakh policies as on 31st March, 1995.

The gross premium income of the general insurance industry in India during 1995-96 was Rs. 6047 crores as against Rs. 4959 crores during 1994-95. It amounted to a growth of 21.9 per cent in 1995-96 over the previous year. The net premium income of the general insurance industry in India during the year 1995-96 was Rs. 5087 crores as against Rs. 4102 crore in 1994-95, representing a growth of 24.0 per cent. The gross profits of the industry during 1995-96 were Rs. 831 crore as against Rs. 503 crores in 1994-95 representing a growth of 65.4per cent over the previous year. The net profits of the industry during the year 1995-96 were Rs. 551 crores as against Rs. 377 crores in 1994-95, amounting to an increase of 46.1 per cent over the previous year.

In pursuance of the recommendations of the Committee on Reforms in the Insurance Sector, an interim Insurance Regulatory Authority (IRA) was set up on 23.1.1996 under the overall administrative control of the finance Ministry. In pursuance of the announcement made by the Finance Minister in his Budget Speech in July, 1996 a Bill on IRA to convert it into a statutory body (insurance Regulatory Authority Bill, 1996) has been introduced in the Lok Sabha on 20.12.1996.

Social Sector Development

The Government has raised substantially the Central Plan outlay for social sectors and anti-poverty programmes in 1996-97 budget with a view to help the weaker sections of the society. The budget allocation for Education increased by about 86 per cent from Rs. 1825 crore in 1995-96 (BE) to Rs. 3388 crore in 1996-97)BE), with the outlay for elementary education going up by about 248 per cent, health by about 22 per cent from Rs. 670 crore in 1995-96 (BE) to Rs. 815 crore in 1996-97 (BE). The Central Plan outlay for Rural Development which encompasses a major programme for poverty alleviation and employment generation was raised by 12 per cent from Rs. 7700 crore in 1995-96 (BE) to Rs. 8632 crore in 1996-97 (BE).

In view of the strong commitment to help the weaker sections of the society, the Public Distribution System (PDS) has been streamlined recently in order to target the poorer Sections of the population. The "Health for All" strategy is being reoriented towards "Health for Under Privileged". A comprehensive Law, "The Persons with Disabilities (Equal Opportunities, Protection of Rights and Full Participation) Act, 1995" has been enforced with effect from 7.2.1996.

FISCAL DISCIPLINE

The Central Government on March 26 brought itself under "fiscal discipline" by signing a Ways and Means Advances agreement with the Reserve Bank of India. This new system of financing temporary mismatches between Government revenue receipts and payments will have an overall limit of Rs. 12,000 crore for the first half of the year (April-September) and Rs. 8,000 crore for the second half (October-March) when the revenue collections start building up. The new agreement will come into operation from April 1,1997. The Ways and Means Advance replaced the over four-decades old ad hoc treasury bills which was originally intended to help the cash balances of the Government. However, the system was misused as the ad hocs were rolled over, creating a permanent source of overdraft from the Reserve Bank. Under the new agreement, there has to be periodic vacation of advances and any excess drawal by the Government will not be permitted for more than 10 consecutive days. However, to help the Central Government to adjust to the new system, a grace period of two years has been provided, which means that after March 1999, borrowings beyond the permissible limit for more than 10 consecutive days would not be allowed.

While the agreement provides for fixing of the limit of advance and the interest rates by mutual consultations between the Finance Ministry and the Reserve Bank, for the current year it has been decided that the interest on Ways and Means Advance would be at three per cent lower than the calculated rate. For any quarter beginning April 1, 1997, the calculated rate will mean the average of the implicit yield at the end of the cut-off prices of 91-day treasury bill auctions held during the previous quarter. For overdraft beyond the Ways and Means Advance, the rate will be the normal interest rate (calculated rate minus three per cent) plus two per cent on the overdraft amount. However, overdraft will not be permissible for periods exceeding 10 consecutive working days after March, 1999.

The agreement was signed in New Delhi on March 26 by the Finance Secretary, Mr. Montek Singh Ahluwalia, and the Reserve Bank Governor, Dr. C. Rangarajan, Mr. Ahluwalia later told presspersons that the Government was confident of managing its finances within the specified limits while Dr. Rangarajan felt that the earlier system had curtailed the monetary authority's freedom to operate instruments of monetary policy for price stability. As for the outstanding treasury bills as on March 31, 1997, it was decided that these would be funded into special securities, without any specific maturity, at an interest rate of 4.6 per cent per annum on April 1. The outstanding Tap Treasury Bills as on March 31, 1997 would be paid off on maturity with an equivalent creation of special securities without any specified maturity, at an interest rate of 4.6 per cent per annum.

FOREX RESERVES ALL-TIME HIGH

The foreign currency assets of the Reserve Bank of India touched an all-time high of $21.16 billion—a result of the bank's aggressive intervention in the forex markets to prop up the dollar for most of the month of March. The foreign currency assets now show an increase of $4.12 billion in the current financial year—$1.47 billion after the budget. The foreign currency assets now cover seven month's import requirement of the country. In an attempt to hedge against the uncertainty before the budget, banks and exporters held on to their dollars. However, the budget offered various sops to attract investment into the country, leading to expectations of good dollar inflows in the medium to long term. As a result, banks that had gone long on the dollar, started unloading. This caused panic among exporters, who started selling their dollar proceeds held overseas.

The result was substantial inflows in both the spot and forward market. The rupee appreciated by 6 paise on March 3, closing at 35.80 paise. The six-month annualised premium for the forward dollar slipped to a low of 6.1 per cent on March 10. The RBI entered the market to support the dollar. The spot dollar now hovers around Rs. 35.87-88 and the six-month annualised forward premium around 7 per cent. The RBI intervention has dispelled apprehensions of a stronger rupee in the medium to long term. "Had the RBI not intervened, the dollar might have weakened by at least 15-20 paise," said a treasury chief. The RBI came in to strengthen the dollar keeping in mind economic fundamentals, particularly the inflation differential between India (7.7 per cent) and the US (3 per cent), the country's major trading partner, he said.

INFLATION

Prices ended the fiscal year 1996-97 on a promising note with the annual rate of inflation falling further to 7.35 per cent for the week ended March

29. Wholesale prices have been showing a falling trend in the last few weeks after touching a 63-week high of 8 per cent in the first week of February. The annual inflation declined by 0.16 percentage points during the week to 7.35 per cent, from 7.51 per cent for the previous week even as official wholesale price index for "all commodities" (base 1981-82/100) also fell by 0.2 per cent to 321.5 (provisional) as against 322.0 (provisional). This is for the 104th weeks that prices have maintained single digit levels. It had got into the single digit orbit in April, 1995. In comparison, last year had ended with an inflation of 4.4 per cent.

The Government had reined in on the inflation with the help of a tight monetary policy after it shot up to double digit levels during February 1995. It had been arrested to the levels of 4.2 per cent during June last year. Inflation has been witnessing a roller coaster ride since the hike in petroleum prices during July last year and touched the 8 per cent-mark during the week ending February 8. The annual inflation rate for the week ending February 1,1997, based on final index calculated on a point-to-point basis, stood at 8.0 per cent as against 7.7 per cent as computed for the week based on provisional index.

BANKING AND FINANCIAL INSTITUTIONS

Government Reviewing Banks' Working

Finance Minister P. Chidambaram said in the Rajya Sabha on December 17 that the government was taking steps to improve the profitability of state-owned banks and was constantly reviewing their performance to reduce fraud. He said the process of reform had been yielding results, which were reflected in the working results of banks. Seeking to distinguish between "commercial misjudgment and culpable negligence of crime" in banking activities, Mr. Chidambaram, while replying to a marathon 200-minute-long discussion on enormous losses incurred by the banks due to irregularities, said the government hoped to put in place a suitable mechanism by this month to prevent *bonafide* bank transactions from coming under investigations. The discussion, raised by V. Narayanaswamy (Congress) and 12 others, mainly focussed on the reasons behind the losses incurred by the Indian banks.

Mr. Chidambaram said the government was also taking measures to reduce fraud and irregularities in the banking system. On the economic reforms, the Finance Minister said the reforms had been yielding results, and this was reflected in the working results of the banks. Operating profits of 27 public sector banks improved from Rs. 3,069 crore in 1992-93 to Rs. 3,696 crore in 1993-94 to Rs. 5,628 crore in 1994-95 and Rs. 7,569 crore in 1995-96, Mr. Chidambaram said, asserting that the burden of provisioning had been exceptionally high as the banks were required to provide for the backlog of provisions in the past years. Consequently, net losses increased from Rs. 3,293 crore in 1992-93 to Rs. 4,349 crore in 1993-94, he added. The public sector banks, as a group, finally recorded a net profit of Rs. 1,116 crore in 1994-95, the Finance Minister said. However, maintaining after making provisions for non-performing assets the PSU banks showed a net loss of Rs. 371 crore during 1995-96. The Minister also stressed on a careful interpretation of these results.

Foreign Equity Norms

The Finance Ministry has revised the guidelines for considering proposals of foreign equity participation in non-banking financial companies (NBFCs). The new guidelines have been framed after a review by the Government of foreign equity investment in NBFCs. Henceforth, all proposals for foreign equity investments in NBFCs will be considered by the Foreign Investment Promotion Board (FIPB), according to an official Press release. The Investment in non-banking financial services to be permitted in (i) merchant banking (ii) underwriting, (iii) portfolio management services, (iv) investment advisory services, (v) financial consultancy, (vi) stockbroking, (vii) asset management, (viii) venture capital, (ix) custodial service, (x) factoring, (xi) credit reference agencies, (xii) credit rating agencies, (xiii) leasing and finance and (xiv) housing finance.

According to the release, the minimum capitalisation has been revised as follows: (a) where the foreign equity is less than 51 per cent or equal to 51 per cent: US $0.5 million; (b) where the foreign equity is more than 51 per cent but is less than or equal to 75 per cent: US $5 million; (c) where the foreign equity is more than 75 per cent: US $50 million; and (d) 100 per cent foreign owned NBFCs would act as a holding company and specific activities would be undertaken by stepdown subsidiaries with minimum 25 per cent domestic equity. The scheduling of capitalisation for foreign equity holding up to 75 per cent will be the minimum capitalisation according to the norms indicated above to be brought up front. For foreign equity holding above 75 per cent and up to 100 per cent, the scheduled capitalisation will be US $7.5 million to be brought up front and the balance to be brought in over 24 months. Domestic equity in the stepdown subsidiaries of 100 per cent foreign owned holding companies may be scheduled by bringing 10 per cent domestic equity up front and the balance domestic equity over a period of 24 months.

FOREIGN TRADE (EXPORTS AND IMPORTS)

Duty Drawback Plan Revised

The Finance Ministry has added 16 more products to the list of items eligible for duty drawback and revised the rates in the case of textile, readymade garments, sports goods, bicycle parts automobile components, food preparations, hand-made tools, leather and certain varieties of packaging material products. The revised all industry drawback rates would come into effect from October 23. Moreover, exporters will be eligible to claim drawback even if the amount claimed is just 1 per cent of POB value of exports. Till now, drawback claims were not entertained only if the amount was less than

2 per cent of the FOB value of exports. The move to lower this limit would benefit small exporters. The scheme for fixing brand rates has been amended to extend the benefit to partnership firms also. Till now only limited companies were eligible for seeking brand rates which are higher than the all industry rates. The Ministry has also introduced seven-digit classification of the entries made in the drawback schedule in order to simplify processing of claims by removing ambiguities. A Press note issued by the Ministry said that in some cases, footnotes have been added to the entries themselves.

In the case of readymade garments, broadbanding of drawback rates has been attempted so as to reduce the incidence of drawal of samples and their testing, besides benefiting a larger section of exporters. Drawback rates are revised every year to reflect the changes made in the Union Budget. This year drawback on a number of items has come down as a result of reduction of customs and excise duties in the Budget. However, in the case of textiles items like made-ups, officials of the Customs Department has taken into account the duties suffered on the fabric. Since inputs imported under the advance licence scheme are subjected to additional customs duty in many case, concerned importer-exporters will be eligible to claim drawback on duties paid on inputs.

Pass Book Scheme for Exporters

The Revenue Department has instructed all Customs Houses to expedite provision of credit to exporters under the Pass Book Scheme, be flexible in dealing with the 'nexus clause' associated with the advance licensing scheme, and treat all instructions issued by the Directorate General of Foreign Trade (DGFT) as the last word while deciding importability of an item. A series of other steps including liberalisation of the EPCG (Export Promotion Capital Goods) scheme have also been initiated to resolve the procedural problems faced by exporters.

To ensure smooth functioning of the Pass Book Scheme, Custom Houses have been instructed to allow credit within three weeks from the date on which claim is filed by the exporter. The process has been simplified to a large extent with a new stipulation. If the exporter concerned produces a contemporaneous bill of entry regarding any import, the value mentioned in it would be accepted. Otherwise, the Custom House would refer to its databank to ascertain value of the material for which credit is claimed but the process has to be completed within three weeks. If this time limit is crossed, then the officials concerned have to accept the value declared by the exporter. All Custom Houses are maintaining their Databank which is updated once in 120 days. In the case of the 94 items which have been put on the negative list for Pass Book Scheme, exporters will be eligible to claim drawback. Credit against these item, is not allowed since they are not being imported at all, even under the Duty Exemption Scheme. To avoid delay on account of debate over importability of items, the Revenue Department has asked Custom Houses to accept all instructions/clarification issued by the DGFT. This move is expected to put an end to exporters' complaints about Customs authorities not accepting amendments made by DGFT in licences.

Rating Scheme for Exporters

The Indian Institute of Foreign Trade (IIFT) on September 4 announced a strategic alliance with Marketing and Development Research Associates (MDRA) to launch a performance rating scheme for exporting enterprises. The IIFT-MDRA performance rating for exporters (PRE) will be available to those involved in services, goods and brands from India. Initially, it will be available for four industry sectors—textiles, garments, computer software, processed foods and engineering goods all of which account for 80 per cent of exports. Next year, it will be extended to other sectors as well.

IIFT Director General P.L. Sanjeev Reddy said at a Press conference that the methodology used in performance rating would involve 105 parameters. "This will help in removing international bias against Indian vendors." The methodology used for independent and credible scheme of assigning rating to exporters would take into account financial soundness, reliability and quality of product, services and sound.

Trade Curbs to go in Five Years

Commerce Secretary Tejendra Khanna on December 2 said that the quantitative restrictions on imports, including on consumer products, would be waived in a phased manner in next five years. Inaugurating a seminar on 'Export Policies and Procedures,' organised by the Confederation of Indian Industry in New Delhi, Mr. Khanna said that restrictions on import of non-sensitive products would be lifted in the first phase and the sensitive products at the later stage. "Of the 123 members of World Trade Organisation, Indian is one of the eight countries, along with Bangladesh, to have quantitative restrictions," he said. Currently, he said nearly 2,000 out of 5,400 tariff lines were restricted on the restrictive list.

The Secretary maintained that a high-level committee under his chairmanship had been constituted to formulate the new export-import policy for next five years—1997—2000. "The new EXIM policy would aim at doubling the exports and achieve at least 1 per cent of total global exports", he said, Mr. Khanna said that the exporters should concentrate more on sourcing equipment from the domestic suppliers. "The new EXIM policy would be prepared in such a way that the exporters would source equipment from the domestic suppliers rather than through imports," the secretary said, adding that the domestic industry has grown up to supply the qualitative products. Referring to the intra-regional trade among the SAARC members, he said the government had decided to waive restrictions on imports originating from the four least developed countries—Bangladesh, Bhutan, Nepal and Maldives. He explained that this decision was taken as part of the Government's commitment.

More Items Off the Import List

Streamlining the export and import policy and procedures further, the Government on August 22 allowed import of 40 items earlier figuring in the negative list. At the same time, 14 items from the negative list of imports were allowed to be imported against the special import licence route, according to a notification issued by the Director-General of Foreign Trade. An official release says the notification also takes care of various representations that some items which were being allowed to be imported earlier without a licence in the past had been restricted.

Through another notice issued by DGFT, the Government allowed import of one two-wheeler (motor cycle/scooter) in place of a car to Indian or foreign nationals of Indian origin coming to India for permanent settlement. The notice further says that supplies made by foreign buyers or procured by Indian exporters on their advice of labels, price tags, hangers and trimming materials to be attached to goods against a specific order placed by them have been permitted to be imported without a licence.

Import Curbs on 69 Items Off

The Commerce Ministry on February 8 allowed free import of 69 more items figuring in the Special Import Licence (SIL) list. At the same time, 92 items have been taken off the restricted list and shifted to the SIL list. A notification to this effect will be issued on February 3. Disclosing this, Commerce Minister B.B. Ramaiah said that the changes were in tune with the current liberalisation process. He said that government was committed to phase out quantitative restrictions on imports in accordance with the commitment made with the World Trade Organisation (WTO). He, however, refused to give a time frame for replacing the quantitative restrictions by price controls and said that the process would depend on the foreign exchange and trade position and would take into account the interest of the local industry.

Terming the relaxation as a normal and gradual process, the Minister said that India still had more than 3,000 items under the restricted list of imports while another 900 items were in the transferable SIL. The present exercise is aimed at moving a number of items which are currently in the SIL list to OGL, and making certain restricted items permissible for import under SIL. Commerce Secretary P.P. Prabhu said that SIL licences valued at about Rs. 2,000 crore were issued in 1995-96 and they now commanded a premium of roughly 13 per cent in the domestic market. Over 3,000 items continue to figure in the restricted list, he added. Mr. Prabhu said that shifting of items from the restricted list to SIL generally gave the Ministry an idea about the demand for such goods, and added that most of the SIL were being used for import of gold and silver.

Among the items that have been shifted from the restricted to the SIL list include sun dust control polyester films, rubber stoppers, finished structures of aluminium, aluminium beverage cans, car air conditioners and other types of airconditioners, toilet deodorants, commercial dish washers, discharge lamps, other photographic flash light apparatus, some kinds of toys, coin-operated game machine, whole range of perfumers, glass statues of metal, colour TVs of less than 14 inch, used postal stamps, cooking and heating apparatus of copper, wide range of office machine, spectacles, goggles, and certain stone items.

Trade Deficit at $5.25B.

India's trade deficit crossed the $5.25 billion mark in the first 11 months of fiscal 1996-97, according to provisional trade date released by the Commerce Ministry on April 3. The huge gap had been caused mainly by imports of crude petroleum, which jumped by as much as 38.23 per cent to $8,761.94 million against $6,338.60 million in April-February 1996. Till February-end of fiscal 1995-96, the trade deficit stood at $4,300.38 million. In the whole of fiscal 1995-96, the deficit at $4.53 billion was more than twice the figure for the preceding year. The deficit in April-February 1997 is notwithstanding reports of softening of crude petroleum prices in the international market. No plausible explanation was available of the factors that had led to the huge deficit as export growth decelerated to 5.61 per cent in April-February 1997 compared to the same period in 1996 and imports grew by a measly 7.81 per cent.

While explaining details of the new export-import policy on March 31, Commerce Secretary P.P. Prabhu had hinted that trade deficit at the end of 1996-97 would be about $5 billion. He indicated that exports would be around $33-$35 billion against the target of $38 billion. Commerce Ministry data shows that the exports during April-February 1997 are estimated at $29,800.31 million compared with $28,218.49 million in April-February 1996. Exports in February 1997 stood at $2,651.68 million which was 1.15 per cent higher than the $2,621.45 million in February 1996.

10

POVERTY ALLEVIATION AND EMPLOYMENT

POVERTY ALLEVIATION

Revamping Anti-Poverty Programmes

The Government is seriously reviewing its rural anti-poverty programmes in the light of lapses noticed and in the context of formulating the Ninth Five Year Plan. The Planning Commission has constituted a steering group and six other groups to look into "poverty alleviation and area development programmes in rural India," according to official sources. So far, scrutiny of the working of the two major programmes—Integrated Rural Development Programme (IRDP) and Jawahar Rozgar Yojana (JRY)—has thrown up some major areas of concern.

While on the positive side, under the IRDP scheme, beneficiaries were selectively chosen for assistance so as not to leave out the really needy, on the flip side, it has been observed that a second dose of assistance given to beneficiaries was very low. Only 2.38 per cent of the total 'old' beneficiaries were given a second dose, while new beneficiaries received less than 2.16 per cent assistance, implying enough attention has not been paid to providing subsequent doses of assistance to eligible families. The steering group will minutely examine the reports and recommendations of the six working groups. Only then will the entire spectrum of issues relating to recasting and restructuring poverty alleviation programmes will be drafted. The groups will broadly look into self-employment programmes, wages, decentralised planning and Panchayati Raj, integrated watershed planning, technology transfer and provision of infrastructure and village amenities.

Lakdawala Method to Assess Poverty

The United Front Government on March 10 adopted the methodology recommended by the Lakdawala Committee as the new method to measure poverty. Accordingly, the poverty ratio stands revised at 36.31 per cent as against the earlier official method, which put the ratio at 19.9 per cent in 1993-94—the year for which latest data from National Sample Surveys (NSS) are available. A final decision was taken at a full body meeting of the Planning Commission, held under the Chairmanship of Prime Minister H.D. Deve Gowda. The meeting was attended by Union Finance Minister P. Chidambaram, Agriculture Minister Chaturanan Mishra, Planning Commission Deputy Chairman Prof. Madhu Dandavate, and senior Commission officials.

As per the new method, while Bihar and Orissa top the list of poorest states, the number of poor in the country increased from 310 million in 1987-88 to 323 million in 1993-94. The proportion of poor was as high as 56.4 per cent in Bihar, 48.4 per cent in Orissa, 42.6 per cent in Madhya Pradesh, 41.5 per cent in Assam and 41 per cent in Uttar Pradesh. Punjab maintained its lead in poverty alleviation with only 11.1 per cent of its population estimated as poor. States that registered impressive performance in poverty reduction included Rajasthan, Gujarat, Andhra Pradesh and Karnataka, where the absolute number of poor as also the proportion of poor declined between 1987-88 and 1993-94.

Going by the new method, in Rajasthan the poverty ratio came down from 34.5 per cent to 27.68 per cent, while in Gujarat, it came down from 32.33 per cent to 23.92 per cent in Andhra Pradesh from 27.02 per cent to 23.08 per cent, and in Karnataka, from 37.33 to 33.18 per cent. The methodology recommended by the Lakdawala Committee—otherwise known as the Expert Group Method on Poverty Estimates—was favoured in place of the earlier official method as the latter was found to be "Inadequate in giving a representative picture of incidence of poverty in the country." As per the earlier official method, the poverty line was defined at Rs. 49.09 and Rs. 56.64 per capita per month for rural and urban areas, respectively, at 1973-74 prices. To obtain the poverty line for any particular year, these figures are updated by using a national average price index appropriately weighted by the consumption basket of the poor. Once the poverty line is worked out, the NSS data on private consumption expenditure is used to estimate the number and proportion of poor.

EMPLOYMENT

Rural Employment need at Rs. 60,000 crore

The working group on the Ninth Plan has projected a requirement of Rs. 60,000 crore for rural employment. The tentative target for the Ninth Plan under the self-employment Integrated Rural Development Programme (IRDP) is to cover 15 million families by 2001-02. However, the target has been nominally raised to benefit 15 lakh rural youth. The panel stressed the need to integrate the rural poor in the new market-oriented framework. It has realised that the growth patterns of the Eighth Plan did not benefit the underprivileged. The panel called for creation of separate budget heads for recurring expenditure. The average level of investment per family is targeted in a manner that it crosses Rs. 24,000 by the end of the Plan period. Agricultural development alone was not sufficient for rural development. The target of 4.5 per cent agricultural growth cannot be achieved unless there was adequate thrust on both fiscal and human resource inputs. The group, therefore, suggested resource mobilisation with local planning.

Access to new technologies was key to increasing productivity and competitiveness. It suggested interaction between corporate houses and scientific institutions. The group has sought 10 bring about a match between the skill and aptitude of the people and the availability of employment through a process of planning. It hoped that the gap between availability of jobs and full employment situation can be bridged. It called for an effective linkage between IRDP, TRYSEM and DWCRA programmes. The Family Credit Plan which is in operation in 213 districts would be extended to more districts. The approach paper has also given priority to the DWCRA scheme with a substantial increase in allocation.

PMRY to be Spruced up

A large gap between the applications sponsored under the Prime Minister's Rozgar Yojana (PMRY) and the loans sanctioned by banks has been identified as a major reason for the slow progress in the rate of employment growth. The annual employment growth rate was 1.78 per cent for the period 1985-92 but it was estimated to have risen by a per cent or so for the years 1992 - 95. However, it is still less than the rate of 2.95 per annum required to generate 940 lakh additional employment opportunities during the period 1995-2002, according to the Industry Ministry. Efforts to speed up the employment growth under PMRY and other employment generation programmes, especially in the khadi and village industries sector, will be discussed at a conference of State Industry Ministers scheduled to be inaugurated by Union Industry Minister Murasoli Maran.

Other programmes, which will be discussed at the conference, include the 125 block development programme launched in 1995 and the district special employment programme to be implemented in 71 identified districts. The national programmes on leather, bee-keeping and handmade paper, expected to provide employment to three lakh people, also will come up for discussion. The number of cases sanctioned under the PMRY during 1993-94-1995-96 was 5,24,454 involving a loan of Rs. 2,979.63 crore. But the amount disbursed was only Rs. 1,619.11 crore for 3,12,812 applicants. The disbursement for the cases sanctioned during the current Financial year is still continuing. They are likely to reach a figure of 2,20,000.

The average loan sanctioned under this scheme has come down from Rs. 64,000 in 1993-94 to Rs. 55,000 in 1994-95 and Rs 57,000 in 1995-96. PMRY has emerged as a major programme for bank lending to micro enterprises through government sponsored programmes. Loaning under IRDP was Rs. 1600 crore while under PMRY was Rs. 1,100 crore during 1995-96.

11

AGRICULTURE INCLUDING RURAL DEVELOPMENT

AGRICULTURE

States Adopt Farm Policy

The conference of state agricultural ministers on February 19 adopted the draft agricultural policy which was completely revised by the United Front Government at the initiative of Union Agriculture Minister, Chaturanan Mishra. Addressing a news conference in New Delhi, Mr. Mishra said the conference suggested some additions and modifications of the draft policy. These would be incorporated into the policy and then the Union Cabinet would also adopt it, he added. Mr. Mishra said the Centre would shortly circulate a note among the states, soliciting their recommendations for achieving the targeted 4.5 per cent agricultural growth rate during the Ninth Plan. To achieve this target, he added, it was necessary to have regional plans of action. He said the state ministers wanted a foodgrains pricing policy to provide farmers with adequate incentives. They also wanted that all available technological options be evaluated and taken to the fields for improving productivity.

Mr. Mishra said the question was how to absorb prices if the Government consented to increased cost of foodgrains in view of their escalating production costs. On transfer of centrally-sponsored schemes, the views among state ministers were divided. Some preferred transfers, while others maintained that they may coninue to be administered by the Central Government. Mr. Mishra who has put agriculture on the front-burner of political discussion was emphatic that held the key for prosperity of the largest number of people in future.

Inaugurating the conference, Prime Minister H.D. Deve Gowda said that Indian farmers were "among the most exploited lot". Their exploitation could end only by bridging the gap between agricultural and non-agricultural sectors, he added. Addressing a conference of state agricultural ministers, Mr. Gowda said the Government wanted to tilt the balance in favour of agriculture by according it the highest priority. Urging state ministers to adopt the revised agriculture policy draft, he said it was necessary to follow a clear-cut policy in view of the fact that investments made so far in this sector had not been commensurate with the size of this sector in the economy and in employment generation.

Funds for Farm Research

The Consultative Committee of the Agriculture Ministry has endorsed the recommendations of the Parliamentary Standing Committee to earmark one per cent of the agricultural GDP for research in the Ninth Plan. In his introductory remarks at the meeting of the Committee on July 31, Agriculture Minister Chaturanan Mishra said there was an urgent need to increase productivity in which farm scientists and researchers will have to play an active role. He further said the Indian farmers will have to increase yields to remain competitive in the market against the eventual removal of quantitative restrictions on imports under the new world trade rules.

The members felt that the allocation for agricultural research was insufficient especially when other countries were allocating between 3 and 5 per cent of their agricultural GDP to research. It was also felt by members that there was a need to give incentives to researchers to attract and retain them in Government institutions in the new liberalised economic environment. This talent is also being wooed by multi-nationals and private Indian companies. Members also suggested that laboratory facilities in many research centres are obsolete and funds are needed for their modernisation. Some members also felt that dissemination of new farming techniques have to be more effective and the small farmers should be the focus of research.

Rabi Prospects Brighten

The recent winter rain has brightened rabi prospects so that the optimistic estimate is for a wheat production of about 65 million tonnes in 1996-97, as against 62.62 mt last year. Besides, there has been about one to two per cent increase in the area under wheat this year raising hopes of higher production. The Minister for Agriculture, Mr. Chaturanan Mishra, considers it 'premature' to officially declare the rabi prospects now after last year's experience when the production figures fell by about three million tonnes owing to late rainfall in March-April. Experts, however, estimate foodgrains production in 1996-97 to be around 192 million tonnes, which will be about seven million tonnes more than last year's output. In 1995-96, the production was 185 million tonnes, including 62.62 mt of wheat and 69.69 mt of rice.

Last year's overall production was affected not only because of shortfall in wheat but also in rice, pulses and coarse grains. Some acreage was lost to cash crops like sugarcane. From initial sowing reports a crop weather watch group in the Ministry of Agriculture has estimated foodgrains production this year to be about 191.5 mt Bihar, UP and Madhya Pradesh, where sowing was delayed, have gone in for late breeding variety of wheat. The availability of water in reservoirs is said to be 15 per cent more than the last 10 year's average. A rabi conference last September had set the wheat target at 66 mt in 1996-97, while the Planning Commission had set the final Five-Year Plan's target at 193.5 mt.

India's Achievement in Rice Production

India has reached a plateau in its irrigated rice yields, yet in the coming years it is expected to play a critical role in international rice production and technology. In particular, it will have to bear the burden of meeting the growing needs of the rice-eating populations in the developing world. For this the focus has to be on tapping the production potential of the north-eastern region of the country and extending the hybrid varieties beyond the frontiers of South India, where it has been adapted more favourably than in the North. Technology will have to be developed for checking the loss of nearly 30 per cent rice yield on an average in a year in the country. These were some of the observations made at a Press conference in New Delhi on September 26, addressed jointly by the Director-General of the Manila-based International Rice Research Institute (IRRI), Dr. G.H.L. Rothschild and the Director-General of the Indian Council for Agriculture Research (ICAR), Dr. R. S. Paroda, on the eve of a three-day "India-IRRI Dialogue" here. In the next three days scientists from both the institutes will review the two-decades old India-IRRI collaboration in rice research and development.

Dr. Rothschild said India has the potential to become the number one rice producer in the world. At present it has the largest area under rice cultivation but is behind China in world's top producer, with a total production reaching 122 million tonnes. "China has reached its potential in irrigated rice production. It cannot be squeezed any more. India has been potential, which needs to be tapped," he said, Dr. Rothschild said India will have to crack the yield ceiling per hectare which has been about 10 tonnes per hectare since the green revolution. New varieties will have to be bred to enhance the yield per hectare. One such hybrid variety being developed at IRRI is nicknamed 'super rice', but its potential in tropical countries like India is yet to be developed. This variety, if successful, could enhance yield by at least 25 per cent hectare, he said. While emphasising the biotechnological collaboration between IRRI and in India. Dr. Rothschild said water and nutrient management will have to be the key to better in India.

Low Agricultural Output—Soil Degradation

About 26 per cent of India's annual agricultural output valued at Rs. 23,200 crore will be hit this year as a consequence of soil degradation, according to figures released by the Tata Energy Research Institute (TERI). Speaking to newsmen, Director R.K. Pachauri, said about 57 per cent of the total area of the country or 1880 lakh hectares was affected. Erosion has rendered 1180 lakh hectares or 36 per cent of the total area of the country uneconomical for cultivation because of a significant loss in productivity, while a further 150 lakh hectares have been rendered unmanageable and uneconomical. Water and wind erosion are the most significant contributor to the economic loss due to soil degradation and accounts for about 87 per cent of the total degraded area. This category alone accounts for up to Rs. 21,600 crore of the total estimated losses per year. Water and wind erosion have been accelerated in recent times by vegetation removal, over exploitation, overgrazing and such poor agricultural practices as cultivation on steep slopes in other vulnerable areas.

Whereas the area under soil erosion has increased by only 80 lakh hectares, the area under erratic erosion has almost doubled in 18 years since 1977. In 1981, estimates should that soil was being eroded at an average rate of 16.5 tonnes per hectare per year. Nearly 29 per cent of the total eroded soil is permanently lost to the sea and about ten per cent is deposited in reservoirs which get silted up as a consequence adding to the many problems of total environmental degradation. 64 per cent of the eroded soil is contributed by highly eroded to very severely eroded areas namely the shiwalik hills, ravines, the western ghats, black and red soils and the north-eastern states. Wind erosion is a serious problem in the arid and semi-arid regions and in the coastal areas.

Another cause of soil degradation is deforestation especially where land is steeply sloped or the soil is shallow or otherwise easily erodable and secondly when the land thus cleared is not managed properly afterwards. Deforestation has been cited as cause for 98 per cent of the area affected by wind erosion. The loss of natural vegetative cover resulting from felling, excessive grazing and extension of agriculture to marginal areas and the depletion of organic matter through bad cropping patterns. Salinity and water logging are the other major kinds of soil degradations and account for upto 30 per cent of the total losses estimated at up to Rs. 2700 crore annualy although they affect only eleven per cent of degraded areas. Waterlogging affects vast tracts of land in the Ganga and Brahmaputra basins and the irrigated areas of Punjab. Haryana and Andhra Pradesh while salinization effects the dry regions of the Indo-Gangetic plain, parts of Rajasthan and Gujarat and the black-soil regions.

RURAL DEVELOPMENT

Rural Population under Poverty Line

Staggering 16 per cent of the rural population of India have access to less than Rs. 3 a day which is less than the price of potatoes. Another 18 per cent are slightly better off—they can scrape togethor Rs. 5 a day. The National Council of Applied Economic Research, after four years of study of 33,000 rural households in 16 States looking at 300 parameters has come out with a human development profile of rural India that should shudder down the spines of development authorities and the affluent who are putting down hard cash for their second Cielo, their third BPL television set or the latest micro oven. The 1994 report, which was released in Bhopal on November 30 at a Government of Madhya Pradesh/UNDP workshop on State level Human Development Reports reveals that 39 per cent of the rural population is living below the poverty line or earning less than Rs. 2,444 per capita per year. It may be recalled that the Planning Commission about a year go head claimed that the population living below the poverty line was 19 per cent and not 36 per cent. Subsequently it had to retract. According to the Government those earning less than Rs. 11,000 a year are said to be below the poverty line.

According to the NCAER survey, however, the all India annual income in Village India is Rs. 4,485. In Orissa and West Bengal, which have never been included in the BIMARU category, the annual per capita is Rs. 3,028 and Rs. 3,157 respectively. It is considerably lower than Bihar's Rs. 3,169 UP's Rs. 4,185, MP's Rs. 4,166 and Rajasthan's Rs. 4,229. Experts who had gathered at Bhopal said Orissa and West Bengal should be included in the list of BIMARU Status so that they could receive the special attention needed to bring them out of the poverty trap. A great deal of surprise was expressed at the low income and high poverty level of West Bengal, a State that had introduced panchayati raj or people's rule at the grass root as far back as 1978.

The survey shows that 55 per cent of the rural population of Orissa is living below the poverty line and in West Bengal 51 per cent of the population is in the poverty trap. Dr. Abusaleh Shariff, principal economist and head of the Human Development Programme Area—NCAER, says "the poor are everywhere—even behind palaces. They are frightened, ignorant, insecure and lack direction They survive without knowing where the next meal will come from and their families are not cohesive units." Poverty like beauty cannot be defined. The highest per capita in rural India is in Punjab Rs. 6,380, followed by Haryana—Rs. 6,368. But even these affluent States have pockets of rural poverty. Thirty-two per cent of the rural poor in Punjab and 27 per cent in Haryana live below the poverty line. The survey shows relatively higher poverty estimates from Punjab which most people will find unacceptable, says Mr. Shariff.

Rural Infrastructure to Get More

Finance Minister P. Chidambaram said on December 19 that the Government would allocate Rs.. 2,500 crore for development of rural infrastructure in addition to the Rs. 2,000 crore already provided to the Rural Infrastructure Development Fund (RIDF). At the same time he also pointed out that the speed of utilisation of the funds allocated to RIDF-Phase-I was slow and there was an emergent need to speed up the same. Only hafl of the Rs. 2,000 crore allocated for first phase of RIDF has been disbursed so far. On its part the Government is taking steps to augment credit flow in order to increase agricultural production, the Finance Minister said while inaugurating a seminar on role of financial institutions in promoting farm exports. The seminar was organised jointly by the Indian Institute of Foreign Trade (IIFT) and National Bank for Agriculture and Rural Development (NABARD). Defending the economic policies of the United Front Government, the Finance Minister also hinted at further steps to liberalise external trade, especially in the case of farm sector goods. Noting that there was no need to lose sleep over the slowdown in exports since the policy directives were taking the economy in the right direction. He also argued in favour of liberalisation of the agriculture sector which contributed more than 30 per cent of the country's GDP.

He estimated the credit needs of the farm sector during the Ninth Plan period to be around Rs. 2,30,000 crore. As much as 1,50,000 crore of this amount is required for short-term projects. On its part, the Government would allocate Rs. 55,000 crore in three years for areas like plantation, horticulture, dairies, animal husbandry and fisheries which have been identified as thrust areas. The price competitiveness of commodities like rice, cotton, onion, bananas and grapes should be exploited fully to boost agriculture exports, Mr. Chidambaram said. In the case of aquaculture and floriculture products, it was possible to achieve annual growth of 30 per cent. The same was the case with items like sugar, molasses, rice, spices and tomato paste, he added. NABARD Chairman P. Kotaiah and IIFT Director General Sanjeeva Reddy also addressed the seminar. They stressed on the need to boost farm exports and formulate strategies for this purpose in the near future since the Ninth Plan and the next long-term Exim Policy were currently being finalised.

12

DEFENCE

NATIONAL SECURITY ENVIRONMENT

The global scenario has been undergoing repid changes since the beginning of the decade, delineating in the process, trends of an emerging world order. The end of the Cold War has not resulted in a peace dividend. Expectations of a peaceful transition from tension and violence to negotiation and cooperation have not materialised in many parts of the world. The existing stockpiles of nuclear weapons by declared nuclear powers continue to pose a threat to international security. On a smaller but still very lethal scale, the proliferation of small arms has been sustaining international terrorism and organised crime, and posing severe challenges to regional and global security. Against this backdrop, India's commitment is to cooperation with like-minded states in ensuring that the world order which is to emerge, rests on the principles of universality, democracy and non-discrimination.

Viewed globally, the failure of the Comprehensive Test Ban Treaty (CTBT) to include within its framework a credible assurance, or modality, for achieving universal nuclear disarmament within a specified time-frame has serious implications for the international community's proclaimed desire to achieve a nuclear weapon free world. India has always maintained a principled and consistent position on the CTBT. At the resumed 50th Session of the UN General Assembly, India voted against the resolution on the CTBT because the treaty, as it now stands, is no longer an instrument for the accomplishment of nuclear disarmament. The CTBT neither enhances global security nor benefits the security environment of our region. The inexplicable reluctance of the nuclear weapon states to pursue earnest and time bound negotiations for nuclear disarmament is not in consonance with the universal abhorrence of these weapons of mass destruction and unrelated to recent geopolitical developments. The irony inherent in the situation is evident from the fact that while negotiations for a CTBT were underway in Geneva, two nuclear weapon states continued to conduct nuclear tests in total disregard of world public opinion.

India has refused to sign the CTBT because it is not a measure for nuclear disarmament. Nor is the treaty truly comprehensive, as it does not arrest the qualitative development of nuclear weapons. Sub-critical testing and computer simulated nuclear tests are not prohibited under the treaty, giving the nuclear weapon states the opportunity for refining and developing new nuclear weapons. The proposed Fissile Materials Cut-off Treaty (FMCT), negotiations for which might start soon, has to be placed in the context of a universal and comprehensive disarmament framework. Unless this is ensured, the proposed

FMCT will only serve to perpetuate the supremacy of the nuclear weapon States. India draws a clear distinction between the provisions of the existing Non-Proliferation Treaty (NPT) and the objectives of genuine non-proliferation. While maintaining reservations on the former, India is fully committed to the goal of curbing nuclear proliferation. However, mere preventive or punitive actions, on a selective and ad-hoc basis, cannot be expected to achieve the desired results.

As in the case of India's nuclear capability, it has also had occasionally to withstand international pressures brought to bear on its missile programme. The indigenous development of missile capability by India is in response to the evolving security environment in its region. China has supplied M-11 missiles to Pakistan and is aiding it with technology and manpower as well in the development of its indigenous missile programme. There are also credible reports about China continuing to assist Pakistan in its clandestine nuclear weapons programme.

Those who have been seeking to impose restraints on India, have in the meanwhile themselves continued their nuclear weapons and missile research programmes. Research on programmes such as the Theatre High Altitude Area Defence (THAAD) missile programme and anti-ballistic missiles programme are receiving new impetus. Nearly all arms control agreements between the USA and the Russian Federation, and treaties such as the Conventional Force Reduction in Europe (CFE), signed between NATO and the erstwhile Warsaw Pact countries have lagged behind in their implementation schedule. While viewed globally the expenditure on arms has registered a decline in recent years, in contrast to the international trend, the area around India has been characterised by continued high spending on defence.

India stands for total elimination of all nuclear weapons and the ushering in of a nuclear weapon free world. However, till such time as this is achieved, India will be constrained to keep open her nuclear option.

In pursuance of its commitment to the international community, India deposited the Instrument of Ratification of the Chemical Weapons Convention (CWC) on September 3, 1996. By doing so, it has become 62nd country to deposit its Instrument of Ratification, and is among the first 65 countries the deposit by whom of their Instruments of Ratification was essential in order to allow the CWC to enter into force. It is a matter of great regret, however, that major possessors of chemical weapons, and several other countries, including countries from this region, have failed to ratify the Convention. India hopes that the principle of universality, which underlines the CWC, will be adhered to by all countries which have supported and signed it.

India remains opposed to ad hoc export control regimes, which it believes are in the nature of discriminatory technology denial regimes. There have been efforts to strengthen these regimes by expanding their scope and seeking greater harmonization in their implementation. India believes that such regimes should be based on the principles of universality and non-discrimination, allowing for easy access to dual technology for legitimate civilian purposes.

Regional developments having a bearing on India's national security can be divided into four areas, viz., (a) Gulf and West Asia; (b) Central Asia; (c) Asia Pacific and South East Asia; and (d) the Indian Ocean Region. These regions which are located in India's strategic vicinity, are of immense interest to India from its national security perspective. India has an abiding interest in the Gulf and West Asia region because of its traditionally close linkages with it, substantial dependence on imported oil, the large Indian community living in it, and the geographical proximity to it. India supports the on-going Middle East peace process which is aimed at the restoration of a just and comprehensive peace in the region. Compared to the relatively steady progress made in recent years, the Middle East Peace Process witnessed this year a more turbulent and erratic phase. Given the irreversibility of the process and the high stakes involved, as well as the preference of the Gulf States for the maintenance of *status quo* in the area, the overall situation is expected to remain stable in the near future.

Another vitally important strategic region is the Central Asian Republics (CAR). India's relations with these Republics in all areas, including the area of military-technical co-operation, are underpinned by geo-political proximity, historical affinity and shared perceptions about the need to build a secular and peaceful society. India and the CARs both believe that the phenomenon of terrorism and extremism in all forms not only vitiates the security environment but also poses threat to multi-ethnic and secular states. While these Republics are grappling with economic challenges, they are also conscious of the dangers of religious fundamentalism, which is occasionally fuelled externally. India is opposed to any outside intervention and seeks all round development of these States through bilateral economic, political and cultural initiatives. India and these States share the principles of respect for territorial integrity and non-interference in each others internal affairs.

The Asia-Pacific region is the most economically dynamic region in the world. Several countries in this region are continuing their efforts of enhancing their military power by the acquisition of modern weaponry. The increasing defence outlays of the countries of this region, both in value terms as well as percentages of GDP, are noteworthy. The Asia-Pacific region is beset with territorial and maritime disputes, such as the South China sea dispute, the Korean peninsula problem and the Kuriles Islands dispute. These issues, if not appropriately addressed may well serve as potential flash points, and can have a destabilizing effect on the economic growth and security of the entire region. A notable development in the Asia Pacific region has been the strengthening of the US-Japan security alliance following the visit of President Clinton to Japan in April 1996. Japan, which has the largest defence budget in Asia, is now taking increasing interest in matters of Asian security.

South East Asia with which India has extensive traditional and historical links, has emerged as one of the fastest growing regions of the world. India seeks closer economic engagement with her ASEAN neighbours. India is also interested in developing mutually beneficial security linkages with the ASEAN countries, by promoting exchanges such as ship visits, training of Service personnel, provision of repair facilities for military equipment, the supply of spare parts, and the joint development of equipments and technologies required by the Armed Forces. India has become a full dialogue partner of the ASEAN, and has been admitted as a member of the ASEAN Regional Forum (ARF). The ARF has the potential of emerging as an important platform for the promotion of peace, security and stability in the region. Membership of ARF would enable India to participate in the political and security related dialogues of the Asia Pacific region, and contribute towards its stability.

India has a vital stake too in the security and stability of the littoral and Island States of the Indian Ocean region. India's maritime security is dependent on its capability to effectively patrol, monitor, and counter illegal activities in this region, be they attempted by national entities or by sub-national groups. India has extensive and growing political and economic cooperation with the Island States of this region, particularly with Maldives, Mauritius and Seychelles and would oppose any move to subjugate and destabilise these States.

Within the subcontinent, India's national security interests are intimately linked to peace, progress, stability and security of Afghanistan, Myanmar and other neighbouring countries.

In Afghanistan, foreign interference and the continuing civil war has denied peace and harmony to the people. As in the past, there is once again a risk of Afghanistan being embroiled in regional and international power games. India strongly opposes such prospects and continues to closely follow events in Afghanistan having a bearing on its national security. India would prefer to see an early end to the present political and military conflict in the country, and it supports the U.N. initiative to engage the warring factions in discussions aimed at restoring the political unity of Afghanistan.

Our relations with Myanmar have improved over the years, and the two countries are committed to ensuring that their respective territories should not be used for nefarious activities by the insurgent elements in either country, who often cross the border at will. Steps have been taken to increase cooperation in border management which have succeeded in curbing the trans-border activities of such insurgent elements.

India maintains close, cordial and cooperative relations with Sri Lanka. India has always stood for a peaceful solution to the ethnic issue in Sri Lanka within the framework of the unity and integrity of that country. While being hopeful that the moves to find a political settlement would soon bear fruit, India is determined to prevent the continuing conflict in Sri Lanka from spilling over into India.

As regards its other neighbours, India has close and friendly relations with Bhutan, Nepal and Bangladesh. With their assistance India expects to successfully oppose outside attempts to create internal security problems. The recently concluded Mahakali Treaty with Nepal, and the amicably decided sharing of the Ganga waters with Bangladesh, reflect India's commitment to remove irritants which have stood in the way of strengthening its bilateral relations with these countries. Anti-national elements operating clandestinely from these countries are now, with the improvement in relations, facing renewed pressure from the respective Governments. The Governments of these countries are strongly opposed to the use of their territory by forces that are inimical to the security of India. The policy has been clearly enunciated during recent high level exchanges with these countries.

A significant development in India's bilateral relationship with China was the signing of the 'Agreement on Confidence Building Measures in the Military Field along the Line of Actual Control in the India-China Border Areas' which is aimed at preserving peace and tranquillity in the border areas. This Agreement was signed during the visit of the President Jiang Zemin to India in November 1996. The Agreement *inter alia* stipulates that neither side shall use its military capability against the other side, and includes provisions for negotiating the reduction or limitation of forces from mutually agreed geographical zones along the Line of Actual Control (LAC), the prior notification of military exercises, the prevention of dangerous military exercises in border areas, and service to service contacts. India's concerns regarding China's defence cooperation with Pakistan, its assistance to Pakistan's clandestine nuclear programme, and the sale of missiles and sophisticated weapon systems by it to Pakistan, were conveyed to the Chinese side. The progress that China has made in the recent years in augmenting her nuclear arsenal and missile capabilities will continue to have relevance for India's security concerns. Upgradation of China's logistic capabilities all along the India-China border, for strengthened air-operations has to be noted. China's posture in the South-China Sea has implications for the regions.

China's strengthening defence relations with Myanmar, need to be carefully watched, in view of the geo-strategic location of Myanmar.

Pakistan's proxy war against India continues, the ISI continues to push in arms and militants into India through the Rajasthan and J & K borders, as well as through India's other borders. Pakistan also continues to interfere in India's domestic affairs by sending in covert agents to many parts of the country to engage in subversion and sabotage. The ISI is known also to be actively supporting anti-India militant groups in the North-East, who have clandestinely set-up camps in some neighbouring countries. These groups are receiving funds, training, and arms and ammunition from Pakistan so as to be able to vigorously pursue their anti-India activities, and to de-stabilise the North-East region. In Kashmir, having failed to thwart and sabotage the elections in the State, the ISI is now attempting to forge a common understanding amongst the various militant groups. The ISI continues to be involved in the operational planning and coordination of terrorist activities in the Kashmir valley, both directly as well as indirectly, through the use of foreign mercenaries. There have besides been repeated attempts by Pakistan to highlight the Kashmir issue in international forums, and to spread disinformation about alleged human rights violations by India. The objective is clearly to de-stabilise the popular Government and revive the seeds of insurgency in the State. The

Indian security forces have done a commendable job in defeating such efforts by the exercise of constant vigilance.

Pakistan's attempts at interference in the internal affairs of States in her neighbourhood have not been confined to Punjab and Kashmir alone. It has meddled actively in Afghanistan too. The September 1996 offensive of the Taliban—which overthrew the Rabbani Government and captured Kabul—was widely believed to have been part of Pakistan's larger game plan to extend her influence in Central Asia. The supply during the year of a package of sophisticated US arms, ammunition and spares to Pakistan, made possible by an incomprehensible waiver off the Pressler Amendment, despite her declared nuclear weapons status, was a negative development for peace and tranquility in the region.

India is committed to the bilateral resolution of all issues between India and Pakistan through discussions, within the framework of the Shimla Agreement. The Government of India has conveyed to Pakistan its readiness to resume dialogues on this basis, at appropriate levels. The Government have also taken several unilateral initiatives with the objective of creating a positive environment and for the promotion of people-to-people relations between the two countries. With the installation of the newly elected Government in Pakistan, India has reiterated her offer for a resumption of a bilateral dialogue.

India's contacts with the US in matters relating to defence continue to be marked by positive developments. The second meeting of the Indo- US Defence Policy Group took place in Delhi in October, 1996. The two sides had a frank exchange of views on security perceptions concerning the Asia-Pacific region, and on other issues of mutual concern. They reiterated the importance of continuing, and gradually widening, the Indo-US dialogue on matters pertaining to defence, so that they could combine to make a positive contribution to security and stability in Asia. Both sides have agreed on an Action Plan within which to promote mutual cooperation in high priority areas, and to define potential areas for future joint ventures in the field of defence research and production.

The traditional cordial and friendly relations between India and the Russian Federation continued to strengthen further. Both countries share common perceptions on the prevailing geo-political situation and possible future trends. The Russian Defence Minister visited India in October 1996. An Agreement on Service to Service cooperation was signed during that visit. Russia is today a dependable source of supply for the modernisation of our armed forces. The availability of spares support for equipment earlier supplied has showed a marked improvement, and the contracting and delivery process has been streamlined. A major acquisition contract was concluded with Russia in November 1996, for the supply of 40 SU-30 aircraft for the IAF, with provisions for subsequent manufacture in India.

In the current geo-political environment, the basic principles and objectives of the United Nations have become even more relevant. While India continues to actively participate in efforts to strengthen the UN, such as through its various peace keeping initiatives, India also believes that the time is appropriate for the introduction of changes in the present composition, and decision making mechanism, of the UN Security Council. India believes that there is a need for broad basing the present composition of the Security Council so as to reflect the legitimate claims of other nations.

Finally, the importance of the internal situation in determining the shape of India's overall national security cannot be overlooked. The reprehensible activities of various divisive forces continue unabated in some parts of the country. India's major law and order concerns centre around Pakistan sponsored insurgency in Jammu and Kashmir, the often externally supported subversive activities of militant groups in the North-East, and the proclivities of such extremist groups as the Peoples War Group in Andhra Pradesh and the Naxalites in Bihar and West Bengal. These extremist groups have been able to exploit populist and emotive issues in some states in their efforts to destabilise the Indian polity. The tensions generated by ethnic, linguistic, chauvinistic and parochial groups too occasionally impinge on the internal security scenario. While there is no immediate threat to the nation's integrity on account of these activities, these do intermittently pose problems for the Government.

In the preceding paragraphs an attempt has been made to present an overview of the various factors affecting India's national security. With the passage of time new challenges to its security may well emerge. A constant evaluation is, therefore, undertaken of the factors relevant to India's security so as to enable timely and effective steps being taken for the maintenance of appropriate levels of defence preparedness.

SELF-SUFFICIENCY IN DEFENCE PRODUCTION

India will emerge self-sufficient in indigenous defence production, from the present 40 to 70 per cent by the year 2005. The Union Ministry of Defence had evolved a 10-year Defence System Self-reliance programme in 1995 and they were working towards achieving this goal in 10 years. Announcing this to newsmen in Tiruchi on March 9, Dr. A.P.J. Abdul Kalam, Scientific Adviser to the Defence Minister, the Secretary, Department of Defence R & D, Ministry of Defence, said the press projected area about the imports of defence equipments rather than the phenomenal strides made indigenously in the defence production area domestically. He said the manufacturers of defence equipments abroad were working three shifts to dump their products in India.. Dr. Abdul Kalam said by the year 2003, these foreign manufacturers would lose their business since Indian defence producing units would operate three shifts to produce equipments, light combat aircrafts, missiles etc. to the tune of over Rs. 30,000 crore. "We are on top now at the global level in missiles, space and satellite technologies," Dr. Kalam added.

Dr. Kalam said the Defence Metallurgical Research Laboratory at Hyderabad had now evolved an indigenous technology for converting the titanium into titanium sponge. This titanium sponge had tremendous opportunities for use in the medical field, especially in the dental tissue transplantation, and in the area of biomedical applications. Mr. N.V.N. Somu, Union Minister of State for Defence said he had received a request from the Tamil Nadu Government to transfer the Defence grounds in Tiruchi Khajamalai, belonging to Territorial Army, 117 infantry Battalion to the State Government for constructing a massive bus stand complex. Mr. K.N. Nehru, State Minister for Food and Cooperation had personally represented to him on this account. The Tamil Nadu Chief Minister had also mentioned this subject. "I am personally interested to help Tamil Nadu to the best of my efforts. The request of the State Government is being examined by the authorities concerned. I am confident of a favourable decision," he added.

13

EDUCATION AND CULTURE

1. EDUCATION

Education for All

Education for All (EFA) continues to be the focal point of the programmes in education during 1996-97. For achieving EFA, a two pronged strategy of universalising adult literacy and universalisation of elementary education in a mutually supportive manner is being followed.

The Government has resolved to make the right to free and compulsory elementary education a Fundamental Right and to enforce it through suitable statutory measures. Realising that the resulting proposal has enormous implications, the Department of Education constituted a Committee of State Education Ministers chaired by the Union Minister of State for HRD (Education) to consider the financial, administrative, legal and academic implications of the proposal. The Committee has since submitted its Report which is under consideration.

(i) Primary Education

Elementary Education

Universalisation of Elementary Education (UEE) has been accepted as a national goal since 1950. In order to achieve the goal, concerted efforts have been made and as a result, the elementary education system in India has become one of the largest in the world with 150.74 million children enrolled in 1995-96 in the age group of 6-14 years covering about 91 per cent of the children in this age group. Of these, 109.73 million children were enrolled in 5,90,421 primary schools and other 41.01 million in 1,71,216 upper primary schools. There are 2.90 million teachers—1.74 million employed in primary schools and 1.16 million in upper primary schools. 95 per cent of rural population living in 8.26 lakh habitations have a school within a walking distance of 1 km. and 84 per cent have upper primary schooling facility within a walking distance of 3 Kms. The percentage of girls enrolled is 43.11 per cent at primary stage and 39.42 per cent at upper primary stage. Recent trends in drop out have shown significant decline. The retention rate has improved and it is 64 per cent at primary stage and 47 per cent at upper primary stage.

Universal access, universal retention and universal achievement are broad parameters to achieve UEE. Greater focus is on school drop outs, working children, girls who cannot attend formal schools, particularly those belonging to SCs/STs and other disadvantaged groups. Special attention has been given on removal of caste, sectional , regional and gender diparities in UEE.

The major initiatives in the form of Operation Blackboard, National Programme of Nutritional Support to Primary Education (Mid-day Meal Scheme), Non-formal Education Programme, Teacher Education and adoption of Minimum Levels of Learning have continued to be accorded priority. In addition, the Government announced a new scheme in the Budget for 1996-97 to assist voluntary agencies in the establishment of residential primary schools for the rural poor, irrespective of caste or creed.

With a view to cushioning the impact of the rising cost of text books and exercise books, the Government has exempted writing and printing paper supplied to all State Text Book Corporations from excise duty in the Budget for 1996-97. It is understood that this measure has provided relief to students, especially those belonging to the weaker sections of the society.

National Programme of Nutritional Support to Primary Education

A nationwide Mid-day Meal programme was launched from 15th August, 1995 to give boost to UEE by improving enrolment, retention and attendance in primary schools and also to improve the nutritional status of children. Over a period of three years, all the Government, Government aided and local body schools are to be covered benefiting 11 crore children. During 1996-97, 5.57 crore primary school children are being covered in 4426 blocks and urban slums in all States and UTs.

The Central support under this programme is on the following:-

(i) Provision of foodgrains free of cost to the implementing agencies.
(ii) Reimbursement of transportation cost to District authorities for moving of foodgrains from Food Corporation of India godowns to schools/villages;
(iii) Besides, remuneration for conversion of foodgrains into cooked food as well as expenditure on construction of kitchen sheds. will be eligible for coverage under the Poverty Alleviation Schemes being administered by the Ministry of Rural Areas and Employment.

The expenditure towards the cost of foodgrains (payable to Food Corporation of India) and reimbursement of transportation cost will be incurred by the Ministry of HRD (Department of Education).

The Programme has commenced in all the States/UTs. Five States namely, Gujarat, Kerala, Madhya Pradesh, Orissa and Tamil Nadu and U.T. of Pondicherry are serving cooked meals. In Delhi processed food is being served. In rest of the States/UTs, foodgrains are being distributed.

District Primary Education Programme

The District Primary Education Programme (DPEP) is another thrust area in primary education. The DPEP is distinct from conventional projects as it takes a holistic view of elementary education, emphasises decentralized management, community mobilisation and undertakes district and population specific planning. The DPEP is characterised by loftiness of its objectives, the nature and the intensity of the planning process, the integration of professional inputs, participative planning and management. It emphasises on capacity building and integrated and locally relevant curriculum. A system of concurrent evaluation as well as monitoring of learner's activity has been set up to evaluate the impact of implementation on the objective of evaluation, retention and achievement. The programme has already been launched in 59 low female literacy districts in 11 States and the objective is to cover 120 districts by the end of the 8th plan

Besides, a number of externally assisted projects such as—Uttar Pradesh Basic Education Programme, Bihar Education Project. Shiksha Karmi and Lok Jumbish Projects in Rajasthan, Mahila Samakhya Project and Andhra Pradesh Primary Education Project are also under implementation.

(ii) Women's Education

Women's education has always been a priority area and NEE envisages the entire educational system to work for women's education and empowerment. It has been emphasized that gender concerns must be built into all educational processes. Emphasis has been laid on enrolment and retention of the girl child in formal schooling, recruitment of rural women as teachers removal of gender bias in the curriculum. Special provisions and have been incorporated in various schemes; e.g. the revamped Blackboard scheme provides that atleast 50 per cent of the teachers recruited should be women under NFE programme. 90 per cent assistance is given for centres exclusively for girls. A scheme for strengthening of boarding and hostel facilities for girl students of secondary and higher secondary schools is continuing with the objective of boosting retention of girls.

Free education is provided to girls by various State Govts./UTs while education is free for girls upto Class XII in Kendriya and Navodaya Vidyalayas. Vocational programme with emphasis on entrepreneurship are being designed for girl drop outs. In Major thrust areas-DPEP and TLC, women are a special focus. Steps are being taken to increase women's participation in educational process, nationwide gender sensitization programme of educational personnel and parental awareness programmes for generating a positive climate for girls' education.

Mahila Samakhya Programme (Education for Women's Equality) is a Women's empowerment project which aims at creating an environment for women to seek knowledge and information with a view to bring about a change in their perception about themselves and that of the society.

Mahila Samakhya was launched in March 1989 as a pilot project through Dutch assistance in 10 districts of Uttar Pradesh, Gujarat and Karnataka. In 1992 the programme was extended to two districts in Andhra Pradesh. The Mahila Samakhya approach and strategy has been mainstreamed with other basic education programmes in the country like the Bihar Education Project where it covers 7 districts and Districts Primary Programme in Madhya Pradesh and Assam. The programme is spread over 2574 villages in 15 districts in 4 states.

The programme has addressed issues like drinking water, health service and developed local accountability for women's needs. MS has provided training for development of indigenous herbal medicine systems, Panchayati Raj and spearheaded activism on social issues like violence against women, institution of Devadasis and the jogini system, etc.

Education has been one of the key areas of focus under Mahila Samakhya. MS has initiated several interventions in Non-formal Education, Pre-school creche support facilities which are managed by Women's groups themselves. MS village women manage 529 NFE centres and 241 ECCE centres. Another innovative intervention in MS has been the "Mahila Shikshan Kendras" (MSKs) for illiterate women who have never joined the formal school system and school drop-outs who seek to plug back into the educational mainstream. 7 MSKs have been established and 5 are being set up currently.

(iii) Adult Education

Literacy has been a priority on the national agenda as a tool of information and knowledge and as an instrument of social change. The initial target of National Literacy Mission (NLM) was to make 80 million persons in the age group 15-35 years functionally literate and to cover 345 districts of the country by the end of the year 1995. This target was revised to 100 million persons by the end of the 8th Plan. NLM is now committed to make 100 million people literate by 1998-99 and to bring about total literacy by 2005.

The Total Literacy Campaign (TLC) has become the principal strategy of the National Literacy Mission for eradication of illiteracy in the country. Against the over all target, as on date, 417 districts have been covered under TLCs and 178 districts under Post Literacy Campaigns (PLCs). Since the launching of the campaigns, approximately 80 million persons are reported to have been enrolled under TLC's, out of which 38.10 million persons have been made literate. The enrolment under PLCs is 18.44 million, of which 10.22 million neoliterates are participating under Post Literacy phase. Since the inception of National Literacy Mission in 1988 57.96 million persons have been made literate under all Adult Education Schemes.

Keeping in view the fall-out of the implementation of various literacy programmes, both achievements and weaknesses as evidenced through evaluations, new strategies have been developed for effective implementation of the programme during the 9th Plan period. Some of the major initiatives include decentralisation and delegation of powers for approval/implementation of literacy programmes to State Literacy Mission Authorities; Strengthening of State Directorate of Adult Education to act as nodal agencies for better and effective monitoring of the programme; establishment of strong linkages between literacy campaigns and Panchayati Raj Institutions and involvement of Panchayati Raj functionaries in the literacy movement; establishment of strong linkage between the literacy programme and other development programmes; restoration of projects which could not achieve desired results and the Scheme of Continuing Education for neo-literates.

(iv) Secondary Education

Secondary Education is being strengthened through various schemes, such as the Schemes for improvement of Science Education, Environment Education,

Population Education, Culture and Sports. In addition, the NCERT has been providing resource support in crucial areas of educational research and training at school level.

Kendriya Vidyalayas and Navodaya Vidyalayas are promoting education with a national identity throughout the country. The Government has accelerated the process of creating buildings, laboratories, libraries and teacher training facilities so that these chains of schools act as pace setters for other schools in the country.

The National Open School (NPS) has been assigned the responsibility of promoting open schooling in the country with a view to provide distance education to deprived and socio-economically backward sections of society in the remotest parts of the country.

NOS has a large and diverse student profile covering learners from 14 years and above without restriction of age. Most of the students are young adults between 18-24 years. In the last registration year of 1995-96, students from educationally and socially disadvantaged categories, comprised women (32.5%), SC and ST (23%), Ex-servicemen (0.36%) and Handicapped (0.70%).

Technological advancement has played a vital role in the expansion of education, particularly in distance education.

As a recognition of the meritorious service of teachers working in Primary, Middle and Higher Secondary Schools, 278 awards were conferred by the President during 1996-97.

A Task Force under the chairmanship of Director, NCERT has been constituted to study the functioning of private schools and evolve a Model Code for the service conditions of teachers and other related matter, transparency in the administration of private schools and their admission policies and a mechanism for the disposal of grievances and possible punitive measures.

Under the centrally sponsored scheme of vocational education for students at the +2 stage, emphasis continued to be given to upgrading the skills of students in more than 6000 schools so as to enhance their employability. A collaborative venture with the National Institute of Fashion Technology for introduction of fashion technology in schools is being mapped out.

(v) University and Higher Education

The Higher Education system in India has witnessed a steady growth since independence. At the time of independence in 1947, there were only 20 universities and 500 colleges in the country. At present, there are 166 Central/State Universities, 37 Deemed Universities and 9278 colleges. The students enrolment in institutions of higher education is estimated to the approximately 64.26 lakh students. The teaching staff strength in universities and affiliated colleges stood at 3.10 lakh at the end of 1995-96.

The Mahatma Gandhi Antarrasthtriya Hindi Vishwavidyalaya Act, 1996 and the Maulana Azad National Urdu University Act, 1996 have recently been enacted to establish and incorporate two new Central Universities at Wardha (Maharashtra) and Hyderabad (Andhra Pradesh) respectively. It is expected that these universities would start functioning from the next academic session.

UGC asists, on a selective basis, science and technology departments in Universities for acquiring highly sophisticated equipment to enable them to become internationally competitive in frontier areas of post-graduate teaching and research. Such Departments are selected on the basis of very stringent norms laid down by the Standing Committee of UGC. The departments supported under the above schemes have been given functional autonomy.

The UGC launched new programmes of Vocationalisation of Education at the first degree level w.e.f., academic session 1994-95. The Commission identified 35 vocational courses out of which 1-3 courses can be introduced by the identified universities and colleges.

The UGC has set up Inter-University Centres, as autonomous organisations to provide common facilities, services and programmes to a group of universities or the universities in general for research in the frontier areas of science and technology. Inter-University Centres set up by the Commission from 1986 to 1994 are in the areas of Nuclear Science, Astronomy and Astrophysics, Atomic Energy, Educational Communication, information and Library Science Network and Humanities and Social Sciences.

The UGC has launched specific target-oriented programmes for the educational development of students belonging to weaker sections of society, especially those falling within SC/ST categories.

The Distance Education system has also become very popular as it is not only cost-effective but easily accessible for upgradation of educational skills, particularly in remote areas. Electronic media has played a very constructive role in this area. The Indira Gandhi National Open University acts as the focal point of the system. It is expected that by the end of the 8th Plan, there would be additional enrollment of one million students under Distance Education System.

In pursuance of the provision of NPE, 1986 (as modified in 1992) and POA 1992 regarding rural higher education following a pattern on the lines of Mahatma Gandhi's philosophy of basic education and 'Nai Talim', the government has set up a National Council of Rural Institutes (NCRI) at Hyderabad.

NCRI has encouraged the setting up of Swami Ramanand Tirth Rural Institute at Pochampalli for which State Government of Andhra Pradesh transferred 17 acres of land and has agreed to provide 15 per cent of annual expenditure. NCRI has provided seed money of Rs. 10.000 lakhs to SRTRI during 1995-96 and Rs. 100.00 lakhs during 1996-97.

The Council has received proposals for setting up a Rural Institute, each in Assam, Bihar, Madhya Pradesh, Maharashtra and Orissa. The Budget provision of NCRI during 1996-97 is Rs. 300.00 lakhs.

(vi) Technical Education

With a view to bringing the benefits of Techno-Economic advances and large scale investments in the Technical Education system to the poorest of poor in the country, the Government of India has been running an institutionalized and structured scheme of Community Polytechnics functioning all over the country along with its Extension Centres in remote/inaccessible areas.

In order to achieve self reliance and maximum autonomy, a new pattern of funding has been introduced in the Centres of Excellence like IITs, IIMs and IISc., Bangalore, IITs and IISc., Bangalore have launched Technology Development Missions in seven generic areas with the participation of industry. While 6th IITs in Guwahati has started functioning, three new Central Institutes including two IIMs—one at Calicut and the other at Indore and an Indian Institute of Information Technology and Management at Gwalior have been approved for being set up. In the two new IIMs at Calicut and Indore, the academic session is starting from July, 1997.

The National Apprenticeship Scheme has been extended to engineers and technicians of SAARC Member countries.

A High Power Committee was constituted in June, 1996 to review the progress made by the RECs and also suggest further changes to strengthen their working. The report is expected by 30th April, 1997.

In addition to advanced department like Aero-space, Bio-mass, Bio-medical, Chemical, Metallurgical and other Engineering Sciences, the Indian Institute of Science, Bangalore has also set up Super Computer centre with an Interest hookup. More than 43 departments/centres/units covering a wide range of Engineering and Basic Science disciplines have been connected to the super computing facility.

The Super Computer Education and Research Centre (SERC) in the institute is engaged in research on the development of computer Aided Design tools to assist in designing sophisticated high speed digital signal processing chips. The research activities include : real-time and database systems, VLSI systems, high performance algorithms, computer graphics, Braille printer design (DOW), computer architecture, software engineering, operating systems and high performance numerical computing.

Further, the Centre has several ongoing/completed sponsored research and consultancy projects such as,

— Multimedia Applications
— LSI/VLSI Design Centre (DOE)
— System and VLSI Design for Digital Television (DOE)
— Technical Advice and Guidance on Information Technology Plan
— System Evaluation (C-MMACS)
— Multimedia and visualization techniques
— Software engineering with special emphasis on issues like specification, design, integration maintenance, testing and management of large software, information integrity.

2. CULTURE

During the year 1996-97, the Department of Culture continued with its multifarious activities of promotion, preservation and dissemination of art and culture through various schemes and projects implemented by it directly or through the network of its institutions working in such diverse fields as archaeology, archives, museums, libraries, anthropology, performing, literary and visual arts, etc.

Archaeology

The Archaeological Survey of India (ASI) is the pioneer organisation in the field of maintenance, conservation and preservation of centrally protected monuments and sites. At present, there are 3593 centrally protected monuments declared to be of national importance which include 16 World Heritage Monuments. As some large monument complexes comprise a number of structures, the total number of individual structures being maintained by the ASI is over 5000.

Some notable work done by the Survey during the year is recapitulated below.

(i) Excavations at Satdhara, District Raisen (M.P.), have led to the discovery of a headless elephant figure bearing an excellent Mauryan polish over it. A large number of iron nails and clamps have also been found during the excavation of monasteries and apsidal temples. The restoration of the (Buddhist) Stupa No. I has since been completed.

(ii) 7 archaeological sites of importance have been discovered in the exploration of Basti and Siddartha Nagar districts of Uttar Pradesh. These belong to the Kushan period.

(iii) At the Taj Mahal, Agra, conservation work is continuing for providing the missing inlay pieces on the south-east corner and at the eastern facade of the main gate. The work of under pinning, plastering and pointing of Lakhauri brick walls and arches of the Khan-a-Alam nursery complex is also underway. Missing inlay bars on the outer facade of the main mausoleum and south-western minar of the Taj have also been provided. The work of providing missing red sandstone chhajjas and filling up of joints of stone veneering in the south-western Saheli Burj has also been completed. Barbed wire fencing to the Mehtab Bagh site at the Taj Mahal has since been provided.

(iv) Under the Indo-US Joint Project for restoration of Mehtab Bagh at Agra, excavation was started and an area measuring 5.5 mts. was earmarked for the digging. Test pits have been taken at a spot near the eastern wall where structures have been noticed.

(v) Conservation works at the Agra Fort, Akbar's Tomb (Sikandra), Fatehpur Sikri (Agra), Jageshwar Group of Temples (Almora), Rudranath Temple (Chamoli) are in progress. The missing red sandstone roof on the main gate of Ram Bagh at Itmad-ud-daula's Tomb (Agra) and red sandstone railing to gaves in Zanana Rauza at Fatehpur Sikri have been provided.

(vi) The Epigraphy branch copied 14 Perso-Arabic inscriptions from various districts of Madhya Pradesh. 18 gold coins secured from the Agra Circle and photos of ten copper coins from the Chandigarh Circle relating to Khilji and Tughlaq rulers are under examination.

Museums

(i) An exhibition entitled "Jewels from India" was sent to Italy in February, 1996 under an MoU signed between the National Museum, New Delhi and the La Rinascente, Milan (Italy). 164 original items of jewellery and some other objects studded with precious stones belonging to 17th-20th centuries were exhibited at La Rinascente from 7the March to 13th April 1996. The exhibition was later shifted to the National Museum of Oriental Art, Rome.

(ii) The National Museum received a gift of 32 rare art objects belonging to the Kashmir region dateable to 6th Century A.D. from the 8th Rajputana Rifles. These antiquities were recovered from Kashmir militants through a surprise raid on 8th and 9th October, 1995 at Srinagar, Kashmir.

(iii) The Indian Museum organised a Mass Communication Programme and a contemporary exhibition "Images off Man" displaying 84 life-size images of tribal and rural people of India from the collection of the Anthropology Section.

(iv) An Orientation workshop on 'Care and Maintenance of Museum Objects' was organised by the National Research Laboratory for Conservation of Cultural Property, Lucknow, from 7-16 August, 1996.

(v) Austria is celebrating 1000 years of its civilization this year. An exhibition of Austrian Contemporary art was organised at the National Gallery of Modern Art (NGMA), New Delhi on this behalf.

Archives and Libraries

(i) The National Archives of India, New Delhi (NAI) is the custodian of Central Government records of enduring value for permanent preservation and use by the administrators as well as scholars.

(ii) In the month of July, 1996, the NAI acquired 34 files donated by Smt. Santosh Thapar. These files contain information about the life and activities of the martyr Sukhdev. The collection also contains 44 books on freedom fighters and 3 xeroxed volumes of records of the proceedings conducted by special tribunal in the Lahore Conspiracy case.

(iii) The National Archives of India acquired 34 xerox pages (1906-1947) and a pamphlet relating to Mahatma Gandhi's political activities from Shri E.S. Reddy, U.S.A.

(iv) The National Library, Calcutta has installed an oil painting on the poet Rabindranath Tagore in the exhibition Hall of their main building.

Anthropology and Ethnology

(i) During the year, Anthropology Survey of India organised various activities as a part ;of its Golden Jubilee Celebrations : A 2-day seminar on 'Ethnic Situation : Fields and Frontiers' at its Western Regional Centre at Udaipur. At the Sub-Regional Centre, Jaddalpur, a new gallery on Terracotta and an exhibition on 'Panorama of Tribal Culture' were inaugurated. A conference on Claude Levi Strauss and a book exhibition on his publications were organised by the French Consulate, Calcutta, in collaboration with the Anthropological Survey of India at the Survey's Conference Hall in Calcutta on 14th October.

(ii) In the month of July, 1996, a significant initiative was taken by the Indira Gandhi Rashtriya Manav Sangrahalaya for promoting a new Museum Movement based on regional cultural traditions. Work is on progress for investigation and revitalisation of the roots of forgotten traditions, ethnosciences and knowledge systems of the Baghelkhand area, specially in the tribal pockets.

14

ENERGY (COAL, PETROLEUM AND POWER)

COAL

Coal Price, Distribution Decontrolled

The Union Cabinet on February 11 approved a new coal policy, lifting price and distribution controls from practically all grades of coal and ushering in private sector participation in coal mining and exploration. The private sector is now only allowed to mine coal for captive consumption. The Cabinet approval paves the path for free exploration, mining and sale of coal and lignite by Indian companies, that acquire blocks through competitive bidding. The Centre also decided to locate new power plants at the pitheads and increase use of lignite in power generation. The ministries of power and steel will be told to adopt appropriate know-how to ensure better utilisation of coal. The surface transport ministry will be told to augment coal handling facilities at the ports. While coal exploration and mining in the private sector is subject to legislative amendments by the Parliament, coal prices and distribution can be decontrolled almost at once, The measure will imply that power plants that consume 70 per cent of the roughly 300 million tonnes of coal produced in the country and still buy their fuel at controlled rates, will also have to pay market-dictated prices in the near future.

Cooking coal and the A, B and C or finer grades of non-cooking coal were taken out of the purview of administered pricing and distribution this month last year. The prices of D, E, F and G grades of coal, consumed primarily by power plants continued to be regulated by the Centre. The Cabinet also gave green signal to the K.S.R. Chari Committee recommendation that all grades of non-cooking coal be decontrolled in a phased manner. Union Minister of State for Coal Kanti Singh, told newspersons, that the Centre had decided to deregulate the prices and distribution of D grade on non-cooking coal, hard coke and soft coke with immediate effect.

Investment in Coal Sector

India will need $26 billion worth of investment in coal and mineral sectors to increase the production capacity and meet their overgrowing demand. In the coal sector, the production capacity needs to be more than doubled to meet the demand of the power sector alone which is one of the prime users of coal. The power sector consumes about 57 per cent of 255 million tonnes of coal mined annually in the country. The power sector needs will shoot up further with the planned addition of over 85,000 mw generation capacity over the next six-seven years, according to a government estimate. Similarly, the mineral sector would need an additional investment off about $10 billion during the next decade, a mineral institute study has estimated.

The total value of mineral production is estimated at $7,970 million in 1994-95. This would entail an increase of 3 per cent over the previous year in the value of mineral production. Of the total of $7,970 million, fuel minerals account for $6,780 million, metallic minerals $545 million and non-metallic minerals $645 million. Due to the vast requirement of resources and the recent financial crunch in India, the government has opened up the sector to private and foreign investment. The government liberalised the mineral sector by a comprehensive—National Minerals Policy 1993—and also amended the Coal Mines (Nationalisation) Act 1973 which allowed coal mining by private companies engaged in power generation, washing of coal and output of iron and steel.

PETROLEUM

Rs. 300,000 Crore for Crude Exploration

An investment of Rs. 3,00,000 crore would be required in the area of crude oil exploration and production, refining and downstream marketing facilities to meet the growing demands of petroleum products in India which is currently extimated at 81 million tonnes and is expected to reach 150 million tonnes in 2006-2007. This was stated by Chairman of Indian Oil, R.K. Narang in his keynote address at the sixth international aviation seminar which has been organised by Indian Oil Corporation in Mumbai on 15 January. Mr. Narang further pointed out that the consumption of aviation turbine fuel (TAF) which is currently at two million tonnes is expected to reach 3.2 million tonnes by 2006-2007. Besides, the world oil consumption which is currently at 68 million barrels per day will rise to 94 million barrels per day by 2010, he added.

He also informed that Indian Oil which meets over 67 per cent of the country's aviation fuel needs from its 96 aviation fuel stations has drawn up a comprehensive plan to set up additional refuelling facilities to cover even the new feeder routes of the various airlines. With aviation fuel constituting nearly 30 per cent of the operating costs of the airline, Mr. Narang said that there was a clear case for airline operators to optimize the use of aviation fuels by adopting various conservations methods such as improvement in airframe design and development, besides, aeroengine and operational improvements.

Indian Oil Corporation Limited (IOCL) has decided to go for major diversification with an investment of Rs. 30,000 crore during the Ninth Plan period. IOCL Chairman R.K. Narang who came to Paradeep to inaugurate the Paradeep Lighterage terminal complex, told newsmen that the company had identified sectors like hydrocarbon, refinery, power, exploration and petrochemical complex besides marketing and operation in abroad to be taken up during the Ninth Plan.

HPCL Turnover

Hindustan Petroleum Corporation Ltd. (HPCL) is confident of exceeding a turnover figure of Rs. 16,500 crore in the current fiscal year ending March 1997. This would ensure its 20 per cent market share. HPCL has revised its projected investments during the Ninth Plan period from about Rs. 9,000 crore to Rs. 11,500 crore and has given notice for conversion of detachable tradeable warrants issued along with the equity shares allotted in the February 1995 public issue, to mop up Rs. 589 crore. Each warrant would be converted into one equity share at a price of Rs. 340 per share (nominal value Rs. 10 plus premium of Rs. 330) payable in four instalments of Rs. 85 each over a period of one year, HPCL Chairman-cum-Managing Director, H. L. Zutshi told a Press conference in Mumbai on February 19. With full conversion of 1.73 crore warrants, the shareholding of the Government would go down to 51.06 per cent from 55-30 per cent.

According to Mr. Zutshi, the corporation's growth, in terms of sales, has exceeded that of the industry by 2 per cent during April 1996 and January 1997. "We experienced an 8.8 per cent growth, as against 6 per cent achieved by the industry," he added. However, the corporation expects its interest burden to increase sharply by Rs. 32-35 crore over the previous year's figure of Rs. 46.21 crore. In the first half of the current fiscal, the company's interest cost doubled to Rs. 37.52 crore. HPCL has undertaken ambitious expansion-cum-diversification plans, with investments planned to the tune of Rs 11,500 crore over the next five years. The investmment plan of the corporation up to 2001-02, include Mumbai refinery (Rs. 1,524 crore), Visakh refinery (Rs. 2,541 crore), marketing (Rs. 5,297 crore) and investment in joint ventures (Rs. 2,138 crore). Mr. Zutshi said that the cost of expansion activities would be met largely through internal resources. "Since HPCL has a low debt-equity ratio, the corporation may raise the required debt from the market."

ONGC to Invest Rs. 25,000 Cr.

Oil and Natural Gas Commission (ONGC) has envisaged to invest Rs. 25,000 crore during the Ninth Plan period (1997-98 to 2001-02) in implementing various projects for exploration and production of hydrocarbon. There is likely to be a shortage of Rs. 8,000 crore and for this ONGC would have to make special efforts for mobilisation of this amount. Disclosing this at a Press conference at ONGC headquarter at Nazira, Mr. B.C. Borah, Chairman-cum Managing Director (CMD) said recently that ONGC expected to meet 80 per cent of this whooping amount of Rs. 25,000 crore through internal resource generating and the remaining gap would have to be filled up by raising fresh equity or borrowings depending upon prevailing condition in the capital market.

Besides this, the ONGC will also have options like external commercial borrowing, expansion of its equity to raise loans in capital market and placements in American and European capital markets. The ONGC CMD informed media persons that ONGC also envisaged a massive diversification programme which includes refining of imported crude oil, production of liquified natural gas

(LNG) for generation of power and production off LPG in collaboration with Oil India Limited (OIL) and Gas Authority of India Limited (GAIL). He added that ONGC would give a major thrust on "high risk" and "high-production" exploration and production activities in the next two years. Meanwhile the ONGC, which has explored vast reserves of natural gas in Tripura and invested huge amount in a project, is worried over its poor return.

Oil Consumption to Reach 81 MT

The consumption of petroleum products in the country during 1996-97 is expected to be around 81 million tonnes based on the current growth rate or 10 per cent. The demand is expected to reach 110 million tonnes by the year 2001 and 150 million by 2006. According to Mr. A.K. Arora, Director (Refineries & Pipelines), Indian Oil Corporation (IOC), country's existing refining capacity of 60 million tonnes is expected to double to 120-125 million tonnes by the year 2001-02. This, however, is not very satisfactory as an additional refining capacity of 40 to 50 million tonnes will be needed by the year 2010. Mr. Arora, while inaugurating oiltech '96, an international symposium on opportunities in India's petroleum refining and marketing sector, said in New Delhi on August 19 that Indian petroleum refining and marketing sector offers excellent scope for large-scale investment by Indian and foreign companies.

Delegates from over 70 companies in India and abroad are attending the two-day symposium organised by the leading oil industry journal, Oil *Asia.* The future scenario thus envisages massive investments by both Indian and foreign companies in the development of refining and marketing infrastructure by way of setting up of new grassroots and export-oriented refineries, development of existing port infrastructure and minor ports, receipt and storage facilities for crude oil and products and cross-country pipelines for transportation . Taking into consideration the men and machinery required to execute these projects, the job can only be accomplished by exploiting the country's full potential in all areas, he said.

Oil Import Bill

India's oil import bill is slated to touch over $9 billion during the current fiscal year and is expected to soar higher in the Ninth Plan period. Petroleum Secretary Vijay Kelkar told newsmen on January 6 that demand for crude and petroleum products was fast outstripping supplies due to general increase in industrial activity. He said domestic production was not rising in proportion to the demand and stress on the need to intensify deep offshore exploration for which massive investments would be required. Besides tapping domestic oil reserves, India would also venture into exploration activities abroad, he said. Dr. Kelkar made these observations while releasing the details of the upcoming second Petrotech conference beginning on January 9. The four-day conference will expose young Indian engineers in the hydrocarbon sector to the frontline technology for exploration and drilling for oil.

Representatives of global oil majors—Chevron Overseas Petroleum, Command Petroleum, Enron Development Corporation, Haldor Topsoe, Hyundai

Heavy Industries, Marubheni Corporation—are among the delegations from among over 100 countries who will be attending the Petrotech '97. The conference jointly sponsored by the Petroleum Ministry and the ONGC will be a show window of the latest technology in equipment and services available worldwide both in upstream and downstream petroleum sector. Petrotech '97 will be inaugurated by Minister of State for Petroleum and Natural Gas T.R. Baalu, said ONGC Chairman B.C. Bora. Mr. Bora said that around 1,500 delegates and experts from more than 30 countries would be participating in the conference. Starting with a focus on the event in the world oil and gas industry in the last decade, this conference would deliberate on petroleum and global energy cooperation, exploration, development and reservoir management, drilling technology, production and platform engineering, transportation, tankerage and pipeline engineering.

Rs. 20,000 crore Oil Pool Deficit

The oil pool deficit is expected to touch Rs. 20,000 crore or even more as against the projected Rs. 15,000 crore halting the development of the oil industry, Union Petroleum Natural Gas Minister of state T.R. Baalu said in Chennai on January 7. Oil prices have gone up by one to one and half dollars a barrel in the past few days alone, Mr. Baalu told reporters after visiting the Seismic survey vessel western horizon at he Chennai harbour. Asked whether oil prices would be raised in view of the mounting deficit, Mr. Balu evaded a direct answer and said the Finance Ministry, which had drawn huge sums from the oil industry development fund to cover general deficit four years ago, should come to the rescue of the oil industry as the issue was very critical.

Mr. Baalu said the seismic survey being done by MV Western Horizon in the joint venture between the Directorate General of Hydrocarbons and Western Atlas which owns the seismic vessel in the eastern offshore, from the mouth of the Ganga to Cauvery offshore, would be over by April next. Geophysical studies would then be done by experts of western geophysicals and directorate General of Hydrocarbons the data packages would be available for marketing worldwide so that oil companies could negotiate for exploration work in India, he said. According to one estimate, gas hydrate resources in the eastern offshore area including the Bay of Bengal could be of the order of 1000 trillion cubic metres of natural gas. This could be the future source of energy for the country in the 21st century, he said. More extensive work would be carried out in this area by our national oil companies such as ONGC, GAIL and oil, he added.

POWER

Power Regulatory Authority Approved

Prime Minister Deve Gowda has approved the much publicised Common Minimum Action Plan (CMAP) for power sector which envisages setting up of an independent Central Electricity Regulatory Commission (CERC) which will fix retail tariff for all categories of consumers. After two rounds of discussions with the State Chief Ministers, Gowda approved this major policy initiative of the United Front Government for power sector. Accordingly, the Minister of State for Power S. Venugopalachari has asked all the Chief Ministers to implement the CMAP immediately. The nodal Power Ministry will pilot a legislation in the budget session of Parliament bringing about an amendment in the Indian Electricity Act of 1910 and Electricity (Supply) Act of 1948 to facilitate setting up of CERC and State Electricity Regulatory Commission (SERCs).

The approved policy has given CERC the mandate to fix, revise and rationalise power tariff to all categories of consumer periodically. The Regulatory Commission to be set up shortly will work out bulk tariffs for all Central generating and transmission utilities. It will also have the authority to resolve all issues relating to inter-State flow and exchange of power. In effect the CERC will virtually take over most regulatory functions hitherto discharged by the Central Electricity Authority (CEA) with regard to grid operation as well as tariffs.

Power Sector Rules Further Relaxed

The Government on January 10 announced another set of relaxations for the power sector. The Ministry of Power has now laid down that in case of expansion and extension of existing projects set up by independent power producers (that is, the private sector), the selection of the promoter for the second phase should be done by following the memorandum of understanding (MoU) or the letter of intent (LoI) route. But the procurement and construction contract will have to be framed on the basis of international competitive bidding. Similarly, the mandatory provision for selection of independent power producers throught the competitive budding route for captive power plants has been relaxed. According to the Power Ministry, these measures have been announced with the intention to maximise the benefit which would accrue in terms of powers project cost, reduced tariff and smooth operations and maintenance of the composite plant and to avoid the accord of the extension project to a promoter other than the original developer of the project which could lead to loss of advantages to the states and the Consumers.

It has also been stipulated that extension projects through MoU or the LoI route and having a project cost of more than Rs. 100 crore would require techno-economic clearance from the Central Electricity Authority (CEA). The tariff would, however, need to be negotiated between the developer and the State Government to ensure availability of the benefit of the extension project to the State and the consumer. The Power Ministy has also advised that allowing for the time gop between the development of the two phases of the project and the global market for power plant equipment, the tariff for the extension project should be worked out to lower than the tariff as per the two part tariff notification of the Centre.

Team to Study Hydropower

The government has constituted a five-member committee under the Chairmanship of M.K. Sambamurti, former Chairman of Central Electricity Authority, to suggest measures to promote and accelerate clearance of hydro power projects in the private sector. The committee will review the guidelines issued by CEA and Central Water Commission for preparation of cost estimates of electrical, mechanical and civil work of hydro power projects besides suggesting methodologies to arrive at the completed cost. The mandate of committee includes the study of the civil work logistics of the CEA and Central Water Commission as well as any other issue which would facilitate development of hydro projects in private sector. The committee is to submit its report within 45 days from the date of its first sitting. Other members of the committee include ;the NHPC Chairman and Managing Director S.R. Narasimhan and NTPC CMD Rajendra Singh .

$171 Billion Investment in Power Sector

Power generation capacity to the tune of 100,000 to 150,000 mw, involving an investment outlay of Rs. 600,000 crore ($171 billion), was needed in the next 10 to 15 years, a study jointly conducted by the Canadian Energy Research Institute and the Tata Energy Research Institute said. According to the study, integrated resource planning was the most preferred mode of development plan that could give an added thrust to the power sector. However, to achieve this, the study pointed out that a radical change must take place in the structure, operation, regulation and decision making practices which currently govern the Indian power industry. The Indian power sector at present was facing the dual problem of increasing capacity to match the fast growing demand on one hand and the environmental challenges that arise from large-scale generation on the other.

Estimates showed that a new generation capacity of 100,000 mw to 150,000 mw would be needed within the next 15 years. Since coal would probably continue to remain as the mainstay, clean and more efficient coal technologies must be introduced into the Indian market, said the study. It also emphasised on cogeneration as a means of reducing emissions and increasing generation efficiencies, as well as to strengthen the transmission and distributing network. The various SEBs, which were deep in the red, should be turned around for a successful adoption of various supply and demand and planning options for power sector growth in the country.

Additional Power Capacity

The Ninth Plan working group on power has projected 55,761 mw additional capacity to get over the prevailing peaking and energy shortages. The working group headed by Power Secretary P. Abrahim has said that 12,378 mw will be added through new schemes, while the rest would be either from ongoing projects or those cleared by the Central Electricity Authority (CEA) . However, going by the past record, the projected capacity addition during Ninth Plan may not be a realistic proposition. It may be mentioned that the actual capacity addition during Eighth Plan is less than 20,000 mw as against a projection of 38,000 mw. Having seen slippages to the order of 50 per cent, the ambitious proposal to add 55,761 mw afresh is bound to remain a pipedream. "With the synchronised capacity addition of 55,751 mw during the Ninth Plan period, it would, by and large, meet the peaking and energy requirement of the country except in the northern region where few more short gestation schemes are required," the working group report said.

With such huge capacity addition, the peaking and energy shortages are expected to be brought down to 0.3 per cent and 6.2 per cent, respectively. This is against the peaking and energy shortages of 9 and 15 per cent, respectively. However, the working group has recommended to the Government that these shortages could be met through 15 per cent unallocated share from central projects. A major chunk of power, i.e., 26,439 mw is expected to be added by corporates through independent power projects (IPPs). The central sector's contribution will be the lowest at 9,570 mw and state sector expected to add 19,742 mw.

Power Transmission to Private Companies

The Cabinet on January 21 took major decisions for opening up the power transmission sector to private Indian and foreign companies. However, it deferred decision on distribution following objections from some SEBs. Clearance was also given to power project of Energy Works costing $ 1 billion. Kalinga Power of Public Power International's 100 per cent foreign venture with an investment of $ 787 million was approved and GMR Vasavy was allowed to increase stake in its Chennai project. The decision would further curtail the powers of the Central Electricity Authority (CEA). The cabinet draft has also once again called for review of CEA role. The changes long sought by the Power Industry will not only bring in Major reforms in the power sector but also increase flow of foreign investment, it is hoped. This would come as a major support activity for projects like the pithead $1 billion Valley projects for which such lines would be a necessity to evacuate power to Gujarat.

The Centre would soon come out with detailed guidelines for states on how to implement the changes in the transmission sector. And ordinance would be promulgated in a day or two to amend sections 12 to 19 and section 27 of the Indian Electricity Act, 1910 as well as relevant sections of Electric Supply Distribution Act, 1948 to allow licensing in transmission with immediate effect. The Cabinet Committee of Foreign Investment (CCFI) has also cleared the draft of the amendments to the two acts. These would be presented in the ensuing budget session for formal approval of Parliament. As per the amended act transmission will be accorded a district activity like generation. Earlier, it was considered an extension of the generation activity.

Renewable Energy Target

The Planning Commission has set a target of about 4,5000 mw of grid power generation from renewable energy in the Ninth Plan period. By April this year renewables would have a share of only 1.5 per cent of the total installed power generation capacity—around 1,400 mw—out of a total 88,000 mw. The Commission has a target of generating additional 3,000 mw of grid power from renewables by the end of the Ninth Plan in the year 2002. According to the Power Ministry, grid quality power generation from renewables has attained maturity during the Eighth Plan period, reaching the total annual turnover of about Rs. 2,000 crore in this sector. The Ministry said that considerable progress had been made over the past decade in harnessing renewable energy. Installation of wind power capacity of about 820 mw placed the country among the top three countries in the world in harnessing this resource. Production of solar energy, one of the important segments in renewables sector, has reached 8 mw per year compared to a total world production of around 85 mw per year in 1995.

The Ministry said as many as 12 companies have been engaged in the production of solar cells and modules. Besides, 70 companies are in the business of designing and supplying solar photovoltaics (PV) system. Over 3,00,000 solar PV systems totalling about 22 mw have so far been installed in different parts of the country. The emphasis in PV so far has been mainly on decentralised off-grid extension. However, the programme is now being expanded to cover grid-connected voltage support systems on weak, rural grids and roof-top peak saving systems in urban centres.

Liquid Fuel for Power Plants

With a view to increasing the power generating capacity as quickly as possible, the Government has decided to allow usage of liquid fuels on a provisional basis in upcoming power plants. Recognizing that the proposals for power plants based on liquid fuels far exceeds the sustainable capacity, it has been decided to restrict usage to power generation capacity of about 12,000 mw as an emergency one-time measure. "This decision has been taken on account of inescapable need for creation of some liquid fuel based power generation capacity which could be brought on stream very quickly to meet the immediate power requirements," stated an official release in New Delhi on December 23. Following this decision, States have been allocated incremental power generation capacity based on liquid fuels on the basis of present and likely levels of shortages to be faced by them at the end of the Ninth Five Year Plan.

States have been asked to ensure that wherever possible projects should be designed as dual fuel projects. Further, priority should be given to projects that have got off the ground. They should have taken steps such as acquiring land, obtaining clearances, preparing detailed project reports, tying up finances etc. The projects which will be allowed to use liquid fuels such as naptha, furnace oil etc. are public sector projects, joint sector projects, independent power projects and even those located in eco-sensitive areas. States have been asked to send the proposals for provisional allocation of liquid fuels to projects to the Centre. Based on this recommendation, provisional fuel linkages to these projects would be issued.

15

ENVIRONMENTAL CONSERVATION AND PROTECTION AND FORESTRY

ENVIRONMENTAL CONSERVATION AND PROTECTION

The ministry of Environment and Forests is the nodal agency in the administrative structures of the Central Government, for the planning promotion and coordination of environmental and forestry programmes. Some of the programmes under taken by the Ministry are as follows :

Environmental Impact Assessment

— A total of 415 projects were appraised for environmental and site clearance during the year, out of which 170 were granted environmental and/or site clearance.

— An Inter-Ministerial Group has been set up to examine the issues of delegation of powers for according environmental clearance for thermal power projects.

— In accordance with the directions of the Supreme Court, all the States and UTs have submitted Coastal Zone Management Plans (CZMPs) which have since been approved by the Central Government with certain conditions and modifications.

— The coastal States have also been delegated powers to take decisions on proposals exceeding Rs. 5 crore falling under CRZ II category as per the approved CZMPs.

— A Dahanu Taluka Environmental Protection Authority has been set up on 19-12-96 under the Chairmanship of Justice C.S. Dharmaadhikari for the protection of ecologically fragile areas of Dahanu Taluka, Maharashtra.

— Through a Notification issued on 5th July 1996 in the Gazette of India, the area within a radius of 15 km. of the petroleum refinery of M/s IBP Co. Ltd., at Numaligarh (East Kaziranga) has been declared as a "No Development Zone".

— A study of the upper Yamuna Basin has been taken up to prepare Natural Resource Accounts so that resource accounting corresponding to economic returns can be correlated and a more consistent and better stream of benefits can be derived from the same resource base.

Prevention and Control of Pollution

— Several activities such as organisation of training programmes, preparation of manuals etc. were undertaken to make Environmental Statement and Environment Audit more effective and comprehensive. Form V of the Environmental Statement has been revised.

— Under a 5 years long project sanctioned to National Institutes of Sciences, Technology and Development Studies (NISTADS), production of computerised maps and preparation of zoning Atlas for siting industries have been taken up. About 150 base and thematic maps have been prepared for different districts of the country.

— Under the scheme "Adoption of Clean Technologies in Small Scale Industries", several training and awareness programmes were organised for personnel in Small Industry Development Organisation.

— Several Authorities have been set up during the year by the Ministry such as the National Environment Appellate Authority, Environmental Impact Assessment Authority for the National Capital Region, Loss of Ecology Authority for the State of Tamil Nadu, Authority for Environmental Planning for Thane, Dahanu Taluka Environment Protection Authority and Aquaculture Authority with the ultimate objective of prevention and control of pollution. The most important authority is the Environment Appellate Authority which deals with representations, complaints and appeals against decisions of competent authorities under the Environment Protection Act. The authority—consisting of persons of national eminence and expertise in relevant areas of development and consertation—to be constituted soon will give environmental clearance to projects covered under the Environment Impact Assessment Notification. The Union Cabinet also made public hearings mandatory before any environmental clearance is given under the EPA for projects and activities included in the notification. This has been done with the objective of not only ensuring transparency in the process of environmental impact assessment but also facilitating environmental decision making based on socio-economic and environmental considerations. Henceforth, people directly affected by developmental and industrial projects as well as non-governmental organisations working in the area would get ample opportunities to present their points of view. This would also help in avoiding unnecessary delays arising out of protracted litigations, it is felt.

— Fifteen Waste Minimisation Circles (WMCs) have been established so far in different industrial clusters across the country.

— Low lead petrol with a maximum lead content of 0.15 gms/l, has been introduced throughout the country.

— Low-sulphur diesel (Sulphur content of 0.5% or less) has been introduced in the four metros of the country.

— High priority has been accorded for control of vehicular pollution in Delhi. A high-level Task Force has been set up under the chairmanship of the Lt. Governor of Delhi for formulation of plans and implementation of time-bound programmes to improve the environment of Delhi.

- Several actions have been initiated to control pollution in the Agra-Mathura Trapezium and to preserve the Taj Mahal and other monuments of Agra. A special cell has been constituted in the Ministry for implementation of a green belt development plan around the Taj Mahal.
- Three Specific authorities have been constituted in the States of Tamil Nadu, Maharashtra and the NCR, under the Environment (Protection) Act, 1986 in compliance with various Supreme Court orders.
- Effluent and Emission standards for 15 categories of industries were finalised and notified in the Gazette of India during the year. National Ambient Air Quality Standards were also notified.
- Out of 1551 industries belonging to the 17 categories of highly polluting industries, 1259 industries have already installed adequate pollution control facilities and 112 have been closed down.
- Under Section 5 of the Environment (Protection) Act, 1986, show cause notices have been issued to 189 units all over the country.
- During the year, 568 industrial pollution complaints were received and attended to.
- The Ministry of Environment and Forests is the National Focal Point for India for the NETTLAP of UNEP, which consists of institutions and individuals active in environmental education and training at the tertiary level in the Asia-Pacific region.

Central Pollution Control Board

- Monitoring of the rivers Ganga and Yamuna have been taken up at 13 locations falling in the Himalayan segments.
- Monitoring of river Yamuna during 1996 has revealed that the stretch of the river between Wazirabad and Etawah is highly degraded and does not meet the desired water quality standards.
- The monitoring programme of River Cauvery was reviewed during the year to rationalise and optimise it.
- A detailed study on the water quality profile of the river Rapti has been carried out.
- Ground water monitoring conducted at four potential sites of Kanpur have shown that the groundwater at all 4 sites contain excessive levels of fluoride, chromium, coliforms, DO, iron and significant amounts of lindane and DDT.
- Monitoring of ambient air quality was continued under several programmes such as the National Ambient Air Quality Monitoring, continuous automatic air quality monitoring in Delhi, ambient air quality monitoring in NCR etc.
- CPCB is authorised to check the calibration of the instruments and checking procedures being adopted by the Pollution Checking Centres (PCCs) authorised by the Delhi Administration. Twenty six PCCs were inspected by the CPCB during the year.
- A survey was carried out in 23 metropolitan cities to ascertain status of municipal solid waste generation, their collection and disposal.

- A comprehensive study of Jammu city was undertaken during December 96 for monitoring the total environmental quality.
- Forty eight water testing kits were distributed to NGOs and schools throughout the country and financial assistance were provided to 10 NGOs for organising mass awareness programmes.
- Two video films were produced during the year and a set of VHS cassettes has been provided to all SPCBs and PCCs. Twenty publications were brought out.
- Inventorisation of hazardous waste generation in the States of Orissa, Kerala and Maharashtra has been completed.

FORESTRY

Village Panels to Protect Forests

Village-level committees have been formed around the country to involve the people at the lowest level in the forest and environment protection activities. The Minister of State for Environment and Forests, Captain Jai Narayan Prasad Nishad, said that 12,000 such committees had already been functioning in the country. In the Rajya Sabha on August 30, the Minister stated that the Government policy on the environment had been enunciated in the National Conservative Strategy and the Policy Statement on Environment and Development, 1992 and the National Forest Policy 1988. The Policy was also in consonance with the socio-economic development of the country.

The Minister said the policy is given effect through a well-established statutory framework and various programmes implemented by the Central and State Governments, polluting control boards/committees, governmental and non-governmental agencies. Capt. Nishad stated that the forest area in the north-east has been on the decline due to various reasons. But in other parts of the country the forest area has been on the increase. He further stated that the Government strictly pursued the complaints about violation of the environment protection measures by the industries and suitable action was initiated in such cases. The Minister said the national awareness campaign is being run in the country each year since 1986 which covers various programmes on the subject.

16

INDUSTRY

INDUSTRIAL DEVELOPMENT

Industrial Growth Slides

The cumulative growth rate of 24 selected industries, which include the infrastructure sector, dropped down to 4.8 per cent for the April-December period as compared to 10.3 in the previous year, according to provisional production performance released by the Economic Advisor, Ministry of Industry, in New Delhi on February 19. Quick estimates for the month of December showed a growth of 4.5 per cent for the industries which account for a total weight of 50.37 per cent in the index of industrial production (IIP).

The growth rate during the first nine months of the current financial year for the six infrastructure industries comprising electricity, coal, saleable steel, crude petroleum and refined petroleum products and cement fell to 3.3 per cent as compared to 8.8 in the corresponding period of the last year. The six industries have a total weightage of 28.77 in the IIP. The percentage change during December as compared to November, respectively, for different industries was electricity 3.8 (6.5), coal 3.5 (7.9), saleable steel 3.6 (-2.3), crude petroleum -7.1 (0.1), petroleum refined products 8.9 (19.6) and cement 1.1 (12.6). For other industries the figures were: sugar -8.0 per cent (-41), salt -11.5 (7.1), cloth mill sector -5.5 (-7.1), cars 16.4 (3.4), commercial vehicles 17 per cent (0.8), nitrogenous fertilisers 0.3 (6.4) and phosphatic fertilisers 23.1 (17.2).

Industrial Output Up

Major industries comprising the Index of industrial production showed a cumulative growth of 7.83 per cent during April-December, 1996. According to a Government release, the computation took into account 172 industries contributing 88.1 per cent to the index. The cumulative growth figure showed wide variation. The pig iron industry grew by 37.7 pre cent during the period. The autorickshaw industry grew by 35.6 per cent to 1,58,000 units from 1,16,000 in April-December, 1995.

Many other industries also registered high double digit growth. The apatite and phosphorite industry grew by 30.4 per cent to touch 11.8 lakh tonnes from 9,08,000 tonnes in the previous year. The machine tools industry grew to Rs. 1,141 crore in the April-December period from Rs. 799.3 crore. The auto ancillaries grew by 29.3 per cent to Rs. 5.062 crore from Rs. 3,745 crore in April-December, 1995. The polyster fibre industry grew by 35.6 per cent in the first three quarters of 1996, production went up from 151 tonnes in 1995 to 205 tonnes in 1996.

PERFORMANCE OF MAJOR INDUSTRIES

(i) Automobile Industry

MUL Expansion Plan

Maruti Udyog (MUL) will increase the production of Zen from 60,000 cars to 75,000 cars during 1996-97. Output of the Omni will also be boosted to 58,000 from the existing 45,000 vehicles. However, there will be no change in the production capacity of the Maruti 800 at 1.8 lakh cars annually, said Director, marketing and sales, MUL, K. Senga in Mumbai on March 8. He said MUL planned to expand capacity as its Gurgaon plant at an approximate cost of Rs. 2,500 crore. "We would need more investment as the company is chalking plans to increase production and develop various components", Mr. Senga said. The company has targeted greater exports during 1997-98.

To date, the company has exported more than 1.4 lakh vehicles to over 100 countries including Germany, the Netherlands, Italy, France and Hungary. Speaking at the inauguration of MUL's Rs. 4.51 crore pre-dispatch quality inspection facility at Jawaharlal Nehru Port (JNP), MUL Managing Director R.C. Bhargava said that the company's products have been well-received all over the world. The vehicles have a brand image and have performed well in exports, he said. In India the company has succeeded mainly due to Suzuki Motor Corporation's good dealer network, Mr. Bhargava added.

Auto Maiors Record Negative Growth

The entire automobile industry barring the passenger car segment is showing negative growth as per figures available from the association of Indian automobile manufacturers. For the period between April and July 1977, the heavy commercial vehicle (HCV) segment has recorded a negative growth vis-a-vis the corresponding period last year. Telco has seen a drop in sales by 27 per cent for the above mentioned period, while Ashok Leyland saw a fall of 28 per cent in the HCV segment. The same scenario prevails in the light commercial vehicle (LCV) segment where the sales of all majors barring Mahindra and Mahindra have shown a negative growth. Telco's sales have dropped by 30 per cent during this period and Bajaj Tempo has recorded a slump of almost 60 per cent. Other majors like Eicher and Ashok Leyland too have been no different.

The only exception has been Mahindra and Mahindra, which has recorded an increase of about 18 per cent in the LCV segment. The passenger car segment, however, continues to show a positive rate of growth. The overall sales of the industry rose from 117,526 in April-July 1996 to 127,050 for April-July 1997. Maruti Udyog continued to record impressive sales with sales going up from 77,533 units to 84,589 units. Apart from Maruti, General Motors and Premier Automobiles were the other players to see an uptrend in the first four months of 1997. Premier Automobiles has seen an increase in sales by about 5 per cent. On the other hand PAL Peugeot has seen a drop in sales by about

2 per cent. In the motor cycle segment, Hero Honda has displaced Bajaj Auto as the number one in the segment. Bajaj Auto witnessed a decline in all the segments barring the three wheeler segment. Hero Honda recorded an increase in sales to 1.23 lakh units for the period April-June 1997 as compared to 84,000 recorded in the corresponding period last year. Bajaj Auto also witnessed a decline in motor cycle sales to 89,000 in the first three months as compared to 93,000 sold in the corresponding period last year.

HM to set up New Plant

Hindustan Motors is setting up a new and modern car plant near Madras to manufacture the latest model of Mitsubishi Lancer. Hindustan Motors with its partner Mitsubishi Motor Corporation, are working closely to set up this facility quickly so as to launch the new Lancer in January 1998. Vendor development and localisation activities are in full swing at the project and so is the detailed planning of the manufacturing facility. The selection of the plant and machinery is nearly complete, says a press release from the company. The new plant, being set up at an investment of over Rs. 300 crore, will manufacture 8,000 cars in the first year. Later, the production will be raised to 30,000 units annually.

Fiat to Invest $1 Billion

European auto giant Fiat on October 12 announced that it would invest $1 billion in the production of trucks, tractors, cars and civil engineering. Fiat's "increased interest in India" stemmed from the seriousness with which both the Centre and the state governments were pursuing liberalisation. Fiat chief executive officer Paolo Cantrella and his team, during their five-day visit to India, reviewed the group's ongoing operations at Ashok Leyland and at New Holland (the farm equipment arm of the group) in Delhi. They also visited Premier Auto Workshop in Mumbai that has recently been licensed to produce the Fiat *Uno*.

The Fiat team also met Prime Minister H.D. Deve Gowda and described the interaction as "positive". The Fiat CEO promised full support to the expansion plans of the diesel engine and cargo truck assembly operations at Hosur. Meanwhile, the US-based aircraft maker, McDonnell Douglas, is on the look-out for Indian suppliers of aircraft components. Addressing a Press conference in New Delhi on October 11, MD Vice-president Allen C. Haggerty disclosed that his company was sending letters of inquiries to Indian companies for the purpose of identifying potential supplier of components.

(ii) Cement Industry

Cement Production to Increase

India is expected to have surplus of 20 million tonnes of cement by 2002 AD with the demand expected to touch 120 million tonnes while the production capacity reaching 140 million tonnes. The per capita cement consumption is expected to rise to 100 kg from the present level of 71 kg, according to a survey conducted by FICCI. Cement industry is expected to have a 9 per cent growth during the Ninth Plan provided economy grows by 6 to 7 per cent. However, if the growth rate slumps and the capital expenditure goes down, the growth would be less than the projected with demand also going to slacken.

The entry of private sector has considerably changed the demand pattern. The role of private sector is anticipated to boost demand with Government offtake likely to decline. Presently 35 to 40 per cent of the total demand is accounted by the Government. India' share in the world trade was only 4 per cent in 3.2 million tonnes in the global trade of 80 million tonnes. It, however, has a good potential for export as it has 11 major ports and 200 minor ports with major production capacity of cement created near ports. The delicensing of cement industry in July 1991 gave boost to the dormant industry with the availability of cement greatly improved and price checked.

(iii) Drug and Pharmaceutical Industry

(a) The Pharmaceutical Industry of India is today one of the largest and most advanced among the developing countries, Indian pharmaceutical industry manufactures bulk drugs belonging to several major therapeutical groups requiring various manufacturing processes and has developed excellent facilities for production of all dosage forms like tablets, capsules, liquid orals, injectables etc. This achievement is strengthened by an assurance with regard to the quality of the products. Today India is in a position to meet 70 per cent of the country's requirements of bulk drugs and almost all the demand for formulations. The setting up of the Penicillin factory at Pimpri, Pune in the early 50's and the construction of Indian Drugs & Pharmaceuticals Ltd. (IDPL) plants at Rishikesh and Hyderabad in the 60's have been milestones in the history of the pharmaceutical industry in the country . These have been the building blocks on which the structure of the pharmaceutical industry in India has been built. The public sector investment in the pharmaceutical industry has been the catalytic engine for the growth of the industry in the last three decades.

(b) Creation of National Facilities for New Drug Development

To be globally viable in R & D high level expertise and adequate human resources as also modern facilities in specified areas of drug developments are required. It was, therefore, decided that the DST programme, beside new drugs development projects, should also support creation of facilities that were essential for new drugs development. Accordingly, facilities that were needed urgently and that would be cost effectively created namely : (a) DNA gyrase screening facility, (b) Quantity-structure-Activity-Relationship (QSAR) facility, (c) Immunomodulators Modelling and Screening, and (d) Pharmacological testing were identified. Proposals on these were invited from institutions having background and expertise in the area. One proposal has already been received, referred to and considered by the Committee in March, 95.

(c) Export

From a meagre Rs. 46 crores worth of pharmaceutical exports in 1980-81 the figure has risen to over Rs. 2337 crores during 1995-96. Bulk drugs constitute about 60 per cent of exports.

During April 1995—March 1996 total exports (excluding castor oil) amounted to Rs. 2337 crores which was 7 per cent higher than the performance during 1994-95.

During the first six months of 1996-97 also, the export performance has been encouraging

(Value in Million US Dollars)

	Exports April '96/ Sept. '96 (1)	*Exports April 95/ Sept. 95 (2)*	*% age Change (1/2)*
Basic drugs	163.7	166.1	(-) 1.40
Finished formulations	248.0	174.7	(+) 42.00
Total	411.7	340.8	(+) 20.80

(*Source* : CHEMEXCIL).

(d) WTO Agreement and the Pharma Industry (WTO)

India was among the 111 Member nations that signed the Final Act embodying the results of the Uruguay Round of Multilateral Trade Negotiations at Marrakesh on 15th April, 1994. The Agreement establishing the World Trade Organisation (WTO) concluded at the Uruguay Round incorporates various Agreements negotiated under the Uruguay Round including the Agreement on Trade Related Aspects of Intellectual Property Rights (TRIPs) which has a bearing on the Indian pharmaceutical industry. The WTO Agreement came into force on 1-1-1995. The TRIPs Agreement provides for a transition period of 10 years from 1-1-1995 to India for granting product Patent. During the transitionary period. India will have to provide exclusive marketing rights for drugs patented after 1-1-1995 subject to various conditions stipulated in the TRIPs Agreement. There have been apprehensions that signing of the GATT accord would lead to sharp increases in the prices of drugs in the market which are incorrect and unfounded. The GATT Accord will not have any impact on the prices of drugs that are currently in the market. The impact of the GATT Accord on the pharmaceutical industry would be confined to only those drugs which came into the market on the basis of the patents granted after its coming into force. However, the likely impact on the prices of patented drugs, which will come into the market in the beginning of the next century, will also depend on a number of factors like the licensing and marketing strategies including local manufacturers by the patent holders and availability of therapeutic equivalent substitute non patented drugs.

In order to meet the challenges of the Post Urguay Round era, the industry has to gear itself to the new patent *regime.* Various measures have been initiated by the Council of Scientific and Industrial Research (CSIR) in this regard.

(e) Review of the Drug Policy, 1986

The first ever Drug Policy was announced in 1978 based on the recommendation of a Committee known as Hathi Committee. This policy was revised subsequently and a new policy was announced in December, 1986 . In 1989 it was decided to review the policy in response to a large number of representations from Members of Parliament mainly relating to the list of price controlled drugs and later on, it also took into account the impact of the Industrial Policy announced in July, 1991. A Standing Committee constituted by the Government on February 5, 1990 considered all matters connected with the review of Drug (Prices Control) Order, 1987 (DPCO '87) and the representations made on various issues concerning price control, including inclusion/exclusion of drugs in the scheduled categories. Also to assess the situation in realistic terms, discussions were held with various interest groups like Consumer Association. Indian Medical Association, Voluntary Health Organisations. Trade and Industry at the Ministerial levels. The views expressed were further debated in inter-Ministerial meetings. On the basis of these deliberations a background note was laid on the Table of both the Houses on 12-8-1992 for eliciting the views of Members of Parliament as desired by the Prime Minister. The matter was discussed in the Monsoon Session of 1993.

After having considered all the viewpoints and after broad based discussions at various levels, the Government finalised the "Modifications in the Drug Policy, 1986" in September, 1994 and new Drug (Prices Control) Order, 1995 within a record time of less than 4 months, on 6th January, 1995.

(iv) Chemicals, Pesticides and Allied Industries

The Chemical Industry in India is well established. The Country has recorded a rapid growth in the manufacture of Chemicals during the last few years. Prominent among these are Caustic Soda, Soda Ash, Carbon Black, Phenol, Acetic Acid, Methanol and Azo Dyes. The production and availability of Chemicals are by and large sufficient and imports have been curtailed. However, some of the inputs for the industry are in short supply. In certain cases of chemicals, the existing capacity is not sufficient to meet the demand.

The Government is supporting modernisation of the industry so as to improve its efficiency by lowering operating costs, since technology obsolescence is one of the prominent features of the chemicals sector.

In keeping with the liberalised industrial policy, industrial licensing has been done away with for all chemicals industries except for a small list of hazardous chemicals. It is expected that the closely held technologies for various chemicals would now be available.

The current Import-Export Policy 1992-97 eliminates licensing, quantitative restrictions and other regulatory discretionary controls. The majority of chemicals can now be imported or exported through simplified procedures.

(a) Chemicals

The country has recorded a rapid growth in the manufacture of chemicals during the last few years. Prominent among these are Caustic Soda, Soda Ash, Carbon Black, Phenol, Acetic Acid, Methanol and Azo Dyes.

(b) Dyes and Dyestuffs

Dyestuff Industry provides important input to many consuming industries contributing to the national economy. It is capable of meeting most of the local demands. In the organised sector, the industry is self-sufficient in terms of most of the inputs. There are around 50 units in the organised sector having a total annual installed capacity of around 49 lakhs tonnes against which the production achieved during 1995-96 was 31.2 lakhs tonnes. The production for various classes of dyestuffs in 1996-97 is estimated to be 30.16 lakhs tonnes. A large quantity of dyes and dye-intermediates is being exported and valuable foreign exchange is earned in this sector.

(c) Pesticides

Pesticides, including insecticides, fungicides, weedicides etc. are used extensively in Indian agriculture and public health. The pesticides Industry in India continues to make impressive progress and today more than 60 technical grade Pesticides are being successfully manufactured in the country. More than 125 units are currently engaged in the manufacture of these technical grade pesticides and over 500 units are making pesticide formulations. As a result of the increased production of pesticides in the country import of technical grade pesticides has declined considerably. The estimated production of technical pesticides during 1996-97 is 102.74 lakhs MT from an annual installed capacity of 139.3 lakhs MT. As compared to this the production during 1995-96 was around 96.5 lakhs MT.

To utilise the idle capacity available with the pesticides units, the country has entered the competitive field of export of pesticides.

The country has started producing some new pesticides but the manufacturers are continuing to import their intermediates in the absence of technology for producing them. Efforts are being made to acquire the right technology to manufacture intermediates for Pesticides like Butachlor, Endosulfan, etc.

(d) Alcohol and Molasses

The molasses Control Order, 1961 under which the prices and distribution of molasses were regulated and Ethyl Alcohol (Price Control) Order, 1971, which controlled the prices were rescinded on 10th June, 1993 with a view to ensure free availability of these products on competitive prices to the downstream industries. However, some problems had arisen in view of some State Governments continuing to regulate molasses and alcohol as also due to the lower production of molasses and consequent increase in prices of molasses and alcohol in the country. Various issues were discussed in the Excise Ministers' conference held on 4-11-93 wherein the Conference had set up a Working Group of Excise Ministers of some States. The report of the Working Group was placed before the Excise Ministers in June 1995. However, no consensus could emerge in the meeting.

The question of power of control of molasses by the State Governments of U.P. and Bihar under their State Molasses Acts is being examined by the Hon'ble Supreme Court on the basis of SL.Ps. filed by some sugar mills.

(v) Petrochemicals Industry

Petrochemicals are chemicals manufactured from petroleum feedstock, such as naphtha, gas etc. Basic chemicals such as Ethylene, Propylene and Butadiene are manufactured from naphtha. Ethylene and Propylene are converted into plastics which are also known as polymers. Butadiene is converted into synthetic rubbers.

The other set of chemicals manufactured from naphtha are basic aromatic chemicals such as Benzene and Xylenes. These are used for making inter-mediates such as Caprolactum and DMT/PTA. These intermediates are used for production of synthetic fibres and yarns such as Nylon Filament Yarn (from Caprolactum) and Polyester Fibre and Yarns (from DMT/PTA).

Kerosene is another petroleum fraction which is used for making Linear Alkyl Benzene (LAB), which is the raw material for detergent powder and cakes.

Petrochemicals can be broadly categorised as :—

(i) Plastics
(ii) Synthetic Rubbers
(iii) Synthetic Fibres
(iv) Intermediates (DMT, PTA etc.)
(v) Feedstocks (Ethylene, Propylene, Benzene etc.)

(vi) Electronics Industry

(a) Electronic Hardware Technology Parks (EHTP)

During the year, no major policy changes were made in the EHTP Notification. During 1996-97, 12 units were approved under the EHTP scheme involving a total investment of Rs. 209.5 crores and foreign direct investment of US $4.28 million, envisaging an export earning of US $ 2,073 million and net foreign exchange earning of US $ 563 million. With this, a total of 165 units have been approved under the scheme, having total investment of Rs. 1,706 crores and foreign direct investment of US $ 52 million, envisaging an export earning of US$ 7,965 million with a net foreign exchange earning of US $ 2,292 million.

(b) Export Processing Zones and 100 per cent Export Oriented Units

The Government has established Free Trade Zones or Export Processing Zones (EPZs) at Mumbai, Kandla, Falta (Calcutta), Chennai, Kochi, Noida and

Vizag. Of these, the Santacruz Electronic Export Processing Zone (SEEPZ) is meant primarily for the development and promotion of the electronics industry. These Zones provide internationally competitive infrastructural facilities, a duly free and low cost environment, including standard designed factories at concessional rates, for export promotion.

100 per cent Export Oriented Units can be established outside the Zones, anywhere in India, and all the incentives available to units in EPZs are also applicable to 100 per cent EOUs. Foreign Equity participation upto 100 per cent is permitted in 100 per cent EOUs and units in EPZs. There is no minimum value addition required for electronic hardware. Access to domestic market, however, is not allowed without a minimum value addition of 15 per cent.

(c) Duty Drawback Scheme

Exporters are eligible for reimbursement of all customs duty paid on imported components of an export product. In few cases, adhoc quantum of duty drawback rates have been fixed to facilitate quick reimbursement. So far, duty drawback rates for 62 electronic items have been fixed to facilitate exporters. The rates for 2 more items, viz., Power Transistor and 14" Monitor Tube FST have been fixed during the year.

(d) Duty Exemption Scheme

Under the Duty Exemption Scheme, duty free imports of raw materials, components, intermediates, consumables, spare parts, software and packing materials required for the purpose of export production are permitted. In order to help the exporters, the standard input/output norms for 291 electronic items (Quantity Based/Value Based) have been fixed so as to facilitate issue of licences, without any delay. During the year, Quantity based norms for Pagers, Computer Line Printers (Band type), High Frequency Electronic Ballast, Disc Thermistors, Negative Temperature Coefficient (NTC) Thermistors, Motor Protection Thermistors, Dish Antenna, Electronic Flash Gun and Value based norms for Compact Disc (Audio)/CD-ROM were fixed.

(e) Consumer Electronics

Consumer electronic products, namely, colour TV, VCR/VCP, CD players and tape recorders which were licensable have now been delicensed. With this, the entire consumer electronics industry has been fully delicensed.

The consumer electronics industry is expected to reach a production level of Rs. 6,500 crores during the year 1996-97, thereby achieving a growth of 12.1 per cent. The colour TV production jumped to 2.4 million nos. As compared to 1.85 million in 1995.

Cassette tape continues to be the most popular media for playback and recording. The CD Players and its combination with compact and component music systems have been gaining popularity.

In order to whip up the demand for TV industry, a number of innovative schemes have been introduced by the manufacturers, In the CTV segment, emphasis was on offering better quality sound. Set top boxes were introduced in the market to enable consumers having TV set with limited channel capacity to receive cable TV programmes. Video compact discs (VCD)/player were introduced in the market by three manufacturers. Number of VCD titles have also been put on the market.

Consumer electronics exports continued to grow. The major products exported are B/W and Colour TV, VCR/VCP and electronic clock/watches. During the year, initiative was taken by the Department of Electronics in promoting exports of consumer electronics products by organising first ever Indian participation in specialised International Electronics Exhibitions namely at CeBIT Home Electronics 1996 at Hannover and at the 16th Hongkong Electronics Fair. Coinciding with Indian participation in Hongkong Electronics Fair, 'Consumer Electronics India: Buyer Guide' was brought out.

(vii) Fertiliser Industry

(a) Fertiliser Production

Fertiliser production during November 1996 is estimated at 7.59 LMT of nitrogen as against the target of 7.32 LMT and 2.42 LMT of phosphate as against the target of 2.24 LMT. Production would have been higher but for a shortfall in the Thal unit of RCF and KRIBHCO, Hazira on account of equipment problems. The capacity utilisation in the month has been impressive at 100 per cent for nitrogen and 103.2 per cent for phosphate, an official release in New Delhi said. The availability of urea in the country during the first two months of the Rabi season has been comfortable. Against an Eca allocation of 109.83 Lakh tonnes for the entire season, the cumulative availability up to November 1996 was 44.47 lakh tonnes.

The availability has been 5.3 lakh tonnes higher than in the corresponding period of last year. During November 1996, priority in berthing of vessels as well as speedy evacuation both from plants and ports was accorded to dap in view of the pressing demand for Rabi sowing. These measures helped mitigate localised shortages especially in Punjab, Haryana, Uttar Pradesh, Madhya Pradesh and Rajasthan. A quantity of 1.45 lakh tonnes of imported urea arrived in November. The cumulative arrival of urea during the period April-November 1996 was 15.04 lakh tonnes.

(b) National Fertilisers Limited (NFL)

The public sector National Fertilisers Limited (NFL) is embarking on a Rs. 3,800 crore capacity expansion programme covering two of its existing plants at Vijaypur and Panipat. It is also planning equity participation in a Rs. 1,400 crore new joint venture project with Syria. While work at the Vijaypur plant is in an advanced stage of completion, a proposal for expanding capacity at the Panipat plant is with the Public Investment Board awaiting clearance, NFL Managing Director, Mr. C.K. Ramakrishnan, said. "The total estimated project cost of these schemes works out to Rs. 3,800 crore against a capital outlay of Rs. 1,027 crore in the current Five Year Plan period of which the actual expenditure is Rs. 606,25 crore till March end."

The Vijaypur expansion project, estimated to cost over Rs. 987 crore, would start production in December this year, he said adding that the plant would add another 7.26 lakh tonnes of urea to NFL's existing capacity of 2.1 million tonnes, Recording its best-ever production of 2.29 million tonnes of urea, NFL posted a higher pre-tax profit of Rs. 225 crore in sharp contrast to the general dip in profitability in the fertiliser industry. The company had recorded a profit of Rs. 204 crore in 1994-95. Discussions were on with the Syrian Government for a joint venture project estimated to cost Rs. 1,400 crore of which NFL would be a 50 per cent equity partner. While declining to give details, the officials, however, said that talks were on for gas price fixation and other fiscal concessions that the Syrian Government would like to extend to the project.

(viii) Food Processing Industry

(a) Food Processing Industry

India is the world's largest producer of fruits and vegetables, yet it commands no more than one per cent of the global food trade with its food processing industry holed up in outmoded technology, inadequate infrastructure and lack of capital. With a production of 39.47 million tonnes of fruits and 65 million tonnes of vegetables, the opportunities for this industry is tremendous. "However, only one per cent of total horticulture produce are presently converted into value added products," says Mr. Rakesh Chopra, Vice President of Escorts Ltd. and in charge of the farm equipment in his study 'Agribusiness in India— an Opportunity'. Only 1.3 per cent of the total fruits and vegetables produced in the country are processed. This is in comparison to 40 per cent for some developing countries and 70 per cent for developed countries.

Due to relatively high profit margin, the food processing industry has been accorded "sunrise industry" status by industrialists and policy makers. "Although the food processing industry has attracted Rs. 61,427 crore private investments in the first five years of reforms, the industry has failed to register the desired level of growth due to various shortcomings," says Mr. Gauri Sundaram of Agriculture and Processed Food Export Development Authority (APEDA). As most of the food processing industry units are in the tiny, small and medium sector with primitive processing equipment, research and development is non-existent and new products are rare. "The processed food industry in India has not yet been organised on modern scientific lines with integration from the production of raw materials to the marketing stage. Methods of production are by and large conventional and that is why efficiency of production is affected," says Mr. Sundaram.

(b) 909 Food Processing Units Approved

Since liberalization, the Centre has given 909 approvals for setting up export-oriented units/joint ventures/foreign collaborations etc. for setting up food processing units with a total investment of Rs. 16,010 crore including foreign investment of Rs. 7,276 crore. The job opportunities envisaged in these proposals are estimated to be 2.52 lakh. From July , 1991 to November, 1996,

3,868 Industrial Entrepreneur Memoranda (IEMS), involving an investment of Rs. 45,696 crore and direct employment of 6.20 lakhs persons, have been filed in various sectors of food industries. During June 1996 to November 1996, 52 Government proposals for the setting up of 100 per cent export-oriented units/ joint ventures/foreign collaborations etc. have been accorded approval envisaging an investment of Rs. 3,863 crore, including foreign investment of Rs. 3,479 crore. The foreign investment approved during the period is around 48 per cent of the total foreign investment approved so far.

During June 1996 to November 1996, 185 IEM with a probable investment of Rs. 1,557 crore and direct employment of 19,512 persons have been filed for the setting up of food processing units. For bringing about a conducive environment, almost all food industries were declared as priority areas, and almost all food products, except brewing and distillation of alcoholic beverages and items reserved for small scale industries, were delicensed. Automatic approval upto 51 per cent foreign equity in food industry was allowed. Procedures for foreign technology agreements were made easier.

(ix) Gems and Jewellery Industry

Gems, Jewellery Exports

Exports of gems and jewellery from India are poised to reach $ 6 billion during the current financial year 1996-97. Exports of gems and jewellery, which account for about 18 per cent of India's total exports, amounted to $ 5.4 billion in 1995-96 and the target for the current year 1996-97 is $ 6,050 million (i.e. a little over $6 billion) According to an official release issued on July 21, the export of diamonds from India in 1995-96 was provisionally valued at $ 4.6 billion. Diamonds account for nearly 86 per cent for the exports in this sector with gold jewellery occupying the second place, accounting for about 10 per cent. In fact, gold jewellery has been identified by the Government as a major thrust area capable of attaining 30 per cent growth annually.

The world market for gold jewellery, both plain and studded, is estimated at $62 billion of which India's share is under than 1 per cent. There is, therefore, much scope for increasing India's market share in gold jewellery, especially studded jewellery. The growth potential of Indian jewellery as a focus area was underlined by the Gem and Jewellery Export Promotion Council (EPC) at the recent meeting of the Commerce Minister Dr. B.B. Ramaiah, with export promotion councils and commodity boards. The council's representative said that while the developed markets were among the major importing countries, serious efforts would be made to tap new markets in South East Asia, in addition to the present major markets.

(x) Iron and Steel

(a) Rs. 50,000 Crore Investment in Steel Sector

Steel Secretary Dr. J.K. Bagchi on February 4 said nearly Rs. 50,000 crore would be invested in the steel sector by the Government and public sector during the Ninth Plan period. The Indian steel industry is on the threshold of a revolution with the production of finished steel set to exceed 23.5 million tonnes during 1996-97, he said while inaugurating a seminar in Calcutta on "Promotion of Steel Consumption, Role of Technology". "The projection of the Ninth Plan indicates that 43.26 million tonnes of crude steel will be produced by 2001-02, making India possibly the sixth largest steel producer in the world. Also new steel plants in the private sector and those proposed will have the latest technology, improving their edge in the international market," said Dr. Bagchi.

Stating that the decontrol of steel prices and waiver of statutory dues as SDF cess and EGEAF cess had motivated more investment in the steel sector, Dr. Bagchi said that this was reflected by the fact that since 1991, financial institutions have cleared 21 projects with an installed capacity of 12.23 million tonnes and an estimated investment of Rs. 22,225 crore. Dr. Bagchi said that six projects, with capacity of 4.85 million tonnes and estimated investment of Rs. 10,105 crore were also being appraised by the financial institutions. "We are hopeful that these will cater to the domestic requirements and also enable us to have a significant presence in the international market," he added.

(b) SAIL Expansion Programme

The steel Authority of India Limited (SAIL) is planning to invest Rs. 5,000 crore for the extension of the Bhilai steel plant at Raughat in Bastar district of Madhya Pradesh. Detailed discussions in this regard were held between the Union Minister of Steel and Mines Virendra Prasad Vaishya and the Minister of State for Housing and Mining Satya Narayan Sharma at Bhilai on September 19, a SAIL release stated. Officials from the steel plant and the state Government also attended the meeting. Mr. Sharma and the principal secretary in the mining department, Mr. S. Laxmi Narayan said at the meeting that the state government had no objection in handing over the iron ore mines at Bailadila to the plant. It was agreed at the meeting the SAIL would give Rs. 50 crore to build a railway line between Rajhara and Raughat for which the National Minerals Development Corporation would provide Rs. 25 crore.

Mr. Vaishya said a meeting between the State Chief Minister Digvijay Singh, the Union Railway Minister Ram Vilas Paswan and SAIL officials would be convened soon to decide on the ways and means to arrange funds for the railway line extension. Mr. Vaishya assured that all aspects of the proposal to hand over the iron ore mine at Bailadila to the Mineral Development Corporation would be considered before arriving at a final decision. He also assured the state government that its demand for hiking royalty for minerals to generate more resources for development would be considered sympathetically. During the meeting, the state government had also proposed the suitable amendment of the Mining Act, 1957.

(c) Sail to Invest Rs. 15,000 Crore

The Steel Authority of India plans to invest approximately Rs. 15,000 crore on modernisation, addition, modification and replacement schemes during the Ninth Plan. The public sector steel major plans to add new facilities at its Bhilai Plant, which is considered to be the best steel plant in the country in terms of blast furnace and labour productivity. The company in the last ten years has already spent Rs. 20,000 crore on its modernisation programmes. SAIL's modernisation programme is almost complete at its Durgapur plant. At Rourkela and Bokaro plants, work is progressing satisfactorily. After the completion of the ongoing modernisation programmes, SAIL's cost of production would decline.

At the Roukela plant, the cost of productioln is expected to come down by about Rs. 1,100 per tonne. The yield of salable steel from liquid steel would improve substantiallly. In Durgapur, it would go up from 75.1 to 84.5 per cent. In addition to this, manpower productivity is expected to increase appreciably. Blast furnace productivity would increase from 0.7 tonne per cubic metre per hour to 1.04 and 0.76 tonne per cubic metre per hour to 1.13 tonne per cubic metre per hour in Durgapur and Rourkela, respectively. Energy consumption is expected to decline due to reduction in coke rate to 653 kg per tonne of hot metal in Durgapur, while in Rourkela from 811 kg per tonne of hot metal to 700 kg per tonne of hot metal.

(d) DSP Modernisation Plan

Modernisation cost of the Durgapur Steel Plant (DSP) of SAIL has gone up to a staggering Rs. 4,854 crore from Rs. 2,668 crore in 1989, according to the DSP sources. Attributing the time overrun to the break-up of the erstwhile Soviet Union, the sources said this adversely affected the pace of modernisation as the Russian steel conglomerate, Tyazpromexort was involved in its update programme. The sources, however, said the completion of such a project in seven years was a major achievement for the project management team.

Referring to the results of the modernisation, the sources said the plant had come up to a level of 1.6 million tonnes of hot metal and 1.5 million tonnes of crude steel which meant that it had attained around 80 per cent of the post modernisation rated capacity levels. Stating that there was a lot of pressure on the plant to reach the full rated capacity within the current financial year, the sources said while it appeared to be a distant possibility technologically, production in some areas was affected by variolus restrictive practices.

(e) Poised for Self-Sufficiency in Steel

New initiatives planned in the steel sector for the Ninth Plan period will raise the steel production in the country to 24 million tonnes and make India self-sufficient, according to Union Minister of Steel and Mines Birendra Prasad Baishya. Speaking on the occasion for the presentation of safety awards for the Steel Industry, where Mr. Baishya presentcd awards to the SAIL and TISCO for best performances in safety related improvement, Mr. Baishya expressed confidence that the new investment in different steel consuming sectors would result in the increased steel consumption in the country. Industry should adopt a total safety culture for sustaining business activities in today's every changing business environment by involving grassroot level workers with the measures undertaken for the same.

India was vulnerable to safety hazards since it was in the process of massive industrialisation and had more labour intensive industries compared to Korea, Thailand, Indonesia, etc. Since these factors were likely to increase the chances of accidents, therefore, it was essential that discipline was infused from a very early age, the Minister stressed. The accident rate per thousand in Steel Industry was nearly one-third of the national figure. The presence of toxic gaseous explosion, radiation, hot metal, fire had created safety hazards in the sector, he said. Commending the role of Joint Committee on Safety, Health and Environment in the Steel Industry in the strengthening safety and health standards and preventing accidents, the Minister urged it to ensure the joint efforts of the management and the union through a broad framework. SAIL Chairman Arvind Pande said maintaining high standards of safety, health and environment was vital to developing employee motivation and increasing productivity.

(xi) Textiles Industry

(a) Textile Fund Approved

The Textile Ministry has secured in-principle approval of the Planning Commission for its proposal to set up a Rs. 5,000 crore technology upgradation fund during the Ninth Plan period, Textile Sectetary Prabhat Kumar said on January 31. "We are now looking forward to its acceptance by the government," Mr. Kumar said, adding that the proposed fund would be managed by a financial institution and the government would pay the difference for concessional loans. The fund would be on the pattern of the Rs. 750 crore fund set up during the Seventh Plan, operated by Industrial Development Bank of India, mainly for upgrading and augmenting spinning capacity. Mr. Kumar said he was confident textile export target of $ 9.9 billion at a growth of about 12 per cent for 1996-97 would be achieved, notwithstanding 1.9 per cent negative growth witnessed during December. He attributed the 13.4 per cent negative growth in the all important readymade garments segment, accounting for over 40 per cent of total textile exports, to sluggish world markets, intense competition and lower per unit value realisation.

(b) Jalappa for Plan to Boost Textiles Production

Union Minister of Textiles R.L. Jalappa on March 15 said an action plan should be drawn up by the textile associations and export promotion council to give fillip to the weaving and processing sector. Speaking at the Cotton Textiles Export Promotion Council (Texprocil) award distribution function in Mumbai, Mr. Jalappa urged the textile manufacturers to reflect on the current level of modernisation in the industry and take necessary steps like setting up of 100 per cent export oriented weaving units and state-of-the-art processing units. The setting up of a technology upgradation fund would add momentum to the modernisation process, he said.

The Minister said export of cotton textiles, the largest net foreign exchange earner for India, accounted for abour 30 per cent of total exports, adding that the export of cotton textiles—cotton yarn, fabrics and made-ups—achieved an outstanding growth of 19 per cent in dollar terms during the last calender year. "Export performance for the current year showed continuation of this trend," he said. "India share in world textile trade is a meagre 2.5 per cent. We have thus a long way to go if we are to achieve a global presence," he said, adding "with the textile industry playing a vital role in our economy and providing employment to a large number of people, there is a need to increase our share in global trade." The need of the hour is an effort from all sectors in the textile industry to channelise their creative energy in the task of increasing export, Mr. Jalappa said.

Mr. Jalappa pointed out that the development of eco-friendly textiles was another related aspect which needed attention while calling upon manufacturers in the decentralised powerloom sector to take steps to develop environment friendly textiles. Changes in international trading regime with the integration of textile trade into GATT and setting up of the World Trade Organisation provided opportunities for increasing exports. The dismantling of quantitative restrictions under the multi-fibre agreement would remove by AD 2004 many barriers in the way of accelerated growth of textile trade countries like India.

17

PUBLIC DISTRIBUTION SYSTEM AND CONSUMER PROTECTION PROGRAMME

PUBLIC DISTRIBUTION SYSTEM

Today the Indian Public Distribution System (PDS) is the largest distribution network of its type in the world. The system is designed to help both the producers and consumers of foodgrains by linking procurement to support prices and ensuring their distribution along with other essential commodities at affordable prices throughout the country. PDS therefore, continues to be a major instrument of Government's economic policy for ensuring food security for the poor.

The Common Minimum Programme (CMP) of the United Front Government stresses the need for streamlining the PDS with the objective of improving the basic minimum services. PDS is one of the services which is sought to be steamlined as follows :

(i) Foodgrains shall be sold to the families below poverty line (BPL) at specially subsidised prices.

(ii) PDS need not cater to the affluent section of society; and

(iii) The management of fair price shops (FPS) shall be entrusted to elected Panchayats and Nagar Palikas.

Restructuring of the PDS on the above lines was discussed in the Conference of Chief Ministers on Basic Minimum Services held during 4-5 July, 1996. Keeping in view the suggestion of the Chief Ministers, a Conference of State Food Ministers' was held on 7th August, 1996 to discuss further the question of targeting PDS. The Conference unanimously endorsed the proposal for targeting the PDS especially the provisions of subsidised foodgrains to the population below poverty line.

The Hon'ble Prime Minister in his Independence Day address to the Nation on 15th August, 1996 announced that 10 kg of foodgrains will be provided every month to the poor families at half the normal price.

The Hon'ble Prime Minister has now made a Statement in the Lok Sabha on 24th February 1997 on introduction of tergeted PDS (TPDS) in the country.

Cheaper Food for the Poor

The Government on February 24 announced that the people living below the poverty line would be provided rice (both common and fine varieties) at Rs. 3.50 per kg and wheat at Rs. 2.50 per kg under the new targeted public distribution system. However, people living above the poverty line will have to pay Rs. 6.50 for fine and Rs. 7.50 for super fine varieties of rice. The affluent sections will be provided wheat at Rs. 4.50 per kg. The total food subsidy under the targeted PDS is estimated to be Rs. 82.90 crore. The announcement of the Central Issue Prices (CIP) for the new ADS fulfils one of the commitments made by the United Front Government in its common minimum programme.

The targeted PDS will benefit 32 crore people living below the poverty line. Initially, the Centre proposes to issue 10 kgs of foodgrain per family per month. About 180 lakhs metric tonnes of foodgrains is likely to be issued under the new PDS. Announçing the issue prices for the new PDS in Parliament, Prime Minister H.D. Deve Gowda said that states which want to cover a large number of people or increase the scale of issue or reduce the price further were free to do so. But, they have to meet the additional requirement of foodgrain and funds from their own resources.

For implementing the new PDS, State Governments must identify the beneficiaries, issue special cards to them and ensure delivery of foodgrains on the basis of norms circulated by the Centre. It is also proposed to continue with the average lifting of foodgrains for the last 10 years by the states for the benefit of affluent sections. The quantity of foodgrains out of this average lifting, which is in excess of the requirement for the population below the poverty line, will be allocation to the states as a transitory allocation at the CIP. The Government also plans to extend the issue of specially subsidised foodgrains to the beneficiaries under the Employment Assurance Scheme (EAS) and Jawahar Rozgar Yojana (JRY). The Centre will issue 1 kg of rice and wheat per person per day under these schemes. Later, talking to reporters, Minister of Food, Civil Supplies and Public Distribution Devendra Prasad Yadav said that the new issue prices would come into force from the date of its implementation by the State Governments.

The last date for implementation has been fixed for May 31. Although several states have taken steps to identify people living below the poverty line for issuing special ration cards, the implementation of the scheme is expected to take time. This is because the Planning Commission is yet to notify the latest estimates of poor people to the states as per the Prof. Lakdawala Committee formula. With the announcement of the new PDS prices, the Centre has quietly effected a revision in the CIP of foodgrains, which has not been touched since February 1, 1994.

CONSUMER PROTECTION PROGRAMME

With the approval of Planning Commission a scheme of one-time financial assistance of Rs. 61 crores to strengthen the infrastructure of consumer courts in the States/UTs was initiated in the year 1995-96. Two installments of the grant amounting to about Rs. 30 crores was released during 95-96. The scheme is being continued during 1996-97 also. Under the Scheme till now a number of States/UTs have achieved clearance of pendency of over 75 per cent cases in consumer courts.

In collaboration with the National Literacy Mission of the Department of Education, the Ministry has arranged the publication of 7 booklets in Hindi on various aspects of Consumer Protection. These include awareness about the payment of correct price, awareness about deficiency of public utility services, filing of complaint against sub-standard goods and services in the consumer courts, not compromise on quality, awareness about adulteration and spurious drugs and necessary tips to the consumers, etc. This measure is meant for educating the consumer at the grass-root level through the trained teachers under National Literacy Mission.

This Ministry is the co-sponsor of an International Conference on Consumer Protection being organised by Consumers' International in the month of January, 1997. This Conference wil be the first of its kind in the South East Asia. Through this Conference, the experience of various countries in the field of consumer protection will be shared and lessons from successful stories would be analysed for taking further necessary action in this field.

Consumer Cooperatives

With the financial assistance of Government of India and the technical support provided by the Consultancy and Promotional Cell of NCCF, a network of successful super markets/Department stores and retail outlets have come up in different parts of the country during the last three decades. They have been the poineers in modern methods of retailing such as, pre-packing, price marking, price display and self-service system. Consumer cooperatives had developed a range image, price image and service image and they are now household names. They sell a wide range of consumer goods comparatively at a cheaper rate. It is a matter of pride that all the top retailers of the country are now consumer cooperatives. Apna Bazar of Bombay and Super Bazar and Kendriya Bhandar of Delhi with an annual sale of more than Rs. 100 crores each, are the top retailers of the country.

The success of the consumer cooperatives and more so the service system especially lin Maharashtra, Tamil Nadu, Kerala, Goa, Delhi, Andaman and Nicobar Islands, etc. has inspired the private retailers and now private super markets are coming up in different parts of the country ushering in a retail revolution.

18

RADIO, DOORDARSHAN AND FILMS

ALL INDIA RADIO

Network

Alll India Radio has at present (as on 10 November 1996) 187 radio stations operating in the country. These include 179 full fledged stations, four relay centres, one auxiliary centre and three exclusive Vividh Bharati Commercial centres. This year two Radio stations at Pauri Garhwal (UP) and Osmanabad (Maharashrta) have been added to the AIR network. AIR presently has 297 transmitters. These include 149 Medium Wave, 52 Short Wave and 96 FM transmitters and provide radio coverage to a population of 97.3 per cent spread over 90.1 per cent area of the country. The growth of the network over the various Five Year Plans and also the coverage by area and population is shown in the graphs on the following pages.

Growth of AIR

	1990-91	*1996-97*	*Growth %*
No. of stations	108	187	73.15
No. of transmitters	197	297	50.76
Radio coverage (area) (%)	84.6	90.1	6.5
Radio coverage (population) (%)	95.4	97.3	02
Broadcast duration on FM Metro channel (in hours)	05.5	24	336
Commercial revenue (Rs. in crores)	39.30	48 (upto 9/96)	22.13 (Appx.)
Budget (Rs. in crore)	355.58	529.53	48.92

In order to bring radio closer to the people, the concept of local radio station was introduced in the Sixth Plan when six such stations were planned as pilot projects. The number of local radio stations in the country to day is 73.

The Computer Division of All India Radio has been engaged in inculcating and spreading the computer culture in the organisation in various areas like MIS, transaction processing and office, automation. It is operating and running of ND-550 computer system with a number of application packages viz., Artist Booking System, Royalty payments, Computer Aided-design, Project Management system etc. These application packages have been developed as per the requirements of users. Bilingual software packages have also been developed for Artist Booking System and Payroll and implemented by EDP

Cell. Training courses were also conducted by EDP Cell for training the staff of AIR and field units in use of application packages.

During the year a number of AIR stations have been upgraded and modernised in its network. These are : (a) 10 KW MW Tr. at Gangtok (Sikkim) has been upgraded to 20 KW; (b) A new 10 KW SW at Gangtok has been installed to provide Short Wave support to the primary Medium Wave coverage in the State of Sikkim : (C) An additional morning transmission has been introduced at Gangtok; (d) The power of the existing 10 KW MW Tr. at Parbhani (Maharashtra) has been increased to 20 KW (e) Studio facilities at Thiruvananthapuram have been modernised and upgraded with latest technical facilities.

AIR has seven stations and 17 projects technically ready. The stations are Kullu, Mt. Abu, Bijapur, Kinnaur, Kargil, Uttarkashi and Pithoragarh and projects are Kurseong 1 KW MW Tr., Calcutta second FM stereo channel, Tawang 10 KW MW Tr., Chandigarh 3 KW FM Tr., Allahabad 2×10 KW MW Tr., Ranchi 2×3 KW FM Tr., (CBS), Ahmedabad 2×5 KW FM Tr. (VB) Mumbai second FM stereo channel, Jabalpur 2×5 KW FM Tr. (CBS), Panaji, Type-III Studios, Panaji two units of 250 KW SW Tr. each Parbhani type-I studios, Jagdalpur 100 KW MW Tr., Bangalore 2×3 KW FM Tr. (stereo), Nagarcoil 2×5 KW FM Tr., Thiruvananthapuram 2 × 5 KM FM Tr. (VB) & Chennai second FM channel.

External Services Division

External Services Division of All India Radio acts as a bridge between India and the world. It is an important link with different regions of the world. The broadcast projects the Indian point of view on matters of National and International importance through its various programmes, broadcast in 24 languages, spanning a period of about seventy hours.

The General Overseas Service (English), Urdu and Hindi Services have been the three major services of External Services Division. The broadcast follow a composite pattern. The Urdu Service continues to project the image of a modern progressive resurgent India committed to the principles of Democracy, Socialism,International Peace and Co-existence. It has been the endeavour to counter false and baseless propaganda launched by Pakistani electronic media particularly with regard to the insurgency in Kashmir. Special inputs were initiated in Urdu, Sindhi and Punjabi Services highlighting Human Rights violation in Pakistan, situation in Sindh and Indo-Pak relations vis-a-vis Pakistan's role in fomenting terrorism in Jammu and Kashmir and Pakistan's role in Narco Drug smuggling. Similarly, General Overseas Service (English) and Hindi Services were geared to mount wide publicity.for the New Economic Policy of liberalization giving all the details of Government schemes and incentives for the new investment climate in India, specially for the non-resident Indians and multinationals. ESD Transmitters directed to SAARC countries, West Asia, Gulf and South East Asian countries continue to carry the 21.00 hours National Bulletin in English, orginally meant for Home Services.

All India Radio

FM Broadcast and other Projects expected to be completed during 1997-98

FM Project	
1. Bhadarwah	2x3 KW FM Tr.
2. Hissar	Local Radio Station
3. Jodhpur (VB)	2x3 KW FM Tr.
4. Lucknow	2x5 KW FM Tr. (Stereo)
5. Dhubri	2x3 KW FM Tr. (Relay)
6. Jamshedpur (CBS)	2x3 KW FM Tr.
7. Siliguri (CBS)	2x5 KW FM Tr.
8. Coimbatore (CBS)	2x5 KW FM Tr.
Other Projects	
1. Delhi (Phase II)	Refurbishing of Studios
2. Bhubaneswar	STI (T)
3. Mumbai	Refurbishing of Studios, (Phase-II)
4. Mumbai	Consolidaton of VB Service (Phase-I)

The Division brings out independently a monthly programme journal, 'India Calling' in English.

Family Welfare

AIR Stations broadcast more than 8,500 programmes on family welfare every month in all the languages/dialects of our country. The main emphasis is laid on small and happy family norms. Important programmes on AIDS, TB, Dengue, Sexually Transmitted Diseases, water-borne diseases, malaria eradication programme, child survival and safe motherhood programme, sterilization, vasectomy, tubectomy ect. are broadcast. Also each station broadcast once a week 'Health Forum' programme of a duration of 15 minutes.

Programme for Children

All India Radio broadcasts from almost all its stations programmes for children of three categories, viz. programmes for children between the age of 5 to 7 years and 8 to 14 years of age. Special programmes are also broadcast for rural children. The programmes are broadcast on a weekly basis. Plays, short stories, features, choral songs, interviews, stories from epics etc. form part of these broadcasts. Children, regardless of their educational and literacy status, participate in these programmes.

Several workshops are being organised from time to time to sensitize the AIR programmers who are involved with production of children's programmes. All AIR stations actively join the celebration of the International Children's Day of Broadcasting every year by arranging envelop and special phone-in programme to give children a platform to express their voices on the various issues concerning them.

Women's Programmes

AIR stations broadcast programmes for rural women as well as urban women at the timings convenient for listening by the respective largest groups. The programmes cover subjects related to socio-economic development of women, health and family welfare, food and nutrition, scientific home management, women entrepreneurship, education, including adult education, gender issues ect. These programmes also aim at creating wide social awareness about rights and privileges of women through the propagation of legal literacy. All India Radio strives, through its programmes, to seek to raise the social consciousness of the country in regard to attitude towards women.

Workshops are conducted regularly by the Staff Training Institute as well as in collaboration with International Organisations for sensitizing the programmes about the latest issues and trends in broadcasting. Recently workshops on "Radio for Women" and "Expanding Partnership for Adolescent Girls"have also been organised.

DOORDARSHAN

Network

From an experimental service started in 1959 at Delhi, Doordarshan, over the years has grown into a giant structure, and in the process, has become one of the major transmitting networks in the world. Doordarshan is presently telecasting programmes on 19 channels with a network of 41 programme production centres and 834 transmitting stations of varying powers, providing service to about 85.8 per cent of the country's population, covering an estimated 68.8 per cent area of the country.

Programmes on all these 19 channels except international channel are disseminated through INSAT satellites (presently 1D, 2A, 2B, and 2C satellites are in operation). Uplinking facilities for the purpose have been established at various Doordarshan stations in the country. The international channel programmes are disseminated through PAS-4 satellite.

Programmes of Primary Channel (DD-I) are being relayed by 784 transmitters of varying power. These are :

(a) High power (10 KW/5 KW/1 KW) transmitters—77.
(b) Low power (300 W/100 W) transmitters—534.
(c) Very low power transmitters/Transponders (10 W)—173.

For terrestrial transmission of DD-II Channel programmes, 43 transmitters including six high power transmitters are in operation in various cities. High power transmitters are in operation at the metropolis of Delhi, Mumbai, Calcutta and Chennai for terrestrial transmission of DD-III programmes. The low power transmitters for relay of Lok Sabha and Rajya Sabha proceedings and one low power transmitter at Srinagar for relay of Kashmir channel programmes are also in operaion.

There are 41 programme production centres presently in operation in various parts of the country. In addition, a Central Production Centre comprising two large studios equipped with modern and sophisticated technical facilities is in operation at Delhi. This centre caters to high quality programme production. In addition there is a production centre at Guwahati equipped with modern equipment which produces programmes for relay by various TV stations in the North-Eastern part of the country.

Thirteen colour outdoor broadcast (OB) vans each equipped with four cameras and other associated equipment and a large OB van equipped with six cameras and nine electronic field productioin (EEP) and 12 mini vans are available in the network. Electronic news gathering (ENG) equipment is available at all the programme producing stations for coverage of outdoor activities.

Development Programmes

For the purpose of expansion of coverage of DD-1 channel about 480 transmitter projects are presently under implementation/envisaged to be set up. With the commissioning of these transmitters, over 92 per cent population of the country is expected to be brought under TV coverage. To extend reach of DD-II channel programmes, four additional low power transmitters are being set up at Panaji, Murshidabad, Port Blair and Pondicherry. At Bangalore and Hyderabad, high power transmitters are being set up in replacement of the existing low power transmitters.

To augment in-house production 31 Studio/Programme generation facility projects are under implementation/proposed to be set up, as part of VIII Plan schemes. In addition, a National Studio Complex at Delhi, viz., Doordarshan Bhavan comprising eight studios of size varying from 50 sq. mtrs. to 600 sq. mtrs. and associated technical facilities, to be housed in an eleven-storeyed building, is under implementation.

The current Five Year Plan (1992-97) of Doordarshan lays stress on consolidation of existing facilities and modernisation/augmentation of facilities at various stations in view of fast changing technologies. The developmental activities taken up by Doordarshan during the current Plan includes computerisation of news system and introduction of multilingual transmission of programmes in a limited way. Besides, a decision to introduce CCD cameras for use in ENG; Studio and OB vans has been taken and Betacam recording format is being adopted in major Kendras in a phased manner. A number of ENG-based production facilities have been envisaged at various locations in the country to augment the programme production from various States. Computerisation of office management has been taken up. Doordarshan is prepared to absorb new technologies in the field of broadcasting.

Consequent upon operationalisation of INSAT 2C additional transponder capacity has become available to Doordarshan. Most of Doordarshan services have been shifted to INSAT 2C Satellite. Satellite news gathering has been introduced. SNG equipment is presently installed at Srinagar. Additional services, viz., regional service in Punjab and Himachal Pradesh and transmission utilising digital compression technique, DTH, ect., are planned to be introduced in future.

During the remaining period of 1996-97, installation of HPTs at Jodhpur (interim), Fazilka (interim), Bangalore (DD-II) and Hyderabad (DD-II), besides a number of LPTs and VLPTs, are expected to be completed.

Sixty-eight projects (studios at Mau and Jalpaiguri; HPTs at Jaisalmer, Barmer (Interim), Mokokchung and Kurnool; 52 LPTs and 10 VLPTs) are presently awaiting commissioning.

DDI National Channel

The main aim of the programmes telecast in the national channel is to promote national intergation, inculcating a sense of unity and making people proud that they are Indians. The National Programme was started on 15 August 1982 and has been extended in stages to include programmes in the mornings, afternoons, etc. At present about 80 hours of programmes are lelecast in the National Network. The programmes include education, information and entertainment roughly in the proportion of 30:40:30.

A large number of topical events are covered live in the National Programmes.

The proceedings in the two Houses of Parliament are available through two low-power transmitters in Delhi and thus can be received within a radius of 10-15 kilometres around Parliament House.

The telecast timings of the National Network were rationalised to make DD-I and DD-II complementary to each other.

Regional Segment

All the Doordarshan Kendras originate programmes in their respective regional languages. The major Kendras originate about 25 hours of programmes each week while other Kendras for one to 10 hours a week. While rural development is one of the major concerns in the regional programmes, subjects like agriculture, health, family welfare and environment are also regularly dealt with. With satellite uplinking it has been possible to provide common programmes for viewers in 13 States.

Educational TV

Doordarshan has given high priority to programmes on education from the beginning. The school telecasts started from Delhi in 1961 itself. As a part of SITE continuity, programmes for school children were started in 1982. At present, school programmes produced by Doordarshan are telecast in the regional segment from Delhi, Mumbai and Chennai and programmes produced by the State Institute of Education are telecast in Hindi, Marathi, Gujarati, Oriya and Telugu for relay by all transmitters in the particular language zone.

The higher education TV programmes produced by UGC and IGNOU are telecast 13 hours each week on the National Network. There is a proposal to have a channel devoted exclusively to educational programmes.

FILMS

Films Division

The aims and objectives of the Division, focused on the national perspective, are to educate and motivate the people towards enlisting their active support and participation in the implementation of national programmes and to project the image of the land and the heritage of the country to Indian and foreign audience. The Division also aims to foster the growth of the documentary film movement which is of immense significance to India in the field of national information, communication and integration.

The Division produced documentaries/news magazines from its headquarters at Mumbai, films on agriculture, defence and family welfare from Delhi and featurettes with rural bias from the regional centres at Calcutta and Bangalore. The Division caters to over 12,623 cinema theatres all over the country and to the non-theatrical circuits like units of the Directorate of Field Publicity, mobile units of the State Governments, Doordarshan, field units of the Department of Family Welfare, educational institutions and voluntary organisations. The documentaries and newsreels of State Governments are also featured in the Division's release on the theatrical circuit. The Division also sells prints, stock shots, video cassettes and distribution rights of documentaries and featurettes in India and abroad.

By organising four international film festivals for documentary, short and animation films at Mumbai, the Division has emerged as a powerful force behind the documentay film movement in the world. The Division is also geared up for the Fifth Mumbai International Film Festival to be held in February 1998.

The 43rd National Film Festival commenced its jury screenings in April 1996. The feature film jury was chaired by Shri Hrishikesh Mukherjee and the non-feature jury by Smt. Vijaya Mulay. Ms. Aruna Vasudev were the Chairperson of the committee set up to adjudge the best writing on cinema. 88 feature films, 68 non-feature films, 12 books and 17 critics were entered for the awards. The President, Dr. Shanker Dayal Sharma, gave away the awards at a ceremony held on 6 August 1996 in New Delhi. The best feature film award was bagged by 'Kathapurushan' directed by Adoor Gopalakrishnan, while Rajat Kapoor's 'Tarana' (Hindi) got the award for the best non-feature film. The award for ;the best book on cinema went to 'Marathi Cinema in Retrospective' (Marathi) by Shri Sanjit Narwekar and Shri M.C. Raja Narayanan was given the best ;film critic award for 1995. The Dada Saheb Phalke Award for 1995 was conferred on the veteran Kannada actor Dr. Rajkumar for his ourstanding contribution to cinema.

International Film Festival

The 28th International Film Festival of India (IFFI) was organised in Thiruvananthapuram from 10 to 20 January, 1997. This was a non-competitive film festival. This festival had as many as 214 feature and non-feature films in various sections from 47 countries, including India. The largest of these was in the Cinema of the world section, 78 from 37 countries, featuring films that have won awards of acclaim at various film festivals. There were 41 films in Retrospectives which included tributes to Shri P.A. Backer, Malayalam film-maker (3 films), Shri Tapan Sinha (one film) and Ms. Smita Patil (2 films).

The Indian Panorama had 14 feature films and 16 non-features. In addition, there were 32 films in retrospective of Malayalam cinema.

Activities Abroad

During the period under report, the Directorate participated in more than 50 international film festivals held abroad. The film titled 'Hkhagoroloi Bohu Door' won the special jury award and the hero Shri Bishnu Kharghoria won the best actor award for the same film in Singapore International Film Festival. The film 'Bandit Queen' won three major awards. Shri Jahnu 'Barua won the best director award for the film 'Hkhagoroloi Bohu Door' and Shri Nandan Kudiyadi won the special mention for his film 'Rasayatra' in the 18th International Film Festival at Brussels, Belgium.

19

SCIENCE AND TECHNOLOGY

RESEARCH AND DEVELOPMENT (R&D)

Prime Minister Deve Gowda called upon industrialists to look upon investment in technology development as non-divestible equity. Inaugurating the 84th session of the Indian Science Congress on January 3, Mr. Gowda assured the industrialists that the government was ready to play its part in this process and would welcome the role of business houses in acquireing technological strengths through their investments in R&D. The government had given many;benefits for investment in R&D and scientific institutions. He wanted the industry to avail these benefits to strenghen the technological base.

The world, he said, was in the midst of a transition form an industrial economy to a global information economy, where power came not form location or control over the factors of production and access to transportation centres along, but from ability to access network. He called upon the scientists to come to the aid of providing basic minimum services such as safe drinking water, primary health services, education and housing. Mr . Gowda said while it might seem that these problems were not in the domain of frontier areas of science and technology these were the real problems of today. While India has a wealth of human resources it still had to capitalise on it by generating skilled persons not only to serve national needs but also to meet the demands of ;the global economy.

ATOMIC ENERGY

Generation of over 8600 million units of electricity by the atomic power stations of the nuclear Power Corporation of India Ltd., cold commissioning of Fuel Reprocessing Plant at Kalpakkam (KARP); commissioning of research reactor Kamini; rolling of turbine at 3000 rpm by the steam from FBTR; commissioning of the New Uranium Fuel Assembly Plant and setting up of Centre for Compositional Characterisation of Materials (CCCM) at Hyderabad, and completion of design and installation of 64-node super computer Anupam, were some of the major achievements of Department of Atomic Energy during 1996-97.

Nuclear Power Programme

Power Generation

The Nuclear Power Corporation of India Ltd. (NPC) earned a net profit of about Rs. 372 crore during the financial year 1996-97, and achieved a gross generation of 8446 million units from the operation of nuclear power reactors during the calendar year 1996-97. The generation from operating units in the financial year 1996-97 is expected to be 8610 million units exceeding the Annual Action Plan target. The cumulative generation from all the units since commencement of commercial operation till end of December 1996 now stands at over 1,07,900 million units. The Atomic Power Stations at Kakrapar (Gujarat) and Narora (Uttar Pradesh) performed very well producing 2683 MUs and 2989 MUs respectively during the calendar year 1996.

All the coolant channels of RAPS-2 were cut and removed before schedule, as a part of enmass coolant channel replacement and system upgradation works.

Power Projects

The atomic power projects under construction progressed as follows :

(i) Kaiga Atomic Power Project-1 & 2 (2×220 MWe PHWRs)

The Reactor Building (RB) —1 inner containment (IC) dome was readied for construction and construction of reactor building R.B.-2 IC dome commenced. In the other main plant buildings, finishing works continued. The Induced Draught Cooling Towers and Waste Management Plant reached 98.5 per cent and 80 per cent of completion stage respectively.

In nuclear piping, 77 per cent erection iin Unit-1 and 46 per cent erection in Unit-2 were completed. Turbogenerator (TG) erecton upto 71 per cent in Unit-1 and 20 per cent in Unit-2 were completed. In Electrical Systems, 220 KV Switchyard creation was completed and 6.6 KV and 415V switch gears were commissioned.

The Unit-1 and 2 are expected to achieve criticality during financial year 1998-99.

(ii) Rajasthan Atomic Power Project-3 and 4 (2×220 MWe PHWRs)

Major civil works except RB-IC wall and Dome were completed and major equipment were supplied at the site. Equipment erection works upto an extent of 60 per cent and 40 per cent were completed in RB-3 and RB-4 respectively. About 64 per cent of the nuclear piping was fabricated. Commissioning of common services system and electrical systems commenced. Turbo-generator and Mechanical Works progressed. The 220 KV Switchyard and start-up transformer for Unit-3 were energised. Around 96 per cent erection of 6.6 KV Switchgears, 415 V Switchgears and MCCs, was completed.

The reactors Unit-3 and Unit-4 are expected to achieve criticality in May 1998 and November, 1998 respectively.

(iii) Tarapur Atomic Power Project-3 and 4 (2×500 MWe PHWRs)

Due to paucity of funds, main plant civil works could not be taken up by NPC so far.

(iv) Kudankulam Atomic Power Project (2×1000 MWe PWRs)

All the mandatory site related clearances were obtained and the site investigations were completed. Land at Kudankulam, both for plant site and township, was also acquired. Negotiations on the supplement to the Inter-Covernmental Agreement were continuing.

Research and Development Related to Nuclear Power Reactors

The research and development relating to power reactors and allied technologies were as follows :

(*i*) *Advanced Heavy Water Reactor*

At BARC, the design study to establish the feasibility of Advanced Heavy Water Reactor (AHWR) reached completion and the AHWR Feasibility Report was under preparation. The work on core-physics design optimization was continued. The Prototype fuel cluster fabricated earlier has been performing satistactorily under endurance test. Assembly or prototype fuel cluster of revised design is nearing completion. Safety analysis for some typical accident scenarios was also completed.

(*ii*) *Reactor Engineering*

Activities regarding management of ageing coolant channels in PHWRs were continued and inputs were provided to NPCIL. The Coolant Channel Replacement Machine (CCRM), developed for large scale coolant channel replacement in PHWRs, was commissioned. Several important tooling systems capable of remote operations were also assembled and commissioned to identify coolant channels needing in-service inspection. BARCIS equipment developed earlier for coolant channel repair technology, was upgraded. Its versions with enhanced capabilities are under development.

Fast Breeder Reactors

(i) *Fast Breeder Test Reactor (FBTR)*

The 40 MWt and 13 MWe Fast Breeder Test Reactor, a major facility of IGCAR at Kalpakkam, was operated at 10.5 MWt. Irradiation campaign with a small core consisting of 25 fuel subassemblies was completed. Maximum fuel burnup of over 26,300 MWd/t, at a maximum linear heat rating of 320 W/cm was achieved without any fuel clad failure. FBTR is using indigenously developed mixed carbide fuel which is first core of its kind in the world. Turbine was also rolled successfully to synchronous speed of 3000 rpm.

(ii) Prototype Fast Breeder Reactor (PFBR)

The conceptual design report for systems and components of PFBR was prepared. Safety classification and seismic categorisation of the components, design basis events, applicable design and construction codes, computer codes for analysis and compilation of material and site data were completed. Other developments were : the core was made compact, shielding requirements were reviewed and R & D in the theoretical analysis and experimental works in the related domain were defined. Also, a three-dimensional core burnup code for use in predicting PFBR subassembly powers was developed.

(iii) Fast Breeder Reactor Engineering

At IGCAR, large Component test Rig (LCTR) was operated successfully for engineering experiments relating to FBR. Studies on heat transfer from sodium surface to the roof slab, and testing of the sodium-to-air exchanger used in rig were conducted. Based on the studies some guidelines for design of exchangers were brought out. Hydraulic studies on the grid plate were completed.

The Annular Linear Induction Pump designed and fabricated indigenously gave satisfactory performance after rigorous tests thereby establishing the design and fabrication capability to high standards.

TECHNOLOGY

Biotechnology

For realising the full potential of Biotechnology, a frontier area of science and technology, an interdisciplinary, inter-institutional and mission approach in some key areas has been adopted by the Department of Biotechnology. Major efforts have been initiated to apply biotechnological tools for efficient and sustainable utilisation of natural resources. The programmes and activities leading to better understanding of structures and functions of cells, molecules and genes have received support.

Considering that this was the last year of the Eighth Five Year Plan, a critical review of the ongoing programmes, the new initiatives to be launched during the Ninth Five Year Plan and efficient institutional mechanisms were all considered by various expert committees and policy making bodies of the Department. A booklet titled "Realising Biotechnology Potential—Some Priorities and Strategies" has been brought out with the help of SAC (O) and SAC-DBT members as also other experts and circulated widely to the scientific community for formulating projects and programmes in the identified areas as we move into the next century.

From various reviews conducted and reports received from the scientists, a large number of R & D leads available through the projects supported during these years have been noted. A special effort was made to consolidate this information, based on which further activities were taken up. Many of the projects in the agriculture and allied fields have made very good progress. Technology transfer activities have been geared up as also filing of patents. The two tissue culture pilot plant facilities created by the department have become fully operational and were dedicated to the nation by the Minister for Science and Technology on January 15, 1997. The foundation stone for the new Centre for DNA Fingerprinting and Diagnostics was laid by the Prime Minister of India, on January 28, at Hyderabad. These mark the beginning of new ventures to be undertaken during the Ninth Five Year Plan in the important areas of micro-propagation technology and DNA Fingerprinting techniques.

The projects supported have displayed an array ranging from fundamental research at the cutting edge of science, demonstration activities, upscaling, validation, field trials and technology transfer. A number of new initiatives were taken; links forged with other agencies while remaining responsive to societal needs in particular of SC/ST and the weaker sections.

Development of transgenic crops, diagnostics and vaccines, human genetics and genome analysis, biodiversity conservation, bio-prospecting, biosafety, patenting and the like were approached with added vigour. The Department has played a pivotal role in supporting biotechnology research and application in the country; bringing together experts for interfacing of disciplines and for evolving new interdisciplinary approaches for obtaining end products.

During the year, there were about 670 ongoing projects. More than 300 project proposals were received during the year. Most of the Task Forces met twice or thrice to monitor and review the ongoing programmes and recommend new projects and avctivities.

The three mission mode projects, specially the biofertiliser and biocontrol programmes have made very good progress and the milestones have been more or less achieved. Due to some administrative problems, the aquaculture mission mode project was slowed down. However, it has subsequently picked up as most of the issues have been resolved. Activity-wise highlights are briefly given below :

Scientific Advisory Committees SAC (DBT)

The Scientific Advisory Committee (SAC-DBT) met on 23rd August, 1996. The Committee took note of the priorities for the 9th Plan. It was recommended that leads obtained should be taken to their logical conclusion and products and processes developed expeditiously. Vaccines for cholera, hepatitis, Japanese encephalitis and malaria need special attention. Prospecting of biological wealth, new mission oriented projects, iPR issues, patenting etc. were identified among others as areas of increased thrust. Development of genetic probes, genetic enhancement centres, human resource development were recommended for continued support. SAC-DBT also recommended the setting up of a Biotechnology Research Council and restructuring of the funding mechanism so as to make it more efficient, transparent and less time consuming.

(i) Scientific Advisory Committees(SAC) (O)

The seventh meeting of the Standing Advisory Committee (Overseas) SAC(O) was organised from 25th to 26th October, 1996. The SAC(O) recommended continued support to basic research on a long term basis, strengthening science-industry interaction and commercialisation of the significant R & D leads obtained in a number of areas. The Committee felt that there should be support especially for DNA vaccines, edible vaccines, protein engineering, genetic counselling, diagnostic kits, biotechnology parks and patenting of research findings.

Research and Development

(i) Basic Research

Further progress was made in the finalisation of a highly efficient and cost effective process for the preparation of large quantities (300-400 mg) of pure native-like recombinant streptokinase from *E. coli.* In a project on molecular biology of human enteric pathogen at IICB, Calcutta toxicological data of a cholera vaccine strain was generated. Scaling upto 10-50 g levels has been initiated as a prelude to full scale industrial production. On purification and characterization of lactotransferrin, an iron binding protein, the purified samples were crystallized and the intensity data were collected upto 2.8 A with 100 per cent completeness. The yield of turmerin by a new method developed at CFTRI, Mysore has been augmented three times compared to the conventional method.

In a project on "Molecular basis of resistance to cycloguanil and pyrimethamine induced *in-vitro* in clones and field isolates of *P. falciparum* malaria." at University of Delhi, a non-gametocyte forming cloned *P. falciparum* line was subjected *in-vitro* to incremental drug pressure, employing a relapse protocol to select porogressively resistant *P. falciparum* lines to pyrimethamine and cycloguanil, the two di-hydrofolate reductase inhibitor antimalarial drugs. Mechanisms of transcriptional activation and cryptification of the *bgl* operon of *E. coli* and transcription of the *bgl* promoter *in-vitro* were studied at the developmental Biology and Genetics laboratory, IISc., Bangalore.

The National Facility for Macromolecular Crystallography at BARC, Bombay, was used for more than 175 primer systhesis, protein purification, DNA amplification etc.

At the Indian Institute of Science, Bangalore, the umbrella support programme will be completed by March, 1997. The centres, facilities and research activities supported have been thoroughly reviewed by the Apex Committee. The overall research outcome was excellent with about 900 publications in leading national and international journals. The work has led to increased industrial interactions involving more than 30 projects and 20 industrial firms/agencies. The facilities provided by DBT have been extensively used not only by the inhouse scientific community, but others also.

(ii) Crop Biotechnology

Two genes viz Cry IA (b) and IA (c) of *Bacillus thuringiensis* were transferred in rice to confer resistance against yellow stem borer. Genetic transformation methods in mustard have been developed and a number of genes transferred. Bt-plants and plants with CpTI were generated at Bose Institute, Calcutta. On the bioassay of transgenic tobacco plants, harboring Bt or CpTI gene now R_2 and R_3 generations are being te l sted at NBRI, Lucknow for stability. In chickpea, parameters for transient and stable expression of foreign gene by microprojectile bombardment with different explants amenable for direct organogenesis has also been standardized there.

Transformed calli of *Vigna mungo* and *V. radiata* were generated. Transformation and integration was confirmed at MKU, Madurai. Further, at

MKU, a plant expression construct containing full length Cry IA (c) gene under CaMV 35 S promoter, gus reporter and nos terminator was developed and successfully used in direct transformation of rice plants.

In order to raise economically important transgenic crops like potato and rice, JNU subcloned the coding region of AmAI in different plant expression vectors under the control of 2 promotors. The gene has been expressed in *Nicotiana* as a model system and rice transformation via particle bombardment is in progress. In the transgenic cotton project, two Bt genes with different host ranges have been synthesized and also a facile method for synthesis and assembly of long double stranded DNA reported.

(iii) Medicinal and Aromatic Plants

The three national gene banks for medicinal and aromatic plants became fully operational. At CIMAP, there were 1282 germplasm accessions of 161 plant species in the field gene bank; 533 accessions of 42 plant species in the seed gene bank and 85 accessions of 30 plant species are being maintained in the *in-vitro* bank. NBPGR, New Delhi, gene bank had 182 accessions of 63 general and 68 plant species in the cryo-bank. In the *in-vitro* bank, cultures were being maintained for a maximum period of 22 months. TBGRI gene bank had 2200 accessions in the field and over 177 accessions of 20 species in the seed gene bank.

In an ongoing R&D project on immunomodulatory and anti-tumour compounds at NII, New Delhi, two active fractions namely NII-30 and NII-47 were isolated from *Piper longum* and *Tunospora cordifolia* which possess enhanced antigen specific cellular and antibody response. At CIMAP, Lucknow, 250 mutants of *Catharanthus roseus* have been isolated and one mutant showed enhanced alkaloid yield. A new variety "Nirmal" was ready for release and a hairy root bank has been developed. In Vinca minor 5 methyltry ptophan-tolerant callus line and high alkaloid producing call line were isolated. In *Duboisia myoporoides,* genotypes with higher alkaloid percentage and desirable alkaloid profile were isolated. Heat stress tolerant and alkalinity-tolerant genotypes were identified. In *Glycyrrhiza glabra* an elite genotype "Mishree" was released for commercial exploitation.

(iv) Horticulture and Plantation Crops

Complete protocols were developed for *Boswellia serrata, Wrightia arborea, Citrus sp.,* coffee, tea, saffron, pepper and kala zira. Field demonstration trials were supported for Coffee. The protocol is being standardized/adapted for large scale production and evaluation trials are being conducted in the farmers' field. Demonstration trials are now being initiated for other crops also. Good leads were obtained on protocol development for Mango varieties. Hardening units have been set up for the eastern region with the main objective of large scale production and plantation of tissue culture raised plants of economic importance. Large scale production has been initiated in arid zone hardening facility also. Two projects have been supported for large scale micropropagation and germplasm characterization of Neem using DNA fingerprinting and RFLP techniques. Studies were continued on the assessment of genetic fidelity and micropropagated plants using DNA fingerprinting and RFLP techniques. At the hardening facility in Regional Plant Resources Research Centre, Bhubaneswar, more than 30,000 tissue cultured banana plants have been supplied to the State Government; more than 3 lakh woluld be produced further.

(v) Seri-Biotechnology

A number of RFLP markers of polymorphic multivoltine and bivoltine strains of silk worm have been developed for genetic map construction. The inheritance pattern of nuclear polyhedrosis virus resistance has been elucidated in multivoltine and bivoltine strains of silkworm. Post harvest processing of silk (degumming, bio-polishing and bleaching) using enzymes is being studied with a view to improving the quality of finished product. The department is initiating a programme on "Silkworm Genome initiative" for systematic map building of the silkworm genome for molecular approaches in genetic improvement of silkworm.

Medical Biotechnology

The screening of 'env' and 'gag' genes on HIV-I isolates carried out at AIIMS, New Delhi suggested existence of sub-types C and B of the virus in the country. Development of diagnostics for Hepatitis E showed promising leads. The coding regions of FI and Pla genes of *Yersinia pestis* (Surat isolates) amplified by PCR have been cloned and expressed. These recombinant proteins are highly antigenic and an enzyme immuno assay using these recombinant antigens is being developed. Sequencing of complete gene of PV9 from *P vivax* has been achieved. The PV 9 encodes gene at significant homology to small heat shock protein of *E. coli.* This is the first heat shock protein of *P. vivax* with metalloproteins activity described in literature. Fetal liver haemapoietic cells have been preserved for eight months at— 80 degrees centigrade and upto 18 months in liquid nitrogen. These cells have been transplanted at AIIMS to reactivate haematopoisis.

The department has supported Phase III clinical trials of the Anti-leprosy vaccine in conjunction with the Standard Multi Drug therapeutic (MDT) regimen. Trials have been conducted in two urban leprosy centres in Delhi and at Kanpur Dehat. In Kanpur Dehat, 820 patients received the full dose of vaccine and 23950 contacts have been immunized. The trials indicated quick recovery of the patients when vaccine was given along with the MDT. The technology for manufacture the vaccine has already been transferred to Cadila. The approval of the Drugs Controller of India is awaited before marketing the product.

As a national facility, a brain bank, the first of its kind has been established at NIMHANS, Bangalore to promote research in neurobiology using precious human material. The facility established a good collection of fresh human brains, as tissue fluids and DNA Bank and is supplying the material to various research centres all over the country.

Immunological Approaches to Fertility Control

After successful demonstration on the potential of *B*hCG as a candidate vaccine for anti fertility in females, efforts were on at National Institute of Immunology, New Delhi to optimize the vaccine using synthetic T-helper peptides as vaccine carrier. This is mainly to enhance the immunogenicity and sustained response against *B*hCG. Recombinant route for the expression of *B*hCG using *Pichia pastoris* system explored at IISc., Bangalore has shown good yield. Efforts are on to increase the yield using fermentors.

Three assay systems were developed for the detection of the HIV I and II infections with the support from the Department. All systems i.e., Western blot, ELISA using synthetic peptides and recombinant reagents for testing with the drop of blood showed encouraging results during in-house laboratory testing. The validation of the test systems has been initiated with the help of five clinical centres covering different geographical regions of the country.

(iii) Human Genetics

In addition to six genetic clinics established for molecular diagnosis and counselling for common genetic disorders prevalent in the country, the Task Force has cleared 5 more centres. Two centres are likely to come up in the North Eastern Region. A comprehensive document on Genomic Diversity and People of India has been finalised with a view to studying the genetic variation among specific groups. In order to initiate programmes on Gene Therapy and Bioethics, guidelines have been finalised for gene therapy research.

(iv) Animal Biotechnology

Embryo Transfer Technology projects in upstream areas have shown significant progress in terms of technology improvements at NII, New Delhi; NDRI, Karnal and CIRB, Hisar. Almost 100 per cent accuracy of fetal sexing using bovine chromosome specific probe developed at NII, New Delhi has been demonstrated. Genome probes and micro statellites have been used for the parentage verification of cattle and buffaloes.

A field diagnostic kit for identification of infections bovine rhinotracheitis (IBR) and other related diseases of overlappling clinical signs is ready for use. Several Blue tongue virus isolates (BTV) have been adopted in BHK-21 cell line and Competitive ELISA has been developed to detect antibodies of BTV. An ELISA has also been developed for the diagnosis of Johne's disease in goats.

Lipase enzyme, isolated from bacteria and fungi has been shown to have potential application in detergent industry as well as in degrading skin or hide. Collagen sheets developed from animal waste products are under going clinical trials. This technology is ready for transfer.

(v) Microbial Biotechnology

New initiatives were taken for rehabilitation of degraded land utilising microbial supports, dissolution of pyritic shells by microial methods to liberate entrapped noble metals like gold, silver etc., and degradation of polyphenolic compounds using microbial approaches. Standardisation of shuttling vectors for *E. coli* and Streptomyces having capabilities of accepting cluster genes of Ansamycins were made. Strengthening of microbial teaching and research in identified universities received special focus during the year.

(vi) Environment and Conservation Biotechnology

A biosensor has been developed for the detection of organo-phosphate pesticide residues in water. This is being field evaluated. Reclamation of degraded ecosystem at Bhatti Mines (near Delhi), coal and manganese mines (near Nagpur) is in progress. Under this project HCN producing microbe has been isolated from grasses that are resistant to termites. A kit for detecton of biological toxins is under development. Studies for removal of heavy metals by bacteria and algae are in progress. Attempts are underway for conservation of endangered plant species of Himalyan ranges (including North Eastern), desert plant species and mangrove species as part of biodiversity conservation.

Under the project on "Isozymes as bio-chemical markers in germplasm characterisation and genetic enhancement in Brassicas" at IARI, for the first time a new methodology has been developed for characterising isozyme variation as Quantitative Traits (QTs). New methodologies have been set up to use isozyme QTs for quantitative fingerprinting of Brassicas and also using the methods developed for improving the yield performance of mustards.

Technology Mission for Cotton

The Planning Commission has approved the Textile Ministry's proposal to set up a 'technology mission' on cotton. Inaugurating an eco-testing laboratory, set up by the Northern India Textile Research Association (NITRA), Union Textile Ministry Secretary Prabhat Kumar said the Textiles and the Agriculture Ministries will jointly implement the mission. He said in the next five years the country will have to produce qualitative cloth and therefore it is imperative for the industry to effect improvements in its weaving and processing sectors. He noted that though the total fabric production touched 30,000 square metres in 1996, there is an urgent need to produce superior quality fabrics in order to make inroads into overseas markets, adding there is as a need for a total restructuring of the industry in the light of the emerging competition and global market scenario.

He impressed upon the industry to adopt the developments in textiles industries across the globe and Secretary assured them all possible cooperation in meeting these situations. The NITRA eco-testing laboratory is one of the 11 laboratories set up in the country by the Textile Ministry in the first phase. It is equipped with highly sophisticated analytical instruments to carry out the analysis and detection of toxic chemicals. Earlier, NITRA Director Jai Prakash in his address had underlined the need for the introduction of modern technology and stressed on training and development of human resources.

Infotech Sector to Cross Rs. 19,300 Crore

The Information Technology (IT) sector is projected to gross Rs. 19,300 crore in 1997-98, registering a 36 per cent increase over the previous year, according to International Data Corporation (IDC), India. The US based IDC, which specialises in market research and consulting for the information technology industry, made these projections at 'Destinations '98', the annual computer industry briefing session. While the exports market is expected to grow by 50 per cent to touch Rs. 75,800 crore, the domestic IT market is projected to gross Rs. 44,800 crore in 1997-98, clocking a 20 per cent growth over 1996-97. The positive influences on the market are economic buoyancy resulting from the easing of the credit squeeze, relaxation in corporate taxes, dilution of the minimum alternate tax and duty cuts, the IDC (India) Vice President Ravi Sangal said. "The strengthening of home and the small business segment and the proliferation of the Internet and the E-mail is also pushing the IT sector towards a higher growth path," he added.

20

SMALL-SCALE INDUSTRY

ABID COMMITTEE REPORT ON SSIS

The export committee on small enterprises headed by Mr. Abid Hussain has recommended abolition of the policy of reservation, scrapping foreign equity limit and enhancement of investment limit of Rs. 3 crore for the SSI sector. The committee in its 54-page report has mooted highly debatable and sweeping reforms in the small scale sector to make it globally competitive. The report was released to the Press by the Mr. Hussain in the presence of Industry Minister Murasoli Maran who said "the government will study the recommendations and implement the non-controversial ones as soon as possible".

The Minister said that he would like a wide ranging debate on the more vital aspects of the report before they are implemented. Mr. Hussain said, the concept of small scale sector should now be widened from the small sector industry to small scale enterprise. The emphasis in future should be on the development policies and programmes which promote accelerate growth and competitiveness rather than protection. For this adequated supply of credit services, technology assistance, infrastructure and low transaction costs are the hallmarks of the proposed strategy for promotion of SSEs.

INVESTMENT LIMIT FOR SSIS

The Cabinet Committee on Economic Affairs (CCEA) on February 3 approved enhancement of investment limit or small-scale industrial undertakings and ancillary and export-oriented industries to Rs. 3 crore from the present Rs. 60 lakh. For the tiny sector, the limit has been raised from the present Rs. 5 lakh to Rs. 25 lakh. The revised ceiling, Industry Minister Murasoli Maran told newspersons, would enable small-scale industries to acquire modern technology to enable them to compete successfully in the market with large units. He said the government would soon come out with a credit package in consultation with the RBI to ensure that the small among SSI sector and the tiny units were not cornered by the larger units in the 40 per cent priority sector credit earmarked for them.

The CCEA had also decided to relax export obligations to 50 per cent from prevailing 75 per cent for the non-SSI units in the 100 per cent export-oriented scheme, Mr. Maran said. The Minister said any decision on de-reserving the list of industries, earmarked for SSIs, would be taken only after a detailed debate on the recommendations of the Abid Hussain Committee. The decision would enable SSIs to grow vertically rather than horizontally or operate under the guise of multiple units as at present, he said.

21

STATE ENTERPRISES

PSU PROFITS

Profits of central public sector enterprises increased by Rs. 978 crore in 1995-96, recording a growth of 20.4 per cent over that in 1994-95, as investment increased by only 3.08 per cent at Rs. 5,336 crore. With four more PSUs turning black, the profits of 134 profit making PSUs increased to Rs. 14,704 crore from Rs. 12,070 crore in 1994-95, the Public Enterprises Survey of 1995-96, tabled in Parliament on May 5, said. The gross margin to the capital employed was higher at 23.31 per cent in 1995-96 as against 20.55 per cent in the previous year while the total investment was placed at Rs. 178,628 crore compared to Rs. 173,292 crore in 1994-95. The number of loss making PSUs also came down from 109 to 101 with total losses slipping marginally to Rs. 4,826 crore from Rs. 4,883 crore, the survey said, adding four of the PSUs were making neither profits nor losses.

While Oil and Natural Gas Corporation topped the list of profit making PSUs with gross profits of Rs. 2,354.32 crore, the Hindustan Fertiliser Corporation posted net loss of Rs. 474.41 crore to lead losers table. Barring Bharat Heavy Electricals Ltd., all the 'navaratna' PSUs figure among the top ten profit-making enterprises which accounted for 62.55 per cent share at Rs. 11,816.24 crore of the total profits of the undertakings. On the other hand, the top ten loss-makers accounted for 51.44 per cent of the total losses at Rs. 2,482.74 crore, the survey revealed. While export earnings of the enterprises recorded a 15.1 per cent increase in 1995-96 at Rs. 13,216 crore, this sector's contribution to exchequer in the form of taxes and dividend increased by Rs. 4,624 crore to Rs. 32,096 crore, a jump of 16.83 per cent. In terms of performance measured by memorandum of understanding, signed by 104 PSUs, 52 were rated 'excellent' and 32 got 'very good' rating, the survey said, adding gross sales of the corporations went up by a shopping Rs. 39,422 crore to reach Rs. 226,777 crore in 1995-96 showing a growth of 21.04 per cent.

Performance of central public sector undertakings also recorded improvement in terms of gross internal resources generated which went up by 21.9 per cent at Rs. 24,371 crore and value added production grew by Rs. 9,788 crore to Rs. 57,774 crore showing a growth of 20.4 per cent. With gross margin increasing from Rs. 33,384 crore to Rs. 40,526 crore, the public sector undertakings retained profits of Rs. 7,672.93 crore after paying a dividend of Rs. 2,205.09 crore in 1995-96.

DISINVESTMENT COMMISSION'S FIRST REPORT

The Disinvestment Commission in its first report issued on February 20 selected three public sector units, Modern Food Industries, Gas Authority of India and India Tourism Development Corporation for divestment of majority of government stake. The Commission which has bracketed the public sector units based on the nature of their operations into core and non-core categories is taking up a case-by-case study for evolving a strategy for disinvestment. The Commission argued for the sale of 100 per cent of the government holding in Modern Food Industries. For the Gas Authority of India the extent of share sale recommended is only 49 per cent. for ITDC the Commission has suggested divestment up to 74 per cent or more. Releasing the report to the Press, the Commission Chairman G.V. Ramakrishna said the losses of unprofitable PSUs have increased in the nineties due to withdrawal of budgetary support as well as increased competition. Most of these losses are cash losses and occur in sectors which have become fully competitive and where they have no special role.

Before releasing the report the Commission submitted copies of the same to the Finance Minister P. Chidambaram and Industry Minister Murasoli Maran. The Cabinet will now take a decision of these recommendations, Mr. Ramakrishna said. Losses in unprofitable PSUs account for about 60 per cent of the total direct budgetary support and will in all probability keep increasing each year, the report said. "This will be a recurring drag on the budget", he said, Mooting a long term strategy for divestment, the Commission has said the exercise should strengthen public sector, protect employee interest, broadbase ownership and augment receipts for Government. An empowered group, the Commission said should be assigned to ensure smooth implementation of the recommendations.

DIVESTMENT OF PSUS

The Disinvestment Commission has recommended divestment of the Government equity in six more public sector undertakings, which include Bharat Aluminium Co. (BALCO) Bongaigaon Refinery and Petrochemicals Ltd. (BRPL), HTL Ltd., ITI Ltd., Madras Fertilisers Ltd. (MFL) and Manganese Ore India Ltd. (MOIL). Addressing newsmen in New Delhi on April 17, Commission Chairman G.V. Ramakrishna said that in four of these companies, the panel has recommended strategic sale, as it believed that the Government need not hold majority stake in those companies, which served little public purpose. While HTL Ltd. has been recommended for 100 per cent off loading of the Government equity, the commission suggested sale of upto 74 per cent equity of BALCO, ITI and BRPL, besides selling 50 per cent shares of MFL and 49 per cent of MOIL.

Keeping in view the real estate and other value of some of the PSU units, the commission has recommended a reserve price for these units. The commission has reclassified HTL Ltd. and BRPL from core to non-core and MOIL from non-core to core. Earlier, in its first report brought out in February this year, the Commission has recommended divestment modalities for three PSUs viz. ITDC, Modern Food Industries and Gas Authority of India Ltd . So far, 50 PSUs have been referred to the Commission. Mr. Ramakrishna said that the Commission would suggest divestment modalities for more PSUs in its third report. It is expected to be submitted in the early June, 1997.

22

TRANSPORT AND COMMUNICATIONS

TRANSPORT

World Infrastructure Conference

During the year, in order to encourage private investment in the development of Roads, Ports etc., the Ministry of Surface Transport organised the World Infrastructure Conference during 23—31 October, 1996 at Vigyan Bhawan, New Delhi. The Conference was held in two groups viz. (i) UN—ESCAP Ministerial Conference on Infrastructure and (ii) World Infrastructure Forum. Forty Ministers from various ESCAP Countries and delegates from 47 Countries all over the World attended the Conference apart from the large number of representatives from Multi-National Companies, Multilateral Agencies, Non-Governmental Organisations and members of Indian Corporate Sector. The Conference was inaugurated by Shri H.D. Deve Gowda, the Hon'ble, Prime Minister of India.

During the deliberations of the Conference an Action Plan on infrastructure development in Asia and Pacific Region for the period from 1996-2006, was adopted which *inter alia* provides for initiatives at the country level, including preparation of regional action programme and resource mobilisation. The Conference also launched a tripartite Asia infrastructure Development Alliance for developing a closer partnership between the Government and Private Sector and Multilateral and Inter-Governmental Agencies in the field of infrastructure development. The need for implementing the Asian Land Transport Infrastructure Development (ALTID) Projects on tripartite basis for developing and strengthening an international and inter-regional land transport linkage to facilitate international bilateral trade and tourism, was also stressed.

It is expected that the initiatives taken, as a result of this Conference, will accelerate the private sector investment in the infrastructure sector in a greater way in the coming years.

Shipping

(i) For the shipping sector in the 8th Plan an outlay of Rs. 3459 crores was approved. During the last year of the Plan i.e. the year 1996-97, an outlay of Rs. 1964.13 crores has been provided for the ongoing programme.

(ii) It is noteworthy that the 8th Plan target of 7 million GRT was achieved much ahead of schedule and the operating tonnage of 7.05 million GRT with 484 ships was achieved by 31-12-96.

(iii) During the year, the performance of Shipping Corporation of India and Cochin Shipyard Limited has been excellent. During the Financial Year ended 31-3-96, the SCI has earned a record net profit of Rs. 323.40 crores and paid a dividend at 20 per cent on share capital aggregating to Rs. 56.50 crores. CSL also posted a total net profit of Rs. 18.16 crores.

(iv) In order to improve the Performance to revive the ailing shipbuilding units, viz Hindustan Shipyards Ltd. and the HDPE, the Ministry is taking the following steps :

(a) Re-introduction of subsidy scheme for shipbuilding industry;
(b) the capital restructuring of HSL; and
(c) conducting a techno-economic commercial study on the long term viability of the Hindustan Dock and Ports Engineers Ltd. (HDPE).

(v) Action has been initiated to amend the Merchant Shipping Act for introducing more liberalisation in the matter of registration, transfer of ships, foreclosure of mortgages, etc.

Transchart (Chartering)

(i) The freight market showed a continued downward slide and recorded the lowest rates during September 1996. About 195.84 lakh tonnes of Government cargoes was shipped through Transchart Wing of the Ministry. Out of this, 51.21 per cent of the shipped cargo was carried by Indian bottoms. The major items handled, under dry/liquid bulk cargoes, included 90.64 lakh tonnes of coking coal, 58.08 lakh tonnes of petroleum products and 31.42 lakhs tonnes fertilizers.

(ii) In addition to extending charter hire of research vessels for exploration of polymetallic nodules in the Central Indian Ocean Basin specialised vessels were chartered for the 16th Antarctic Expedition.

(iii) During the year, Transchart Wing of the Ministry made concerted efforts to provide shipping coverage and the demands for chartering vessels were fully met.

Ports

(i) Over the years there has been a steady increase in the total cargo traffic handled by major ports. During the first nine months of the current financial year the major ports handled 163.9 million tonnes of cargo traffic as against 215.3 million tonnes handled during the full financial year 1995-96.

(ii) In order to decongest the major ports a very ambitious plan, with an outlay of Rs. 17,000 crores has been drawn in the Ninth Five Year Plan, for the infrastructure development at the major ports. It has been proposed to meet about Rs. 10,664 crores from the revenue account of the major ports and balance funds are anticipated from the private sector. The 9th Plan is aimed at increasing the major ports capacity to 424 million tonnes per annum from existing 215 million tonnes per annum.

(iii) In order to achieve these goals during the year, the Ministry has issued policy guidelines to attract private investment in the Ports Sector. The areas identified for private investment are as follows :-

(a) Leasing out assets of Port
(b) construction and operation of more container terminals, multipurpose cargo berths and specialised cargo berths, warehousing, storage facilities, tank farms, container freight stations, setting up of captive power plants etc.
(c) leasing of equipment for cargo handling and leasing of floating crafts from the private sector.
(d) pilotage.
(e) captive facilities for port based industries.

(iv) The Major Port Trusts Act, 1963 has been amended by issue of an Ordinance to provide for an independent Tariff Authority for major ports for fixing and revising the ceilings on tariff rates.

(v) In order to give practical shape to the liberalisation policy the Boards of the Major Port Trusts have been empowered to take investment decisions upto Rs. 50 crores for addition/modifications/new investment and upto Rs. 100 crores in case of replacement/renewal of assets. In addition, they are empowered to exercise full powers for award of contracts and placement of orders in respect of projects/schemes for which the approval of investment decision and sanction of estimates has been obtained.

(vi) Ushering in the era of private investment in the development of the port sector, the Ministry of Surface Transport has given clearance, to the Jawaharlal Nehru Port Trust (JNPT), Navi Mumbai to award the licence for the construction, management and maintenance of a two-berth container Terminal for a period of thirty years on Build, Operate, Transfer basis to the P and O Ports, Australia led consortium which will be investing approximately Rs. 700 crores on the project over a period of thirty six months. The terminal will be developed as per international standards with state-of-the art facilities. With the commissioning of the new terminal, the capacity for handling containers at JNPT will be more than doubled, increasing to over 1 million TEUs per annum.

(vii) To encourage foreign private investment, automatic approval upto 74 per cent foreign equity participation has been allowed. Besides, attractive financial concessions have also been allowed for Lenders/Investors :

Inland Water Transport

(i) The Inland Water Transport is being regulated by the Inland Waterways Authority of India.

(ii) During the period under report in addition to introduction of Experimental Fixed Schedule promotional sailling by M.V. Rajgopalachari between Calcutta and Patna, a scheme for providing 24 hours navigation facilities in Calcutta-Farrakka sector on National Waterway No. 1 has been approved.

— International steamer Route (191 Km) in Sunderbans has been completed.

— Techno-Economic Feasibility studies for development of navigation on identified waterways like East Coast Canal linking Paradeep to Calcutta port, canal system connecting Kakinada and Chennai, extension of NW-3 in north and south, Karimganj-Lakhipur stretch of river Barak etc, are under progress.

— Study on cost effectiveness of IWT for Ganga (NW-1) has been completed while other studies like preparation of DPR for improvement of existing terminals and semipermanent river training works in Patna-Monghyr stretch of NW-1 are also under progress.

(iii) National Conference on development of inland waterways and water transport in India was held on 19-12-1996 which was jointly organised by IWAI and FICCI for interaction amongst the representatives of the Government and various agencies involved in infrastructure development on the one hand and representatives on industry and trade on the other.

(iv) The protocol on Inland Water Transit and Trade between India and Bangladesh has been renewed for a further period of two years w.e.f. 4-10-95 to 31-10-97.

Road Sector

(i) In the Road Sector, the Ministry is primarily concerned with the construction, development and maintenance of National Highways. An outlay of Rs. 3141.73 crores was provided during the Eighth Plan for construction, maintenance and development of National Highways in the country. During the last year of the plan i.e. the year 1996-97 an outlay of Rs. 818.64 crores has been provided for the ongoing programmes.

(ii) The volume of Road Transport in India has been growing at an average rate of 10 per cent and the road transport have emerged as one of the preferred modes of transport in comparison to rail because of certain inherent advantages. The share of road transport for trade traffic has increased from 11 per cent in 1951 to 60 per cent in 1995 and is expected to be around 65 per cent by the year 2000. Similarly, the passenger traffic has increased from 28 per cent to 80 per cent and is expected to be about 87 per cent during the same period. Keeping in view, the traffic load on the roads it has been proposed to remove the deficiencies in the existing National Highway network in a phased manner to meet the traffic needs for next 10 to 15 years with emphasis on four Planing of high density corridors to modernise road construction technology for speedy execution and quality assurance. Measures to improve road safety and conservation of energy, to sufficiently widen the roads leading to industrial centres to encourage industry and exports etc. The total requirement of funds for the Central Sector and centrally sponsored schemes in the road sector for the Ninth Plan has been projected at Rs. 23,000 crores.

(iii) In the past, development of the National Highways has been done by mainly budgetary support from the government. However, the resources required are so huge, that it is essential to encourage private investment in the construction and maintenance of National Highways on BOT basis. Therefore, in order to encourage private investment in the road sector, the Ministry has issued the policy guidelines for private investment in the road sector also.

(iv) These comprehensive guidelines encompass land acquisition, environmental clearance, simplification of procedures, tolling of four lanes/bypasses and bridges, equity participation in the highway sector. Some of the important ingredients of guidelines issued to encourage private investment are as follow:

— Automatic approval upto 74 per cent foreign equity participation.
— BOT documentation and procedures standardised.
— FIDIC conditions for tendering .
— Competitive bidding.
— Two cover tender system—technical and financial.

(a) Financial strength, experience, quality and adequacy of organisation and institutional arrangements (technical bid)
(b) Lowest cost to user (financial bid)

— Transparent evaluation criteria.
— Dispute resolution mechanism under Indian Arbitration Act, 1940 which has been duly amended to provide arbitration procedure in accordance with United Nations Commission of International Trade Laws (UNCITRAL)

(v) During the year, two projects of bypasses (Thane-Bhiwandi) in Maharashtra and (Udaipur) in Rajasthan and one project of road over-bridge (Chalthan in Gujarat) involving an investment of Rs. 42 crores have been awarded on BOT basis.

(vi) Further, during the year, the National Highways Act, has been amended by issue of an ordinance to provide for a speedy process of land acquisition on the lines of Metro Railways Act; delays in land acquisition has been one of the major bottlenecks in the development of National Highways.

(vii) The provisions relating to foreign investment in the road sector have been considerably liberalised. Automatic approval will be accorded for foreign equity participation upto 74 per cent in the construction of roads and bridges. In addition to this, automatic approval would be given for majority foreign equity upto 51 per cent in support services to land transport like operation of highway bridges, toll roads and vehicles.

(viii) During the year 1996-97 it is expected that 227 kms of National Highways will be widened from single lane to double lane, 432 kms. strengthened, 139 kms widened to four lane and 86 bridges (Major and Minor) completed.

Border Roads Development Board

(i) During the year Border Roads Organisation completed the construction work of two laning of NH-4B at Panvel (Maharashtra), a prestigious work of joining Nhava Sheva Port to NH-17 at a cost of Rs. 30.66 crores. In Bhutan one bridge at Thimphu, additional improvement works of India House Complex, Construction of bulk petroleum Depot and construction off Bank building were completed. During 1996 a total of 14 major bridges were completed by BRO.

(ii) The BRO was instrumental in organising National Seminar on Planning and Management of Bridges and Flyovers in New Delhi in May, 1996. The second Conference on Asian Road Safety, Evaluation and Priorities held at Beijing (China) from 28th October to 31st October 1996 was attended by DGBR as official delegate from India.

(iii) In spite of disturbance and militant activities in North Easter and North Western sectors, the overall performance of BRO has been commendable. Its 9 officers and personnel were awarded Param Vishist Sewa Medal, Shaurya Chakra, Vishist Sewa Medal and Jeevan Raksha Padak and 109 officers and personnel were given commendation cards.

Road Transport

(i) The programme to convert government owned petrol driven vehicles for operation on compressed natural gas (CNG) was continued.

(ii) The Transport Development Council meeting was held on 30/31-12-1996 at new Dehli.

(iii) The Eighth Road Safety Week was observed from Ist to 7th January, 1997 throughout the country with the involvement of State Government, Voluntary Organization etc.

(iv) The Delhi Transport Corporation was transferred to the Government of National Capital Territory of Delhi on 05-08-1996.

(v) Grants-in-Aid was provided to various Voluntary Organisations for Undertaking Road Safety Programmes.

(vi) There are 69 State Transport Undertakings having a fleet of nearly 1,11,538 vehicles providing Passenger Transport in the various parts of the Country.

COMMUNICATIONS

Telecommunication

(i) Telecom Sector Is Infrastructure

The Government on January 30 announced that the telecom projects would be treated as infrastructure and decided to extend all fiscal benefits to them, such as tax holiday and concessional project import duty, as were available to other infrastructure sectors like power. The concessional project import duty would be pegged at 25 per cent. The Finance Ministry said that the limit on external commercial borrowing (ECB) for the telecom projects had been hiked to 50 per cent from the present 35 per cent of the project cost. The sanctioning of ECB in this sector would be allowed in due course of time, the Ministry said. It also said that licence fees by the telecom service providers would be treated as revenue expenditure or capital expenditure with a suitable amortisation formula.

Welcoming the Government move, the industry said the decision to treat telecom as infrastructure would provide a boost to the private basic and cellular operators and help them organise the much-needed funds for their capital-intensive projects. "It will facilitate inflow of funds into the telecom sector, particularly from the foreign banks," they said. This is also expected a provide a level-playing field for the private operators vis-a-vis the state-owned telecom companies like MTNL and VSNL. In a few cases, the Ministry recently blocked the disbursement of loan by foreign banks to the private licence holders on the ground that it was in violation of the ECB norms, which disallowed borrowings above 35 per cent of the project cost.

Highlights

* ECB limit raised from 35 per cent to 50 per cent of project costs
* Assignability pact finalised between DoT and FIs
* Telecom projects to be treated as 'infrastructure'
* Five year tax holiday and 25 per cent concessional import duty
* Licence fee to be treated as capital expenditure.

(ii) Telecom Show '97 Inaugurated

In order to achieve the target of GOP growth rate at 7 per cent in the Ninth Plan, there is a requirement of large investments particularly in the infrastructure areas like telecommunications. Stating this Mr. R. Dhanushkodi Athithan, the Minister of State for Human Resource Development, said : "We need to stress more on the quality of telecommunications services which will be very vital for the growth of the economy., "The Minister was speaking at the inauguration of the Global Telecom Show '97 on March 12 in the Capital. "Bills Gates, the network wizard in his recent visit to India had said that worldwide India was recognised as a high quality manpower especially in computer software engineering," said Mr. Athithan. "And as such, India can build on this advantage by linking all the universities and scientific establishments with a high quality communications network," he added. A major objective of the Ninth Five Year Plan was to provide sufficient employment opportunities in the country and as such India's potential to become a leader in software could well help in boosting employment in the country. It was also emphasised that there was a significant need for a broad-based programme to create more employment opportunities for the youth.

(iii) India and WTO Agreement on Telecom

According to Telecom Commission Chairman A. V. Gokak. India stands to gain from the WTO agreement on telecom reached in Geneva Speaking to newsmen in New Delhi on February 18, 1997 Mr. Gokak said the negotiation in WTO for basic telecommunications on market access held nine formal meetings and numerous bilateral meetings and India took part in all the discussions. In April, 1996 India made an offer keeping in view the prevalent policies of duopoly in basic services with one of the operators being Department to Telecommunications (DoT)/MTNL. In cellular services India also made an offer for this service to be provided by two operators. But the Government retained the right of DoT/MTNL to provide this service. Mr. Gokak said the foreign equity commitment was kept at 25 per cent in various subsectors of basic telecommunications services although autonomously India was permitting 49 per cent foreign equity. Also, he said India did not commit about opening of domestic long distance i.e. intercircle and international traffic sectors. M. Gokak said since there were different opinions about the subject on accounting rates being part of GATS. as a matter of abundant precaution. India chose to file MEN exemption regarding accounting rates. This was done as the accounting rates were finalised bilaterally and was not a multilateral subject. Asked if VSNL (monopoly long distance carrier in India) was not over charging when developed countries were charging far less for long distance calls, he said "we have to take into account the cross-subsidisation of providing telecom facilities in the rural areas". He said VSNL has also debunked the cost calculation worked out by FCC of the US which forms the main basis of determining accounting rate between two countries. It may be recalled that the FCC had sent notices to VSNL and also the Government of what it perceived as the actual costing behind the accounting rates.

Mr. Gokak said after series of negotiations with India's trading partner since July 1996, India made certain additional commitments in its revised offer submitted to WTO in February, 1997. The additional commitments were by way of adopting most of the internationally well known regulatory principles like competitive safeguards, interconnection, universal services, public availability of licensing criteria, allocation and use of scarce resources. The Telecom Commission Chairman said the Government's decision of reviewing the opening of inter-circle long distance subsector in 1999 and opening of international service in the year 2004 had also been reiterated. Although there was considerable pressure for withdrawing MFN exemption regarding accounting rates, India stuck to its earlier stand and did not give in to pressure for withdrawal of the same.

23

DIVERSE ISSUES

(i) CENTRAL GOVERNMENT EMPLOYEES FIFTH PAY COMMISSION REPORT

Fifth Pay Commission Report

The Fifth Central Pay Commission has recommended that the minimum salary for government employees be Rs. 2,440 per month and the maximum at the level of Secretaries to the Government of India at Rs. 26,000 a month. The Cabinet Secretary, however, has a fixed salary of Rs. 30,000 a month. A major recommendation is that the allowances and pensions should not be taxed (be paid net of taxes is the recommendation). Also, a shift to six-day week with second Saturday as off day has been recommended, along with the suggestion that overtime allowance should be abolished. It has also been recommended that the revised pay scales, dearness allowance and pension should have retrospective effect from 1-1-96 and all other allowances made applicable prospectively. Besides, the age of superannuation has been hiked to 60 years, except for armed forces and Central police organisations. Also, the increased service period will be applicable from the date it is notified and will not be applicable to those who are on extension.

Increase has been recommended in house rent allowance, which will now be at the rate of 30 per cent of the maximum of the pay scales in A-I cities and from five to 15 per cent of the maximum in other cities. A transport allowance ranging between Rs. 75 and Rs. 800 a month is being permitted to all employees. However, staff cars are to be restricted to top executives and field officers only, all others being served by a pool of hired taxis. On Leave travel Concession (LTC), the new proposals are for three home town LTCs instead of having one all-India and one home town LTC in a block of four years. Also LTC is being allowed by air for some selected senior categories. As for leave rules, an extra period of 60 days is being allowed for accumulation of earned leave which can now go up to 300 days. This can be encashed either at the time of superannuation or in batches up to 10 days each along with the LTC.

The Commission has also enunciated broad parameters for determination of bonus. In this context, an eligibility ceiling of Rs. 4,500 per month has been suggested and the calculation ceiling retained at Rs. 2,500 per month. The maximum bonus has been suggested as 30 days in case of ad hoc bonus and 55 days in case of productivity-linked bonus. On contributions to the General

Provident Fund (GPF), a higher rate of interest at 13 per cent on deposits has been suggested. In a special recommendation, the Commission has suggested that all executives of and above the rank of Deputy Secretary and equivalent should be provided with a Telephone Attendant at their residences. The attendant would be recruited directly by the officer and would not enjoy the status of a Government employee, but the fixed salary of Rs. 1,500 per month for such attendants would be borne by the Government. This facility will not be additionally available to officers who are already entitled to personal attendants by whatever name they may be called.

As in the case of armed forces, the Commission has recommended that for certain specified officers in the civil service, both at the Centre and the States, entertainment allowance ranging from Rs. 600 to Rs. 1,000 per month be paid. The Commission has recommended that the Gazetted holidays be reduced from 17 to three, that is, Republic Day, Independence Day and Mahatma Gandhi's birthday. The reduction of 14 days is to be made up by increasing the number of restricted holidays. It has also been suggested that no holidays be declared on the demise of any leader, except the incumbent President and Prime Minister. The Finance Minister, Mr. P.. Chidambaram, on January 30 held out the assurance that the recommendations of the Fifth Pay Commission would be implemented "as soon as possible". The Pay Commission had been appointed by the Government and it would make available the funds required to implement those recommendations which would be ultimately accepted by the Government, he added. According to the Pay Commission's estimation, the additional financial implications for one year would come to Rs.8,800 crore. However, this figure would be reduced to Rs. 7,300 crore for the financial year 1996-97, if the savings expected from the postponement of retirement benefits is taken into consideration.

The Major Recommendations

The following are the major recommendations of the Fifth Pay Commission :

* Minimum salary for Government employees to be Rs. 2,400 per month and maximum for Secretaries at Rs. 26,000 per month.
* Six-day week with second Saturday as off day.
* Overtime allowance abolished.
* Age of superannuation raised to 60 years, except for armed forces and Central police organisations.
* Revised pay scales to be effective from 1.1.96; Allowances to be prospective.
* Maternity leave quantum enhanced from 90 to 135 days.
* Age of initial recruitment for women raised to 35 years.
* Part-time employment for women on optional basis proposed.
* House Rent Allowance (HRA) at the rate of 30 per cent of the maximum of the pay scales in A-1 cities and from five to 15 per cent of the maximum in other cities.

* Transport allowance ranging between Rs. 75 to Rs. 800 per month.
* Leave Travel Concession (LTC), three home town LTCs proposed instead of one all-India and one home town LTC in a block of four years. LTC being allowed by air for some selected senior categories.
* Leave accumulation up to 300 days.
* House building advance to be raised to Rs 7.5 lakh.
* Golden handshake scheme for departments with identified surplus staff.
* Compulsory medical check-up of employees at Government cost after age of 40.
* Medical insurance to cover hospitalization needs of employees.

(ii) CIVIL AVIATION

Civil Aviation Policy

The Government on January 24 announced a new civil aviation policy which simplifies some of the existing rules and regulations, But, on the controversial issue of allowing foreign airlines to hold equity in joint venture companies in India, the Union Cabinet has referred the matter back to the Civil Aviation Ministry to examine it afresh. Giving out details of the new policy, the Civil Aviation Secretary, Mr. Yogesh Chandra, told presspersons after the Cabinet meeting that 40 per cent foreign equity was allowed in the aviation sector, but whether foreign airlines and airports could hold this equity was a matter yet to be determined. However, non-resident Indian holdings in domestic aviation companies would continue to be permitted.

The immediate implication of this is that the controversial proposal from the Tata group and Singapore International Airlines (SIA) to form a joint venture company with 40 Per cent equity each and the balance with the public remains pending for the time being. The Tata-SIA proposal was cleared by the Foreign Investment Promotion Board (FIPB) as well as the Industry Ministry but was publicly opposed by the Civil Aviation Ministry. Some prominent Members of Parliament, belonging to the BJP, the CPI(M) as well the Samajwadi Party had also opposed the proposal. The other modifications made in the existing policy include free choice of aircraft by the operators by removing the existing ceiling on import of 50-seater aircraft, subject to clearance from the Directorate-General of Civil Aviation (DGCA) and other relevant authorities. Also, the existing constraints on growth in capacity of operating airlines were removed, though there would be overall monitoring of the situation by the Government in order to avoid congestion and chaos at airports.

Significantly, the new policy allows free entry and exit for private airline companies. However, to obviate the functioning of companies with dubious standing, the new policy also enhances the minimum fleet size from three to five aircraft , to be achieved over a period of time. Also, the equity requirement for airline companies was hiked and the small airline companies would now have to a minimum equity of Rs. 5 crore against Rs. 3 crore earlier. For the Larger operators, the increase was from Rs. 10 crore to Rs. 30 crore. Mr Chandra also said that existing route guidelines would continue, including flying on category two and category three routes. The Cabinet also re-emphasised the paramount role the national carriers were expected to play, despite the entry of private operators in the aviation business.

New International Airport

Union Civil Aviation Minister C.M. Ibrahim on Febuary17 declared that the International Airport Authority of India would take up the international airport project at Devanahalli. Talking to newsmen in Bangalore, the Minister said he had at a recent meeting with industrialist Ratan Tata made it clear that the Government favoured taking up of the project on build, operate and transfer (BOT) basis instead of build, own and operate basis. The air traffic control and the landing rights would be vested only with the Government. He hoped Mr Tata would consider the proposal favourably. If the consortium backed out of the project, the Government would not hesitate to go ahead as he was keen that Bangalore should have an international airport, he asserted.

He said he had convened a tripartite meeting on February 20 to take a final decision. Besides the State Government officials and the Minister concerned, the meeting would be attended by the officials of Tata-Singapore consortium and the Union Civil Aviation Ministry. Mr. Ibrahim referring to the Tata-Singapore airlines proposal for running a domestic service, said the Government would not allow an international airlines to take up domestic service. The Government favoured foreign investment in the sector, but it should be a non-international airlines offer, he clarified. Mr. Ibrahim said the Government was for foreign investment in the area but it should not be at the cost of 55,000 employees of the Indian Airlines. Besides providing various concessions, the Indian Airlines was also operating on routes especially in the north-eastern sector.

He said the policy did not mean that the Government was against foreign investment. It welcomed even 100 per cent foreign investment in building airports in certain greenfield areas. But it would be only on BOT basis. Referring to Air India operations, the Minister said it had made Rs. 10 crore profit in January alone. Indian Airlines would emerge as a zero loss operator from March next. He said Air India would give up some of the loss making routes and concentrate on the corridors where the traffic was heavy. He said he had asked the Airport Authority of India to take up the feasibility study for the establishment of an airport in Shimoga in Karnataka

(iii) ELECTION

Election Commission

In a landmark judgement to curb use of black money and to bring transparency in the election funding, the Supreme Court on April 4 ruled that the expenditure incurred by a political party on a candidate in an election would fall within the prescribed ceiling of expenses if the source of the money was not revealed. The Court held that political parties not maintaining books of accounts and not filing income tax returns could not take advantage of the provision exempting the expenditure incurred by political parties on their candidates. "If a political party deliberately chooses to violate or circumvent mandatory provisions of Income Tax Act and Representation of People Act and goes through the election process with the help of black and unaccounted money, the said party, ordinarily, cannot be permitted to say that it has incurred or authorised expenditure in connection with the election of its candidates in terms of Explanation 1 of Section 77 of the R.P. Act, the Court held.

The ruling was given by a division bench comprising Mr. Justice Kuldip Singh and Mr. Justice Faizan Uddin while allowing a public interest petition by "Common Cause", a registered society, headed by Mr. H.D. Shourie. The petitioner was seeking strict enforcement of Section 293A of the companies Act, 1956, Section 13A of the Income Tax Act, 1961 and Section 77 of the Representation of People Act, 1950 as these provisions of law are being violated by the political parties with impunity. Mr. Justice Kuldip Singh, who delivered the 32- page judgement on behalf of the Court, said that any expenditure in connection with the election of a candidate, which according to him has been incurred by his political party, should be presumed to have been authorised by the candidate or his election agent. But the presumption is rebuttable. "The candidate shall have to show that the said expenditure was in fact incurred by a political party and not by him. The candidate shall have to rebut the presumption by the evidentiary—standard as applicable to rebuttable presumptions under the law of evidence." The Judges observed

Setting off the process of implementing the Supreme Court judgment on election expenditure, the Election Commission (EC) on April 7 directed all political parties to submit for scrutiny not later than July 31, 1996 details of expenditure incurred or authorised by them since March 19, when the elections were announced, The EC also directed the Union Revenue Secretary to furnish by April 22, at the outset, details of the income tax returns filed (or not filed) by recognised national and State level parties. After a two-day meeting to deliberate on the implications of the Supreme Court judgment, the EC issued four orders addressed respectively to the Revenue Secretary, all recognised national and State parties and all registered unrecognised. parties, Chief Electoral Officers of all States and Union Territories and to all Election Expenditures Observers. These letters, released in New Delhi, quote the relevant portions of the verdict and are also accompanied by a copy of the April 4 Supreme Court judgement, which seeks to check the misuse of money in elections.

While the first two letters seek information from the Government and the political parties, the second set of letters are directives to the EC officials and staff to keep a close watch on the expenditure incurred by a candidate and his supporters and .political party on him. Although the text of the four letters differs, the basic thrust remains the same— to give action to the Supreme Court judgement and stress the point that under Article 141 of the Constitution, the verdict becomes the law of the land and is binding on all since it was delivered on April 4. There is no doubt that the EC orders, which aim at purifying the electoral process, will also be seen by political parties and candidates as having made their task even more difficult, given the present ceiling on expenditure for Parliamentary and Assembly constituencies. Unless the Government revises it, the Rs. 4.50 lakh and Rs. 1.5 lakh ceiling for Parliamentary and Assembly constituencies would be the touchstone for election expenditure as given by the Supreme Court verdict.

(iv) HUMAN RIGHTS

Government continued to follow a multi-pronged strategy on Human Rights matters—strict enforcement of constitutional and legal safeguards, stern action against officials found guilty of human rights violations, providing necessary financial and administrative support to the National Human Rights Commission to enable it to discharge its functions effectively, promotion of human rights awareness both amongst the law enforcing agencies as well as the common masses and total transparency which had helped the country in projecting the human rights situation in correct perspective and in effectively countering the disinformation campaign of adversaries like Pakistan. Special attention was paid to the need for observance of respect for human rights even in the insurgency and terrorism affected areas. Initiatives taken during the last few years for increasing human rights awareness among the common masses in general and public servants in particular, were further consolidated.

In keeping with its deep commitment to the protection and promotion of human rights, Government have included the setting up of State Human Rights Commissions by State Governments in its Common Minimum Programme. The States of Assam, Himachal Pradesh, Madhya Pradesh and West Bengal have already set up their State Human Rights Commissions. Other States are being persuaded to follow suit. Government is also committed to signing the UN Convention against Torture, and other Cruel, Inhuman or Degrading Treatment or Punishment as reflected in its Common Minimum Programme.

Special attention was given to the training aspects of the police and paramilitary force personnel. The National Human Rights Commission had prepared a three-tier model syllabus for human rights training of police and paramilitary officers of all ranks. Most of the States have adopted the syllabus. Seminars/training programmes on "Human Rights" have been organised by the Central Para Military Forces for their officers in collaboration with the International Committee of the Red Cross (ICRC). Three one-day workshops on 'Human Rights' at Srinagar on 15,19 and 20 July, 1996 and two one-day workshops at Jammu on 22 and 24 July, 1996 were organised in collaboration with the ICRC. Officers of BSF, CRPF and Jammu and Kashmir Police attended these workshops. A presentation on 'Human Rights' was organised by BSF in collaboration with ICRC on 07.08.1996 during the XXV BSF Annual Training Conference held at Frontier Headquarters on 6-7 August, 1996. A debate on 'Security Forces observing Human Rights are better equipped to combat organised violence' was conducted by BSF under the aegis of NHRC in New Delhi on 6th February, 1996. All the Central Police Organisations and members of NHRC participated in this seminar. These efforts have resulted in greater degree of responsibility and sensitisation on the part of security forces.

A three-day Workshop on Concept and Enforcement of Human Rights was organised by the Ministry at Vigyan Bhawan on 3-5 December, 1996. Senior Police Officers from various States and from Central Para Military Forces, who are incharge of training, attended the Workshop. Eminent persons such as Members of NHRC, Retired Police Officers, Academicians, media personalities etc. having wide and long experience in the field of human rights participated as panelists in this Workshop.

In furtherance of its policy of openness in human rights matters, the Government continued to facilitate visits of foreigners, including Parliamentarians and Diplomats to various parts of the country, particularly to Jammu and Kashmir. During 1996, till 30th November, 1996, 161 diplomats, 2 Parliamentarians and 186 foreign journalists visited the State of Jammu and Kashmir

Government cleared a research visit by a four-member delegation of Amnesty International to Delhi, Bangalore and Rajasthan. The delegation visited these places from 4th July, 1996 to 10th August, 1996 for conducting research on custodial death and rights of women.

In furtherence of Government's policy of openness and firm commitment to Human Rights matters, a MoU was signed between the Government of India and the International Committee of Red Cross on 22.06.1995. Under the MoU, Government has agreed to provide to ICRC access to jails and detention centres where persons detained in connection with the situation in Jammu and Kashmir have been lodged.

Mr. Abdelfattah Amor, Special Rapporteur of the UN Commission on Human Rights on Riligious Intolerance was invited by Government to visit India. He paid a two week visit to India from 1-14 December, 1996, during which period he also visited the States of Maharashtra, Jammu and Kashmir, Punjab and Uttar Pradesh. He interacted with Governors, Chief Ministers, Senior Government Officers, eminent persons and NGOs. In Delhi, he called on the Home Minister, External Affairs Minister, Speaker of the Lok Sabha, Leader of the Opposition in the Lok Sabha, Secretaries in the Ministries of Home Affairs, External Affairs, Law and Welfare, and the departments of

Culture and Education. In these meetings he discussed several issues connected with religious intolerance. Mr. Amor was adequately briefed about India's long standing culture and tradition of religious tolerance and of its unity in diversity. He also visited a number of shrines.

The Government continued to follow a policy of full cooperation with the UN System for Human Rights. Information sought by various agencies of the UN System, namely the Thematic Special Rapporteurs and the Working Groups were provided to them promptly. The timely and complete responses provided to them by the Government helped considerably in blunting the edge of the propaganda of International Human Rights Organisation like Amnesty International and Human Rights Watch/Asia at the UN fora.

The National Human Rights Commission constituted in October, 1993 functioned during the year 1996-97, with its full complement of Members. Consequent on Shri Justice Ranganath Misra demitting office as Chairperson on 24.11.1996, Shri Justice M.N. Venkatachaliah assumed charge of the office of the Chairperson of the Commission on 26.11.1996.

Government took steps towards ensuring greater effectiveness in the functioning the National Human Rights Commission. During the Year 1996-97, Government sanctioned 32 additional posts for various divisions of the Commission in addition to the 250 sanctioned posts. There is a budgetary provision for providing grants-in-aid of Rs. 3 crores for the Commission during the current financial year 1996-97 out of which Rs. 2.25 crores has already been released.

During April-October, 1996 the National Human Rights Commission held 114 sittings in which 8,039 complaints were considered. Of these 3,474 complaints were dismissed and 675 complaints were sent to other Organisations/ Ministries/State authorities with appropriate directions for disposal at their end. The Commission took cognizance of 3,276 complaints for purpose of making inquiries. During this period, the Commission concluded 1,060 cases on the basis of reports received from different authorities which included the cases carried over from the previous years.

The Investigation Division of the National Human Rights Commission investigated a number of cases as directed by the Commission. During the period from 01.04.1996 to 31.10.1996, the officers of the Investigation Division investigated as many as 189 cases. Investigations made by the police and other agencies in 372 cases were also monitored. As a result of the investigations made by the officers of the Commission, departmental action has been initiated/taken against large number of erring officials and compensation granted to many deserving victims/next-of-kin of the victims.

A number of foreign dignitaries continued to interact with the National Human Rights Commission. With a view to sensitising various sections of society, particularly, the police personnel, workshops and conferences were held from April, 1996 to October, 1996. A training course on Human Rights for Prison Staff was held in Delhi from 28.07.1996 to 01.08.1996 in which Superintendents of Prison of various States participated. A National Workshop on Human Rights was held at Madras on 3-4 August, 1996 in association with an NGO. The Commission has also constituated a Core Group with identified officers to look into the prevalence of child prostitution and the measures to combat it. The Commission is monitoring the implementation of the projects designed to eliminate child labour. Recently, it has also taken up the issue of abolition of manual scavenging.

One of the functions entrusted to the National Human Rights Commission, relates to research in the field of Human Rights. In order to perfrom this function, a Research Division has been set up within the Commission. It has been associated with the work relating to Research Projects/Studies concerning human rights aspects, which includes examination of the functioning of Custodial Homes/Institutions set up under different statues. Apart from this, all States/ Union Terriories have been requested to report within 24 hours to the Commission the custodial death/rapes occuring in these Homes/Institutions. At the instance of the National Human Rights Commission, the Ministry of Human Resource Development (Department of Education) has also set up a Working Group for coordination in Higher Education to oversee and monitor the human rights education programmes as well as to consider matters relating to international collaboration in this field.

Chairperson and Members of the Commission visited various countries and held wide ranging discussions with National Human Rights Commissions, International Bodies and Human Rights agencies and activists. The Chairperson also attended the First Asia-Pacific Regional Workshop of National Human Rights Institutions held in Darwin, Australia in July, 1996.

(v) HOUSING

Housing and Development Corporation Limited (HUDCO)

Housing and Urban Development Corporation Ltd. released loans worth around Rs. 1,501 crore for 1996-97, 21 per cent more than about Rs. 1,242 crore 1995-96, to finance construction of dwelling, sanitation units and urban infrastructure projects nationwide. Addressing a Press conference in New Delhi on April 10, HUDCO Chairman and Managing Director V. Suresh said that the corporation continued to maintain its tradition of being a profit-making organisation with social focus, with its financial results showing a provisional operating profit of Rs. 83 crore during 1996-97. HUDCO's net woth as of March 31 this year rose to Rs. 844 crore, as against Rs.728 crore in 1995-96. In the housing sector alone, HUDCO sanctioned 764 schemes with HUDCO loan assistance of Rs. 1,206 crore, the CMD claimed.

HUDCO also claimed to have raised Rs. 1,950 crore during 1996-97 as against the target of Rs. 1,558 crore, including Rs. 250 crore through its first public issue of infrastructure bonds issued by a public sector company. The issue was fully subscribed. HUDCO has also been notified as a public financial institution. The recognition puts it at par with other long-term lending FIs, adding a new dimension to its resource mobilisation capacity. In line with the Union Government's decision on disintermediation of foreign currency loans, HUDCO has signed a line of credit with the Overseas Economic Cooperation Fund (OECF). Under this agreement, the entire foreign exchange exposure would be on UHDCO's account, enabling it to take financial asistance directly from OECF, without taking recourse to budgetary support from the Government, as has been done in the past.

This aims at HUDCO emerging as a market leader in supporting urban housing development needs of the 21st century. The plan—HUDCO Vision 2002—envisages financial sanctions and releases of Rs. 14,746 crore and Rs. 12,534 crore, respectively, during the Ninth Plan.

(vi) LABOUR

The 33rd session of the Indian Labour Conference on October 25 adopted Rs. 35 per day as the national floor level minimum wages for unorganised employment, including farm labour. Although the implementation is not mandatory, State Governments are being advised to adopt Rs. 35 per day as the minimum wages for all schemes, including poverty alleviation programmes. The Conference also unanimously adopted a resolution supporting the Government's commitment to eliminate child labour in all industries and occupations and resolved that the Government should provide strong administrative and budgetary support for this. The Conference referred two controversial items on the recognition of trade unions through secret ballot and amendment to the Industrial Disputes Act, 1947, to a Sub-Committee comprising eight representatives each of the unions and employers. The sub-committee, which will be convened by a Ministry official, will submit its recommendations within three months.

On the burning topic of abolishing bonus ceiling for workers, the Conference could not reach a consensus. The Conference discussed the Action Taken Report on the Bill on Workers Participation in Management and authorised the Ministry of Labour to go ahead with the Bill. With 37 million perople waiting for job placement, the Conference resolved to modernise, reorganise and computerise the 895 employment exchanges and vocational training systems. As part of their expansion programme the employment exchanges would be re-named Employment Guidance and Promotion Centres.

The Conference resolved to form an all-India Council for Vocational Training on the lines of the all-India Council for Technical Education on the pattern of CSIR/ICAR. Later, addressing mediapersons, the minister for Labolur, Mr. M. Arunachalam, who chaired the two-day conference, said the national floor level wages have been worked out on the formula recommended by the C.H. Hanumantha Rao Commission on Unorganised Rural Labour and linked to the present level of Consumer Price Index (CPI). Mr. Arunachalam said States are being asked to revise the minimum wages and review them once in every two years based on the CPI, More than 70 per cent of the States were paying less than Rs. 35 per day minimum wages in the unorganised sector, whcih is about 290 million of the entire work force in the country, including over 100 million agriculture labour.

(vii) SPORTS AND PHYSICAL EDUCATION

Sports

Introduction

During the year 1996-97, India participated in the Olympic Games and Leander Paes won a bronze medal in an individual event after 44 years. Arjuna Awards for the 1995 were presented to 9 outstanding sportspersons at Rashtrapati Bhawan on 29th August 1996. Special Awards (Cash) were conferred on 70 Sportspersons/Coaches at Vigyan Bhawan on 7th December, 1996.

A Draft new Sports Policy was prepared and circulated to the States, National Sports Federations and the concerned departments of Govt. of India. It was also discussed during the conference of State Ministers held on 12.2.1997. The proposals received from various sports federations for inclusion in the Public Notice issued by Ministry of Commerce for the purpose of import of Sports goods without import licence were forwarded to Director General of Foreign Trade for inclusion.

Sports Authority of India

The Sports Authority of India (SAI), a corporate outcome of the IX Asiad, 1982, Delhi, was set up in 1984 by the Govt. of India. Over the years, SAI has initiated a number of schemes/programmes and is the apex body in the country for development of sports, SAI has 6 Regional Centres with head office at Bangalore (Southern Centre). Calcutta (Eastern Centre). Chandigarh (Northern Centre), Gandhinagar (Wastern Centre), Delhi (Central Centre) and Imphal (North Eastern Centre). All the centres are well equipped with provisions and support facilities for sports. The Centres provide a conductive sports environment essential for development of excellence. Each Regional Centre is responsible for effective implementation and coordination of sports development programmes of SAI and Central Govt. in the concerned region in collaboration with the respective State Govts./UT Administrations. Apart from the Regional Centres, SAI has two sub-centres: one each at Guwahati and Aurangabad. A High Altitude Training Centre at Shillaroo is in the process of being set up primarily for athletics, hockey, football, basketball, volleyball, boxing, wrestling and weightlifting.

The period under report witnessed a number of activities and achievements for SAI. The SAI trainees continued to make their presence felt in various national competitions. About 40 per cent of the Indian contingent which participated in Atlanta Olympics, 1996, comprised of players hailing from different SAI schemes.

Physical Education

(i) The Lakshmibai National College (now Institute) of Physical Education was established by Government of India, on 17th August, 1957, the centenary year of the first war of Independence. The Institute is located at Gwalior where Rani Lakshmibai of Jhansi had lost her life.

(ii) In recognition of the educational services rendered by the Institute in the field of physical education, sports and research and on the recommendations of the University Grants Commission, the Government of India, Ministry of Human Resource Development (Department of Education) declard this Institute as a 'Deemed to be a University' *vide* Notification No. E. 9-14/92 dated 21-9-95. The Institute has been delinked from the Sports Authority of India and is registered under Societies Registration Act, 1973 at Gwalior. The Institute is fully funded by the Government of India.

(iii) During the year 1996-97, the Institute offered the following full time courses :

(1) Bachelor of Physical Education (3 years' degree course).
(2) Master of Physical Education (2 years' degree course).
(3) MPE (Summer Course) (3 years' degree course) for in-service teachers.
(4) M. Phil in Physical Education (1 year degree course).

The Institute also conducted in-service training programmes in Physical Education for the Pre-Released Army Personnel, U.G.C. refresher/orientation courses for physical education teachers in universities, colleges and schools. The Institute also organised a Certificate Course in games. The Institute attracts students not only from India but also from abroad. Students from Mauritius joined the institute for pursuing Physical Education courses. One Ph. D. scholar from Thailand is undergoing the Doctoral programme. Five girls and five boys joined the Institute during the year 1996-97.

(viii) POPULATION AND FAMILY WELFARE

Population to cross one Billion by 2001

India's population should stablise around the year 2026, according to the latest Census projections. By then, the country's total fertility rate (TFR) would decline to 2.1. This is the replacement level of fertility, when just enough children are being born to maintain the population at a constant level. But there are wide variations between the states in the rate at which they are moving towards the near zero growth 2.1 TFR goal. Kerala achieved it in 1988 and Tamil Nadu in 1993. According to currrent trends, Bihar will reach it in 2039, Rajasthan in 2048 and Madhya Pradesh after 2060. Uttar Pradesh will make it only around the beginning of the 22nd century.

These are the latest projections of the office of the Registrar General, which on January 18 released more data-based on the 1991 Census. The topics covered included employment, fertility and migration. While the data collected in 1991 was still being processed, the preparations for the next once-in-a-decade Census had already begun, Registrar General M. Vijayanunni told reporters. India's population will cross the 1,000 million mark just around the time it enters the 21st century. Going by the trends in both countries, the population of India will be higher than that of China by 2040.

Family Welfare

ECU Grant for Welfare Programmes

India will receive about Rs. 900 crore (200 million ECU) grant from the European Commission for carrying out its various family welfare programmes. This was announced at a joint Press conference by Union Family Welfare Secretary Y.N. Chaturvedi and ECU Ambassador to India M.B. Mcgeever in New Delhi on February 10. The EC grant to be provided in two phases is meant for the preparation of the programme, and to support the nation-wide implementation of family welfare sector services at state and district level. Of the 200 million ECU, 10 million ECU (about Rs. 44.34 crore) will be to cover the cost of support activities, technical backstopping and institutional linkages between India and the EU.

Mr. Mcgeever said the EC decision was in response to Inia's initiative in favour of a policy reform process in its family welfare programme. Following the consensus at the 1994 International Cairo Conference on Population and Development on the importance of a comprehensive family welfare package. An important feature of the programme was the shift in focus from demographic targets to the delivery of a range of family health serves based on the need of individuals. The Government had launched a target-free approach in its family welfare programme last year. EC First Counsellor (Development) AJL Smith said the EC decided to extend its support to India after having got encouraged by the successful education programme.

(ix) TOURISM

Increase in Tourists Arrival

The initial efforts to propagate tourist information about Indian destinations globally through the Internet bore fruit in the form of a 7.7 per cent increase in tourist arrivals during 1996. The number of tourists visiting India during 1996 was 22,87,860 as compared to 21,23,863 in 1995, according to Tourism Secretary M.P. Bezbarua. The largest increase has been witnessed in the case of tourists from Australia and Japan whose number increased by 29.8 per cent and 25.5 per cent, respectively. Arrivals from the US and Germany increased by 11.9 per cent and 10.5 per cent, respectively, while the number of visitors from the UK increased by 9 per cent. However, the number of tourists from other countries increased by only 5.2 per cent.

Various efforts are being made to attract a larger number of tourists and the Tourism Departments' website on the Interet-Http/www. tour India. Comprovides information on a large number of tourist attractions in the country along with infrastructure facilities and immigration procedures. Efforts would be made to project the facilities and infrastructure available in the country, Director General of Tourism Ashok Pradhan said. Upgradation of facilities and better publicity would lead to higher tourist arrivals, he added, since the tourist destinations in India are numerous while the diverse culture makes it more interesting for visitors.

Rs. 10.000 Crore from Tourism

Tourism activities in the country recorded an all round growth during 1996 with foreign tourist arrivals crossing the 2.2 million mark, yielding an all-time high in foreign exchange to the tune of Rs. 10,000 crore. The impressive performance in the tourism sector is particularly noteworthy in the wake of the adverse publicity due to dengue in the northern parts of the country and the election process which generally affects tourist arrivals from abroad. While the foreign tourist arrivals increased by 10 per cent over the last year, the foreign exchange earnings from tourism during the year registered an exceptionally high growth of about 18 per cent. The tourism sector remained an important instrument for employment generation with the number of employed persons in the sector crossing the 8 million mark. A drive to streamline publicity efforts abroad was launched to attract more foreign tourists by relocating some of the overseas offices of the department of tourism. It was decided to shift the Bangkok office to Durban, the Kuala Lumpur office to Seoul and the Geneva office to Moscow. In an effort to tap foreign tourist potential in new places, new offices were opened in Buenos Aires and Tel Aviv.

Information about tourism places in India were also made available through internet by establishing a homepage in the world wide web service. The government also initiated the process for setting up a Tourism Industry Promotion Board to co-ordinate activities amongst industries, trade and infrastructural departments. A strategy paper was prepared to undertake tourism development in an integrated manner. The paper outlines projectons of various tourism activities upto 2000 AD and spells out the sector-wise requirements. However, since the Planning Commission had not yet finalised the plan resources and allocations for the Ninth Plan, it was not possible for them to take any decision on the investments proposed in the strategy paper. The strategy paper enlists a number of activities to be taken up by various departments of the Centre. The state government financial institutions and the private sector have been urged to achieve synergy in the development of tourism.

(X) YOUTH PROGRAMMES

The Youth of India representing a third of our population, constitute a vital and vibrant human resource. The need, therefore, is to create increasing opportunities for them to develop their personality and their functional capability and thus make them economically productive and socially useful. The Youth Policy is directed towards achievement of the following objectives :—

(i) to instill in the Youth a deep awareness of and respect for the principles and values enshrined in our Constitution;

(ii) to promote among youth an awareness of our historical and cultural heritage and imbue them with a sense of pride and national identity;

(iii) to help develop in youth the qualities of discipline, self-reliance, justice and fairplay;

(iv) to provide the youth with maximum access to education which, in addition to developing their personality, imparts appropriate professional and vocational training with a view to enabling them to avail of employment and self-employment opportunities; and

(v) to promote among youth an awareness of international issues and involve them in promoting world peace.

Committee for National Youth Programmes

Government of India has constituted a Committee for National Youth Programmes (CONYP) as per the guidelines of National Youth Policy. This Committee replaces the earlier National Youth Council. It has 50 members with Prime Minister as its chairman. The functions of the committee are to :—

— suggest policy measures and programmes for youth;
— advise Government on implementation of the 'Plan of Action' of the Natonal Youth Policy;
— review the coordination between various Departments of the Central/ State Government and voluntary organisation/other agencies involved therein ; and
— provide a feed-back on implementation the national youth programmes.

National Service Scheme

National Service Scheme, popularly known as NSS, was launched in Gandhiji's Birth Centenary Year, 1969, in 37 universities involving 40,000 students with primary focus on the development of personality of students through community service. Today, NSS has over 13.45 lakh student volunteers on the roll spread over 158 universities/+2 system. From its inception, more than 1.52 crore students from the universities, colleges and institutions of higher learning have benefited from the NSS activities, as NSS volunteers. Due to its overwhelming popularity and demand, the scheme was extended to the students of +2 level in selected institutions.

The National Service Scheme has two types of programmes, viz., 'regular activities' and 'special camping programmes' undertaken by its volunteers. Under 'Regular Activities', students are expected to work as volunteers for a continuous period of two years, rendering community service for minimum of 120 hours per annum. The activities include improvement of campuses, tree plantation, constructive work in adoped villages and slums, work in welfare institutions, blood donation, adult and non-formal education, health nutrition, family welfare, AIDS awareness campaigns, etc. Under 'Special Camping Programme', a camp of 10 days' duration is conducted every year in the adopted areas on a specific theme like 'Youth Against Famine', 'Youth Against Dirt and Disease', 'Youth for Afforestation and Tree Plantation', 'Youth for Rural Reconstruction'. Youth for Development', 'Youth for mass Literacy, 'Youth for Social Harmony', etc. The theme for 1995-96 and 1996-97 was "Youth for Sustainable Development" and 'Wasteland Development and Watershed Management'.

Nehru Yuva Kendra Sangathen

Nehru Yuva Kendra Sangathan (NYKS) is an autonomous organisation under the Department of Youth Affairs and Sports. It is the largest grass-root level organisation in the Asia-Pacific region, catering to the needs of the needs of more than 8 million non-student rural youth in the age group of 15-35 years enrolled through 1.82 lakh village besed Youth Clubs covering, education, training, employment promotion, income generation, self-employment, enterprise creation, etc. In addition, activities for the overall development of the rural communities such as health and family welfare, preservation and enrichment of eco-system adult literacy people's empowerment; eradication of social evils and superstitions, AIDS and drug abuse etc. are organised with emphasis on values, vision and voluntary action. The basic idea is to bring rural youth into the mainstream of national development as active participants, responsible and productive citizens of the modern technological India. Consequently, NYKS has emerged as a mass movement. At persent, about 500 Nehru Yuva Kendras are working all across the country.

Vocational Training Programme

The principal objective of this programme is to update and improve the vocational skills of rural youth so that they may increase their income through improvement in their productivity. The trades include handicrafts, consumer items, tailoring/knitting, embroidery, basket-making, mat and making, cane and bamboo work, book-binding, candle-making, bakery, doll making, fabric painting, nutrition/food preservation methods. Repairing of electronic gadgets, automobiles, household goods, pump-set, radio/TV, agricultural implements, etc. was also covered. From January, to November, 1996, 1320 programmes were organised. More than 50,000 youth were benefited.